AMERICA

Unzipped

AMERICA
Unzipped

IN SEARCH OF SEX AND SATISFACTION

BRIAN ALEXANDER

HARMONY BOOKS / NEW YORK

Published in the United States by Harmony Books, an imprint of the
Crown Publishing Group, a division of Random House, Inc., New York.
www.crownpublishing.com

Harmony Books is a registered trademark and the Harmony Books
colophon is a trademark of Random House, Inc.

Library of Congress Cataloging-in-Publication Data

Alexander, Brian, 1959–
America unzipped: in search of sex and satisfaction /
Brian Alexander.—1st ed.
1. Sex customs—United States.   I. Title.
HQ18.U5A35 2008
306.770973—dc22   2007031710

ISBN 978-0-307-35132-6

Printed in the United States of America

10   9   8   7   6   5   4   3   2   1

First Edition

TO THE MEMORIES OF KURT VONNEGUT AND NEIL POSTMAN,
TO WHOM WE SHOULD HAVE LISTENED

CONTENTS

Because of the nature of this book, some subjects portrayed in it preferred not to use their real names, usually for the protection of relatives or out of concern for their jobs. Generally, use of both first and last names denotes a person's real name. A first name only may or may not be his or her actual first name. All events are real.

You'd be surprised what was going on on the other side of the hotel. They didn't even bother to pull their shades down. I saw one guy, a gray-haired, very distinguished-looking guy with only his shorts on, do something you wouldn't believe me if I told you. . . . Then, in the window almost right over his, I saw a man and a woman squirting water out of their mouths at each other. It probably was highballs, not water, but I couldn't see what they had in their glasses. Anyway, first he'd take a swallow and squirt it all over *her* and then she did it to *him*—they took *turns*, for God's sake. You should've seen them. They were in hysterics the whole time, like it was the funniest thing that ever happened. I'm not kidding, the hotel was lousy with perverts. I was probably the only normal bastard in the whole place—and that isn't saying much.

—J. D. Salinger, *The Catcher in the Rye,* 1951

AMERICA

Unzipped

What Have I Been Missing?

I am still of the opinion that only two topics can be of the least interest to a serious and studious mood—sex and the dead.

—William Butler Yeats, 1936

Fucking and the Trinity are the two most interesting things to talk about.

—Joe Obenberger, adult entertainment lawyer, 2006

T his is my chance to be a "player." And a VIP. A VIP player. I have my fingers wrapped around the invitation and that's what it says: "Player VIP Party." Thanks to the invitation, and many gin and tonics, I can feel myself closing in on the American Dream of being a VIP player.

I am standing here in line facing the huge, black-suited security bravos with my two new friends, Zach and Anna. They're Internet porn entrepreneurs as well as being boyfriend and girlfriend with degrees from the University of North Carolina as fresh and crisp as just-picked heads of lettuce. Befitting our status, we have been placed in the VIP line, meaning we get first dibs on the elevators that will sweep us into the sky to Rain, the nightclub at the top of the Palms hotel and casino, a joint made famous by *MTV*'s *Real*

World Las Vegas and near-constant celebrity sightings: Paris, Britney, rap stars, sports guys—all dressed and looking sexy. Always sexy.

All around us young women are tucked into tight, short dresses or draped with cleavage-baring metal tops. Every one of them is perched on high, spiked heels. Their lips are glistening. They outnumber men. The men who are here, waiting in the line snaking down toward the hotel lobby, look like younger, thinner versions of Tony Soprano.

For the briefest of moments, I feel guilty as we VIPs ooze forward, inexorable as a glacier, while the men and women who have worked so hard to be worthy stand still in the other line, their eyes following us. I admit I haven't worked hard at all. Still, I have put on a nice pair of pants and a decent print shirt and my best leather flip-flops—an elegantly casual ensemble, I think, for Vegas in the summer when it is still ninety-something degrees outside at 11:00 p.m. Zach and Anna are pretty casual, too.

We shuffle forward, myself, Zach, Anna, and a few others from XBIZ, the Internet pornography producers convention we are attending where we obtained these VIP tickets. But just as I reach the enormous gatekeeper, a few steps from the elevator of happiness, he places his beefy hand on my chest.

"I'm sorry, sir. You can't go up without shoes."

He is not sorry. I know that. "But these are my best flip-flops." He shakes his head. I show my VIP pass only to learn how worthless "VIP" can be if you aren't wearing shoes. I have come so close. Now I am banned. I could go to a twenty-four-hour Wal-Mart a few miles away and pick up a pair of shoes, he suggests with sarcasm he would never use on LeBron James, or even K-Fed.

Zach and Anna feel sorry for me. With the wisdom of all that gin, we hatch a plot to have them go on up and then send Anna down with Zach's shoes because, man, nobody could ever possibly notice the switch. But I know in my heart this won't work. I can see into the elevator heading up into the sky, but I won't be allowed to launch.

I retreat into a tattoo parlor located in the hotel lobby near the elevator line. For twenty minutes I watch a boy and girl about eighteen pore over a book of sample art, trying to decide which design would be sexiest on her. The tattoo will cost a couple hundred dollars, cash she is clutching tightly in her fist. "Yeah, it's a lot of money," she says, "but it'll look so hot, won't it?" In a couple of years, she can show off the tattoo in a short, backless dress and her own set of heels, and if her makeup is just right the security guard won't send her away, and up there at Rain, or whatever the hot club of the moment is by then, she will be cool and sexy, sexy and cool, and then she will step into a glossy, candy-colored dreamworld.

Earlier tonight, while walking around the pool deck of the Hard Rock Hotel during an XBIZ cocktail party, I met a girl wearing a miniskirt slung perilously low on her hips, with a hem that did not quite cover her ass. Thin and coltish, she wore Lucite stripper heels and a crop top. I think she thought I could do something for her—impressed by the leather flip-flops and shirt, no doubt—because she made a point of introducing herself to me by saying, "Hi, I'm *con*tent!" with the accent on the first syllable.

"Uh, excuse me?"

"I'm *con*tent."

"Well, hello," I answered. And then we talked briefly about being *con*tent as opposed to con*tent*. She was not con*tent* yet, she said. So I asked her what she hoped to do, thinking I would hear something like "After I make some money in porn, I would like to go into commercial real estate."

"Oh!" she said excitedly, "I wanna be the next teen anal queen!"

I wished her luck, and as she walked away to introduce herself to more people in nice shirts I wondered at what point, when thinking of her life options, she decided against medical school or retail management or working in a tanning salon.

Now, though, watching this girl try to pick out just the right tattoo, and the line outside beginning to nudge forward, I think, Well, why not? After all, I was so happy to be in my VIP line. I wanted to be *con*tent along with all the other pretty people in our own little porn production, bigger and better than life, the glow of disco stage lighting illuminating our belief in American possibility.

Lately I have been spending a lot of time zigzagging across the country exploring sex. I am trying to square encounters like the one with America's future teen anal queen and what seems to me to be a hypersexual culture with the idea that we are also supposed to be in the middle of a new Great Awakening, a time when the nation is said to be turning to the Bible and medieval canon law as the preferred sex manuals, and a conservative view of sex disguised as "traditional values" has become part of the nation's political dialogue. The view from the window of this tattoo parlor makes me think we have come unzipped.

Several years ago, I was sitting in the Atlanta airport, waiting between planes, when my cell phone rang. An acquaintance I knew from my work writing for magazines was calling. She wanted to know if I would be interested in writing a column for MSNBC.com, the online news site financed by Microsoft and NBC through some Byzantine arrangement that has since been explained to me but which I still don't understand.

The column, she said, was about sex, to which I replied that I was not an expert in the subject. I quickly retracted that statement and said, "Well, I do know how it works. I mean to say that I'm not a sex therapist or anything."

No problem, she answered, because in the column they had in mind, I would not speak as an expert. I was to report, to contact experts, sometimes to find answers to questions from readers, sometimes to write short features. It shouldn't be that tough a job, really.

I debated with myself. I have been preoccupied with sex since I was a boy, or at least thought of myself as preoccupied, though, truth be told, I have never been sure if my own expended brain power qualified as preoccupation or just normal guy interest. I have occasionally worried. Maybe I fretted because I was raised Catholic or because other people keep their own similar worries under cover and I felt alone.

On the other hand, I think sex is a perfectly legitimate subject, as legitimate—maybe more—as politics (something else I have covered), which itself has become a sort of porn entertainment in recent years. So I have always been willing to write about it. In the early 1990s, for example, I had a phone conversation with an editor at *Details* magazine, then the very hip downtown New York young men's magazine of choice. The editor wanted me to do an edgy, transgressive first-person memoir, but as he ran down his list of desired topics, I began to feel hopelessly inexperienced.

"Ever had an STD?"

"Uh, not that I know of."

"Okay. Um, ever had a threesome?"

"Well, no, but I can, you know, do some research."

We struggled to come up with some exotic sexual episode until he finally gave up and moved on to other possible topics, saying, "Okay . . . Well, hey, have you ever killed a guy?"

Not long after that conversation, I became a columnist for *Glamour* magazine (where I am now a contributing editor) and sometimes wrote about sex, including some of my own experiences with dates and girlfriends. But I wasn't sure I wanted to take on the title of sex columnist.

Still, when the job was formally offered, I took it. I thought it would be fun. Not long after I started, though, I began to wonder just who was reading this column. People sent in hundreds of e-mails every week, and I was shocked at both the volume and the nature. It wasn't the language. Henry Miller hasn't shocked anybody since the sixties, and these days thirteen-year-old girls in shopping malls sit with bags of new clothes around their feet, each with a cell phone to her ear, successfully using *fuck* as several parts of speech, sometimes in the same sentence.

Rather, I was surprised that so many questions were about sex I always assumed was carried out in real life only by a tiny fringe in swanky apartments conveniently located near the British parliament. The transgressive sex *Details* wanted from me in the early 1990s didn't sound transgressive in the 2000s. If my readers were at all representative, I wondered how it could be that so many people existed in the same country that was experiencing a national freak-out over the possible baring of Janet Jackson's nipple. (I still can't make it out, and believe me, I've tried.) How could a country that said its football-watching children would have to go into therapy to recover from the trauma of seeing Janet's boob also be full of people demanding to know "the difference between same-room swing and soft swing"?

I also wondered why I didn't know the difference between soft swing and same-room swing and had to look it up. I wondered why so many people wrote to ask me—me!—if they were normal because they had an unnatural passion for women's shoes or stuffed animals, or being tied up and spanked, or if their penises took a dogleg to the left, or their labia dangled.

When they wrote, there was an element of striving in their tone, a fear of being left out of something. "My wife and I have heard that a lot of couples in their thirties are playing strip poker, truth or dare and other games that end with someone being naked, as well as skinny dipping with other couples/friends. Any idea if this is a fashionable trend or has it been going on for some time and we never knew it?" "I am interested in bondage and hear that there are secret bondage clubs someplace. Can you help me find them?" "My girlfriend saw a porno with female ejaculation, and now she keeps trying to do it. Is there any such thing?" "I hear Paris Hilton is into fisting, how do you do it?"

Like everybody else, I have an imagination. So of course, being somebody who thinks about sex, and worries about thinking about sex, I have wondered about all sorts of sexual possibilities, but it has almost never occurred to me to ask in any serious way about the more extreme variations. Now I was discovering that many people, from all over the country, from many walks of life, were not simply verbalizing their imaginations but trying to act on them, partly because they thought lots of other people were too. The fact that they were asking me was a little disconcerting, but I didn't get the idea they were loathsome, sad perverts. They were average people who were being bombarded, and so bombarding me, with their bewilderment, consternation, and above all curiosity about sex, including what we used to think of as deviant sex.

The wildest of wild sex seemed to have caught on with accountants, managers, truck drivers, cops, husbands, wives. Something was happening out there, I decided, and I thought it might be important. While I had been pretty confident I was sexually hip, or while I was fooled by what was supposed to be the "culture war" into believing Americans who were sexually exploring were a tiny number located on the coasts, the country had moved on. Average people, people whom we never got to read about, were quietly altering their own sexual lives and the sex life of the nation. They were people who did not testify before Congress or make movies or march with protest signs, but they were there.

I did a little research to see if my instinct was correct. The last scientific survey of the nation's sex life was formulated and taken nearly a generation ago and it didn't ask many questions like the ones I was getting.

Then I looked at Amazon.com. I typed *sex* into the search function and came up with 277,697 books with *sex* in the title or that have sex as their subject matter, many of them promising "mind-blowing" sexual experiences, often through oral sex or anal sex or new sex positions or the use of some tool or other. Lately, the books have been coming even harder and faster. *How to Make Love Like a Porn Star*, the story of porn actress Jenna Jameson, spent so much time on best-seller lists, "Jenna" became a mainstream brand in her own right. We have been treated to overheated and self-important sex books. The *New York Times* declared *The Surrender,* a book about anal sex by a former ballet dancer named Toni Bentley, one of the most notable books of the year in 2004. In 2003 *The Sexual Life of Catherine M* ("My favorite parts describe the gangbangs," wrote reviewer Dr. Susan Block in Alexander Cockburn's *Counterpunch*) made headlines, too.

The sex isn't just literary. Hardly. Gawker Media, parent of popular websites such as Wonkette and the eponymous media gossip blog Gawker, is appealing to young viewers with a site called Fleshbot. The site turns sex into camp with a snarky tone that clues readers into the escapades of, for example, Edouard and Virginie, a French couple documenting their sexual experiments, or a review of the new porn flick *Kill Girl Kill,* an installment in the ongoing "punk-porn" revolution.

Didn't know there was a punk-porn revolution? Never heard of *Art School Sluts* by auteur Eon McKai? It was one of the biggest-selling DVDs in the United States, though you'd never know it from the official entertainment industry listings. Hard-core productions like McKai's are making porn cool again among twenty-somethings—both men and women. Just how cool is reflected in the box office. The adult industry rakes in revenues of somewhere between $11 billion and $15 billion per year, on par with the "legitimate" film industry. We have arrived at the moment when a wannabe starlet and fashion icon like Paris Hilton finds her Q-ratings increased (becoming the Guess girl, being given her own TV series, starring in *House of Wax,* inspiring frequent media frenzies) after exposure in her own porn video.

Porn companies have gone public. They are traded on stock exchanges and covered by investment analysts, industry trade magazines, and the *Wall Street Journal.*

Americans are doing far more than just playing Peeping Tom in the privacy of their own homes. Big-box adult stores are opening in small towns across the country. In Seymour, Indiana, for example, the quintessential midwestern town of about nineteen thousand people made famous by singer John Mellencamp, the Lion's Den sells dildos and platform shoes, X-rated DVDs, and enough lube to supply an Exxon station. Such stores are popping up in places like Chillicothe, Abilene, and Newton, Iowa.

Some of the stores' customers may take their new gear and head for places like Las Vegas, Miami, and Chicago, where hundreds of middle-class men and women strut around hotel swimming pools in thong bikini bottoms during swingers' conventions. They are part of "the lifestyle," a booming phenomenon that has far outstripped 1970s wife swapping. Thousands of these couples now heed the old square-dance call to switch partners. Travel agencies, resorts, clothing companies, websites, dating services, and convention programmers take care of the details.

In Madison, Wisconsin, a "woman-centered" adult toy store called A Woman's Touch conducts regular classes, often using DVDs like *Bend over Boyfriend* as instructional aids to explain how to use a strap-on penis. Lou Paget, a Los Angeles–area woman who describes herself as "very Junior League," conducts no-holds-barred sex seminars that are so successful, she recently moved into a new manse in Beverly Hills—and all because she tells women how to play with a man's rectum.

Dominatrices and their submissive slaves spank their way through fetish soirees in San Francisco, Phoenix, St. Louis, Tampa, Denver. Seminars (Introduction to Flogging, Advanced Pony Play) held in hotel conference centers are standing room only. In cities all over the United States, rubberists slip into latex dresses, pants, and head coverings so total they have to breathe through snorkels, all in excited anticipation of, say, receiving a stern lecture from a woman dressed as a rubberized schoolmarm.

Sexual experimentation has become so mainstream that middle-class women now routinely write out checks at Passion Parties, Tupperware-style gatherings for the vibrator curious. Passion

Parties reports its income has grown by about 73 percent per year over each of the past five years—despite the bust on obscenity charges of a Passion Parties hostess in Burleson, Texas. (The charges were dropped.)

Wives and husbands are not only relying on professionally produced porn and toys manufactured by big companies to boost their sex lives: many have taken up new digital cameras to make porn of themselves. In a growing democratization of erotica, they are posting the images on websites, where they're available to everyone in the world with an Internet connection and the inclination. (One such site, Voyeurweb, claims to receive more than three million hits every day.) These fledgling Larry Flynts hope stimulated people will e-mail back, describing in great detail exactly how the experience of seeing a housewife naked in her kitchen in front of the open Wheaties box has sent them into masturbatory reverie.

Meanwhile, men and women are engaging in new forms of body modification, many inspired by porn. Products from Hair Care Down There help the pubically hair challenged achieve the porn-star look. Plastic surgeries for private parts have spread. One social researcher at UCLA has been studying the trend of "anal bleaching," the use of lighteners to reduce the contrast between the anus and the surrounding skin, so anal sex enthusiasts have pretty rectums.

And yet, at the very same time, the political rise of conservative Christians, many of whom regard sex outside marriage, pornography, fetish, even lust and masturbation, to be sinful, has supposedly become an equally significant cultural phenomenon. Preachers Jerry Falwell and Pat Robertson blamed sexual immorality—as they defined it—for the attacks of September 11, 2001.

Legislators of all stripes now feel they must declare their fealty to sexually conservative "moral values." Newt Gingrich knelt for absolution for his marital infidelity from preacher James Dobson on Dobson's radio show, *Focus on the Family.* Senator Barack

Obama talked up his religious credentials. Former New York mayor Rudolph Giuliani faced questions about his gay friends and his multiple marriages during his presidential campaign.

United States attorney general Alberto Gonzales declared war on pornography, forming an "obscenity prosecution task force" to go after not just child porn but also porn featuring consenting adults marketed to other consenting adults. "The welfare of America's families and children demands" it, he said. Conservative Christian lobby organizations like Concerned Women for America harangued the offices of U.S. attorneys and the FBI, demanding they prosecute more porn cases. A failure to do so may have been an element in the controversial firings of eight U.S. attorneys by Gonzales in early 2007, a move that eventually led to his own forced resignation.

Religiously motivated activists lied to schoolchildren about human sexuality, contraception, and sexually transmitted diseases in an effort to justify "abstinence-only" sex education. Conservative ministers pressured state legislatures and local prosecutors to shut down adult stores selling sex toys. Social conservatives resisted calls to vaccinate young girls against the human papilloma virus that causes cervical cancer, arguing that the vaccine would encourage promiscuity. Some states passed laws allowing pharmacists to refuse to fill prescriptions for birth control while other states passed laws making such refusal a crime.

At first all this sounded to me like the culture wars, but from where I sat as the new writer of a sex column, it seemed lust had quietly won and just failed to declare victory. There were occasional hints of that victory, though. An estimated 50 percent of evangelical pastors have viewed online porn and more than 20 percent of born-again Christians report they have been "addicted" to porn. The conservative Republican mayor of Spokane, who was a vociferous opponent of gay rights, sought out young male lovers via the Internet. Preachers Ted Haggard (drugs and gay sex), Jim

Bakker (booze and adulterous sex with a secretary), and Jimmy Swaggart (sex with hookers) all made headlines, but were thought to be merely high-profile exceptions.

Then one night I sat in a bar eating a pork chop and drinking a glass of scotch when a forty-year-old woman sat down next to me and we started to talk. She was a conservative Republican, she said, loved George W. Bush, and then, when I told her about my new job, she volunteered that "there's something just really great about sport fucking. You know, without any of the relationship bullshit."

I reckoned that contrary to what we have been told, American sex, at least in practice, doesn't have a political ideology or even a religious one, though noisy combatants keep trying to impose both. The Left is as guilty of this as the Right. At sexology conventions you are likely to hear more debates over politics than sex, like "Conceptualizing Sexual Rights," a seminar given at a conference I attended. It promised to "problematize polyamory as it is practiced in the United States by demonstrating how it cannot transform oppressive relationships and family structures without addressing racial and economic inequalities . . . [using] sociological and feminist theories of intersectionality and social justice to provide a critique of polyamory based on qualitative content analysis." Holy cow! I was pretty sure "problematize" wasn't even a word. It seemed to me sex and the way people explored it followed its own logic and was influenced more strongly by something I had yet to define.

I also admitted to myself that my curiosity was not just professional. My own thoughts have always been complicated by being a product of Catholic schools, having a long career as an altar boy, and growing up in a small town in Ohio. I was even, for a short while, the president of the Fairfield County Teenage Republicans. As any other Catholic altar boy teenage Republican will tell you, we think about sex a lot.

Even so, I was a late bloomer, sexually speaking. I will spare you the details of my first time except to say it involved a coed neighbor, a commercial break during *Saturday Night Live,* and a mumbled apology from me about her couch.

My wilder imaginings have usually been more like Einstein's thought experiments. I've engaged in no Bloomsbury literary group spouse swapping, no visits to Bangkok bars where dancers shoot Ping-Pong balls out of their vaginas. I do not own a leather codpiece, and I've never been whipped, gagged, fucked by two women, or arrested for lewd conduct.

I suppose I am libertarian when it comes to consenting adults doing sexually whatever it is consenting adults want to do, but I have never truly been a part of all this letting go and I wonder how other people manage it. I feel both admiring and apprehensive about them. It's fair to say I have always been a little conflicted.

So now I wanted to know who these sexual explorers were; if the scene had really changed as much as I thought, and if so, why so many people were doing what they were doing; what influences were inspiring them; and most important, if they were finding any happiness by doing it.

Sexual explorers don't usually seek publicity, and I wasn't much interested in the loudest voices. So much was happening among the people who could be my neighbors that the only way I could think of to answer my questions, to see if I was correct in my theory, was to go where they were and ask them.

That's how I ended up in Las Vegas meeting the next teen anal queen and nervously looking forward to points east, west, north, and south.

CHAPTER 1

The Sex Mogul of Hillsborough, North Carolina

I EXPLORE PHIL HARVEY'S EMPIRE

Pleasure is so difficult to come by in this culture. I say
fight for your right to enjoy your porn, your sexual fantasies, your masturbation and your orgasms.

—Betty Dodson, 2003

"He may just have been trying to shock me, but out of the
blue, over breakfast, he asked what I thought about
threesomes," Kathy Brummitt told me of a conversation
she had with her fifteen-year-old son. Kathy is a forty-something
brunette from central North Carolina with a short, sensible haircut, a little extra middle-aged weight, and a soft lilt to her
voice. She resembles my Catholic-high-school Latin teacher, the
one I used to torment by choosing to read aloud Roman narratives
about bathhouse prostitutes and by displaying Roman good-luck
drawings of erections.

So normally it would have been easy for me to picture Kathy
dropping a spoon into her heart-healthy Cheerios, grabbing her
minivan keys, and dragging her son to school to demand the

principal explain just what kind of education the kid was receiving. But I was having a tough time imagining Kathy's kitchen, because just as she launched into the details of how she handled this ticklish mothering challenge, I became preoccupied with a pretty brunette sitting naked and open-legged in a love swing.

A scrawny middle-aged guy with thinning black hair had his hands on the two straps attaching the swing to the ceiling of a dreamlike darkened room. He was naked, too, and gently pushing the swing back and forth about six inches at a time as he watched his erection slide in and out of the brunette. She, meanwhile, was wearing a big, satisfied smile. Though the scene on the video monitor just over Kathy's shoulder was running without sound, it had the effect of turning Kathy's voice into so much white noise. I thought I heard her say, "So I asked him why he wanted to know," but I couldn't be sure because—really—I was very impressed by the precision measurements that must have been involved in setting up the swing.

Think about it: What are the chances you could hang a swing from your ceiling while factoring in the critical height differential between a hard and a flaccid penis, the weight of the person in the swing, and a dozen other variables, without making multiple trips to Home Depot? How were those calculations made? Did they consult a carpenter? Was a laser device involved?

Meanwhile, Kathy was chattering away like a concerned PTA mom, seemingly oblivious to the video sex going on right behind her. "And it turned out that a friend of his wanted to have a threesome with my son's girlfriend and his girlfriend . . ."

I tried paying attention to Kathy, but now I couldn't help counting all the reasons why, and I mean never in a hundred million years, I could never have broached this subject with my mother.

"He really said this to you?" I asked, interrupting the story. "I mean, you two actually discussed threesomes?"

The guy on the video screen started moving the swing a little faster, bending his knees as if bearing down on a difficult task.

"Yes, of course," she said.

Then he arched his neck and stood up straight as if struck by lightning. His butt cheeks clenched. Apparently the love swing worked.

"And so then I asked him, 'Well, what do *you* think of three-somes?' I didn't want to appear shocked at all because I think he was testing me, though I do appreciate that he felt free to approach me with such a question, and he said, 'It might be okay.'"

Most mothers would have become hysterical at this point in the conversation, but not Kathy Brummitt. Thinking about three-somes is part of her job. I didn't realize it at first, but Kathy was manning a convention exhibit booth for an outfit called the Sinclair Intimacy Institute, and as I soon learned, she was the director of production on the love swing video, and others, too, for Sinclair, based in the unlikely location of Hillsborough, North Carolina. In other words, it's her job to hire people to have sex, hire other people to film those people having sex, and make sure the whole production looks classy.

"So you make porn."

Kathy smiled. No, she said, she doesn't consider this porn. She knows porn, and porn doesn't look or sound like this. This is education, erotic how-to, an exploration of fantasies and techniques that can forge a deeper bond between loving couples. The way she said all this made the love-swing video sound almost medicinal.

Besides, she argued, the movies she helps create are produced by Sinclair for its Better Sex series, those DVDs and tapes advertised in sports sections of newspapers all over the country, in women's magazines, even in highbrow publications like the *New York Times Book Review* and the *Atlantic*. The ads feature attractive people in each other's arms apparently in the beginnings of foreplay. They are who we would like to be, or at least who we wish our lovers would be. This kind of product, Kathy told me, is far removed from the pizza-delivery-boy-meets-horny-housewife world of porn.

The *Atlantic*!

To me, Kathy was one of the more interesting people at the sexology convention, which, as far as I was concerned, was mostly a bust. I had gone because I had my questions and thought perhaps I could get most of them answered in two or three days of Power-Point presentations. There were seminars and symposia and lectures from Women Going Topless on the Red Mile During the Stanley Cup Playoffs, Calgary, May–June, 2004, to Sex with Animals on the Caribbean Coast of Columbia (76 percent of adolescent boys do it, apparently, usually with a "she-ass"). But an awful lot of the dialogue was opinionated and political and not really about why so many of my readers wanted to know if it would be a good idea to have sex in a car for the entertainment of passing truckers.

One researcher's poster did address a question somebody had once asked me. My reader wanted to know about bukkake. I had never heard of bukkake, so I looked it up, promptly dismissed it as urban legend, and never answered. But as the poster explained, bukkake "is a Japanese term that refers to showering a receiver, male or female, with semen from one, several, or many men." I had seen porn and so I had seen the facial "cum shot," but according to the poster, bukkake was neither urban legend nor a pornography trope. It had "spread across the globe and . . . has gone from cult-like status to an accepted sexual practice." There were now organized bukkake groups that "have generated several popular schools and techniques" of bukkake practice and that have brought bukkake into the sexual "mainstream."

Though I was grateful for such bits of information, I preferred talking with Kathy because she was not a sexologist or a sexuality theorist. She was giving people what she said they wanted—more information on how to expand their sex lives in any number of ways, with any number of accessories. Still, I half expected her to be apologetic. Kathy just didn't fit the part of somebody who works in the sex industry. But she is proud, she said. Kathy believes that helping people find more and better sex is a noble purpose. She is a middle-class mom whose concern for others is expressed by making sex videos.

The DVDs seemed popular among the sex therapists, psychologists, and sociologists. Several stopped by as Kathy and I talked. They like the idea of visual aids, they said, because there is now so much curiosity out in the big world away from sexology conferences. People are asking questions they never asked before. Hearing answers from a therapist in an office about how to slide a butt plug into your ass or how to use your tongue on a woman's clitoris is a far less amusing experience than watching a well-made video with folks who look like more attractive versions of your neighbors.

"We're very successful," Kathy said. "We sell to people all over the country. Big cities, small towns, Midwest, South, West, everywhere."

When I asked her if it isn't difficult to find couples to perform for her, especially considering that the videos didn't seem to hire pros with porn-star names like Allysin Chaynes, she said no.

"It's not really hard at all." Some are indeed porn-industry wannabes, "but most are just couples who like having sex in front of cameras." Kathy had a way of making this sound like taking the dog for a walk. "And thank God for them. They help us promote better sexual health, better relationships."

Kathy made her work seem practically altruistic, but she is not exactly employed by a sexier version of the Maryknoll Sisters. Sinclair is a division of PHE, Phil Harvey Enterprises, of Hillsborough, a porn and sex toy empire founded by, naturally, Phil Harvey.

Despite her insistence that she was exactly what I had thought her to be—a mom, a businesswoman, a churchgoer—despite the way she regarded her work as being as American as the Wal-Mart greeter, I had to ask how others living in the geographical heart of the nation's evangelical revival react to her job. Do they stop her in the produce aisle at Food Lion to inquire how the dildo scene worked out that day? Or do they hug their child close and dash over to canned soups?

"We've all had the 'What do I tell my mother?' moment," she replied, referring to how she and her coworkers explain their careers to friends and family in North Carolina. "But everyone accepts that this is a job I love and that we do a lot of good for people."

"So how did you solve the threesome dilemma?" I asked. Her face lit up with the triumph of mothers everywhere who respond with, "If Jimmy jumped off the bridge, would you do it, too?"

"I just asked him, 'Well, how would you feel if your girlfriend wanted to be with you and another boy?'

"He said, 'Ewww! That'd be really gross. No way!' And so I said, 'I think there's your answer,' and that ended his flirtation with threesomes."

Yes, well, having once been a fifteen-year-old boy I was not quite as confident as Kathy that her kid's flirtation with three-somes was over for good. Actually, I couldn't help feeling a little sorry for him. He is being robbed of one of the three ways kids have to persecute parents. Other than drugs or absurdly fast cars with questionable provenance, sex is supposed to be the great tool of teen tormentors. Most wouldn't even have to come close to sug-gesting a three-way to send Mom dashing for the Valium. At least that's the way it was when I was a kid. Of course, none of us had a mom who was the Harvey Weinstein of sex.

"You ought to come down and see us," Kathy said cheerily as we parted. "We're just regular folks."

Which is how I have come to be sitting in Kathy's office sur-rounded by sex videos and dildos and talking about Jesus Christ. "He is my Lord and Savior," Kathy tells me. That is exactly the sort of statement that brought me here. Kathy seems to be a rich stew of apparent contradiction and the more I thought about traveling to PHE, the more I thought it might provide insight into what was going on around the country and who or what was making it happen.

PHE is the largest online and mail-order sex retailer in America, possibly the world, selling to over ten million customers. It comprises several divisions. The Sinclair Institute positions itself as the progressive, high-minded instructor in sexual happiness. Since 1994, it has sold over four million copies of its Better Sex videos. Its raunchy big sister, Adam and Eve, earns the bulk of the corporate income by selling sex toys, porn DVDs, and cheap lingerie. Adam Male markets to gay men. A video-on-demand arm sells streaming porn online. PHE also has a growing chain of retail store franchises. Adam and Eve Productions is a pornography powerhouse that finances and distributes over one hundred movies per year. Exactly how much money the entire company makes is impossible to know; it is privately held by Harvey and a few close associates. But sales in 2006 amounted to somewhere north of $109 million.

Sinclair is located apart from the rest of PHE in an office park of redbrick buildings vaguely resembling southern plantation architecture. Kathy drives to work, and most every morning she prays while she drives, giving thanks for a new day because it will present her with another opportunity to help people. She is descended from tobacco farmers who believed what they read in the Bible and they read that all people are equal before the eyes of God whether a body is white, black, or green. Everyone, they believed, is to be treated as you would wish them to treat you. Sometimes, during the days when Kathy was growing up, that created a little friction with neighbors who didn't always agree and that friction taught her that one did not always have to live by the prevailing thinking.

After college, Kathy became a buyer at Thalhimer's. For nearly a century, that venerable Virginia department store was an anchor to Richmond's downtown social and civic life. But then, like all other regional department stores, it succumbed to the merging giants of retail and the malling of America.

She wasn't looking to work in the adult industry; things just turned out that way. Kathy is a family person, the kind of woman who makes sweet potato pudding for Thanksgiving. (Long after I have left North Carolina, she will send me a recipe for chess pie, a heart attack on a plate worth dying for.) So she used to commute often from Virginia back home to North Carolina and when a girl-friend told her about a job opening at PHE, she saw it as a chance to come home for good.

Her story makes for a nice American homespun tale, but when I look around the room it is tough to reconcile the penises and porn and the "Jesus is my Lord and Savior" so I ask, "Uh, Kathy, you don't find all this a little strange?"

"Some people would find it strange, where I work, but I see no disconnect at all. Jesus may have lots of thoughts about how some people choose to use sex. But my personal mission fits nicely into Sinclair's vision of helping people."

This is the Sinclair mantra. I am in Hillsborough for most of three days and over and over again I am told about how they help others. From executives and employees at both Adam and Eve and Sinclair, I hear the phrase *permission giving*.

"We are in the permission business," Martin Smith, Sinclair's director of e-commerce, tells me when we meet in a conference room with Sinclair's president, Peggy Oettinger; Kathy; and whole-sale director Susan Yaeger Montani. "The idea I brought to the Web was, 'Let's approach this like we are the Pottery Barn of this space. And it worked because there are certain touchstones people are comfortable with . . . Our customers are older, richer, smarter than the average bear, especially online." What those people are looking for is an upgraded experience and better packaging, what Smith says is "a prettified version of adult, packaged in a way to give people permission to buy it."

When Phil Harvey first bought the original Better Sex video concept in 1991, the company tiptoed around many sexual topics because he wanted the new division to appeal to an upmarket, skittish demographic who would not patronize Adam and Eve or an adult book store. So Harvey named it the Better Sex Institute. Soon, though, Kathy realized that Better Sex didn't sound mainstream enough. Newspaper publishers, for example, rejected ads. So the name was changed to Chapel Hill Institute after the nearby college town, but then that sounded religious, like a Bible college. "Sinclair just sounded like a very dignified, clean, educational name to me," Kathy says, "so I said, 'Let's try Sinclair. We do know a Sinclair, Lloyd Sinclair,'" a famous sex therapist. "I called him up and said, 'Lloyd, would you be offended if we named our company Sinclair?'" She looks at me and says, "It could have easily been called the Alexander Institute." That's a double joke. Sinclair's biggest competitor is the Alexander Institute in Sherman Oaks, California. As far as I know, it is not named after me.

Sinclair's customers have a conflicted relationship with the sex industry. They want what it offers but don't like the idea of wanting it and what that wanting might mean for their self-image. They are both lured and repulsed by the taboo.

I understand. I feel perfectly comfortable at Sinclair, with the idea of Sinclair, and with Kathy and the others because they inhabit, or at least appeal to, my own sexual territory. That land is a safe place from which one can see the adventure without having to live it.

The truth is, I have always felt cowardly in this way. The summer after my senior year in high school I worked as a lifeguard at the swimming pool of a development of low-rent town-house apartments. People who lived there were newly divorced or had a boyfriend who'd been sent to prison or a spouse who'd died. The place was a living soap opera. One night, a few minutes after closing, two girls walked through the gate of the pool as I was cleaning up. They begged me to let them swim even though it was late, and when I said yes, they slipped out of bathrobes to show me how naked they were and how happy they were to be naked. They jumped into the pool, giggling.

"Come in, join us!" they shouted. I was a Catholic boy with an imagination. I knew I was being invited to a threesome.

"Quiet! I'll get fired!" I said, without thinking, almost instinctively. Yet I wanted, more than anything on this planet, to jump in and have sex with both of them. So what if I got fired! The summer was almost over, I was off to college soon . . . But I couldn't. I kept thinking of consequences. Why? To this day I am not sure, but it likely had something to with my belief, honed over years of Catholic education, and hundreds of hours serving Mass on my knees, that something bad always happened if you had too much fun. But I also think it had something to do with my being afraid of them—not literally, like I would come to harm, but afraid of being stuck, like I imagined they were stuck, going nowhere. In my young mind, vaginas equaled quicksand.

"Well, then, come back to our house. We've got beer."

"Uh . . ."

This was all I said. "Uh." I felt like a weenie then; I feel like one now.

I relish the idea of the taboo. Yet I have done much more thinking about it, more observing of it, than doing. Such detachment has allowed me to write about sex without being a sexual radical. This is another reason why I have come here and why I went to the sexology conference. If I just talk to all these people at this big company, I think, I will learn what I need to know. No muss, no fuss.

Sinclair is the shallow end of a swimming pool for those, like me, who are nervous about the deep end. When the first Better Sex videos sold in the 1990s, everyone at the company was pleased but quickly realized there was no "back end," nothing else to sell. Suddenly, they had a lot of customers and no more product. So they gave them products, three thousand of them. Though the name may sound serious and clinical, and though it advertises to educated elites, Sinclair offers many of the same items as Adam and Eve. But they all come with the Sinclair imprimatur, a brand that comforts the uneasy. Once you buy your educational videos, see the toys used, get used to seeing naked people having sex, you can buy the toys and XXX features like *Exxxstasy Island* and *Wicked Sex Party 7* from Sinclair.

"Sinclair videos give customers permission to buy the other items," Smith says.

"You're a gateway drug!" I say, laughing.

"You're right," Montani agrees. "Sinclair comes first, then people get softer features, then XXX, and then they are into bondage!" Montani is kidding a little, but not much. "That is the normal progression for the majority of our customers."

Often Sinclair customers start out feeling afraid of their own desires or their performance or their bodies. Customers often ask the question I most often get: "Am I normal?" "That is why our business exists," Kathy says. "People want to know if they are okay. Is it all right? Is there something wrong with this? Am I not doing something right?" In the Sinclair world, the answer is always "You're fine. You have permission."

Sometimes the Sinclair folks are surprised at what they are giving permission for. Ultimately, almost nothing is taboo. Mark Schoen, the PhD sexologist who directs the action on the videos, told me earlier that oral sex techniques were considered edgy when the division first started and that Sinclair told itself it would never make an anal sex how-to. *The Better Sex Guide to Anal Pleasure* was issued in 2005. Then came a "power play" video. Now, with Sinclair videos, you can learn how to shave your pubic hair, give erotic massages, use sex toys, have sex in "unusual places," try out sadomasochism, indulge in "guilty pleasures."

"My wife and I bought this video and it opened up a lot of doors," one satisfied customer wrote. "She finally let me cum all over her face. Thanx [B]etter [S]ex video series!"

To me it sounds as if Sinclair might be manipulating demand, that perhaps people don't really want anal sex, that they have just heard a lot about anal sex because Sinclair sold them videos with anal sex in it, thus piquing interest for a new product it could produce and sell. How else is a company like Sinclair going to grow except by giving people the idea that everybody else is having more fun?

But when I suggest this to Smith, he admits he and Sinclair often have no idea what the hell is going on in America's sex culture. "My job is to constantly, with different indexes, figure out what people are doing on our website and what they are doing out in the world so I can take that and put it on our site." Sinclair follows, it doesn't lead, and Smith is often shocked by where his customers want to go.

"People are asking for more and more experimental stuff. That told me I have to let them ask questions," and so he created a forum to help build Sinclair's own online community. "I was very surprised at some of the questions I got. It's incredible what people will ask you, like in your column. I get these long notes about what people are saying on the site and I am going, 'Oh my God!'"

This goes to show you, Smith, a Vassar graduate, tells me in his best business-school jargon, that "anything will become a commodity if you give it enough time. What was a boundary yesterday is today's commodity."

Sinclair is trying to figure out the landscape just as I am. "It's no longer Donna Reed out there," Montani says. "People are talking about it. No more missionary position in the dark. And they all think the next guy is having better sex than me, so I had better figure it out."

"Well, it's Britney Spears and her private parts exposed!" Kathy speculates, sounding once again like a concerned mother.

"You gotta get technology in there somewhere, because it is technology that has brought it into every home," Smith interjects with his own theory.

"Yeah," Montani says. "It is, like, in your face whether you want it to be or not."

"But you think you are absolutely mainstream?" I ask.

"Yessir!" Oettinger, a tall, thin woman about sixty, says quickly in her thick southern accent. "We are absolutely mainstream America. Our product line is progressing, but I do not know if it is because people are progressing or if we are driving the culture. I would say the culture is driving me."

Starting about 11:00 a.m. the calls begin flooding into the Adam and Eve customer service desk, an all-day, everyday operation situated on the second floor of PHE's modern three-story building in another office park not far from Sinclair. I sit with headphones on my head and listen to a twenty-four-year-old man order "Sistas" along with the Azz and Tits combo pack, which includes *Booty Talk 45*, *Nice Azz/Tits*, *New X-Rated Sistas*, and a free gift item, *Black Poles and Dark Holes*, all for just $19.95.

A man from Massachusetts buys *Over 40 and Horny as Hell*. A Michigan woman requests Eve's Pearl Diver vibrator as a replacement for a defective Eve's Pearl Diver vibrator she bought a couple of weeks ago. "This one toy doesn't seem to like me," she tells Mary, the operator. "And it is my favorite one, too! They quit after one use."

A sixty-one-year-old Florida man selects several DVDs and a vibrator, and wants them quickly, please. But when Mary asks for his credit card number, he wants her to hold while he calls his wife on his cell phone. "What, honey?" Mary and I can hear him saying. "Yeah, Adam and Eve. Okay." Then to us, "Four one seven . . ."

Often, Mary says, the husband orders without the wife's knowing. The company then sends the catalog to the house, and the wife finds it and calls customer service. "They cuss us out, and say, 'I go to church, God damn it!'"

As if on cue, a Muslim man calls. "Uh, could you please take my name off the mailing list? My wife doesn't like me getting the catalog."

A sixty-three-year-old man in Delaware orders *Black Chunky Chicks 4*, *Hip-Hop Hooters*, and *Pure Pussy 4*, adding a polite "please, ma'am." Mary offers him a selection of a free gift—all customers who buy get something free—and she lists the offers like a tired waitress rattling off the domestic beers. "Okay, you can choose from *Girl Gasms 2; Over 30 and Dirty; Tight and Fresh Part 3;* and *Sistas 21,* with over two hours of mocha lesbian heaven and plenty of booty lickin', or *Booty Call,* with over four solid hours of hot chocolate asses." This guy goes for mass, choosing the four solid hours.

Mary, in case you are wondering, is black. She says she blushed the first few days she worked here, but doesn't anymore.

A seventy-year-old man from a small town in Illinois chooses a *Buckleroos* DVD, a gay title, and a Senso Stroker masturbator. Oh, and how about *Summer in the City?* With the freebie *Dick to Dick* thrown in, he's charged $79.35.

They just keep calling, one after another. A fifty-year-old man in Grosse Point, Michigan, buys Jenna Jameson porn. A fifty-six-year-old Colorado man buys $110 worth of porn and vibrators for himself and his wife. A twenty-seven-year-old woman who calls from Oklahoma wants the catalog so she can start ordering. An Ohio man wants a refund. A thirty-five-year-old man in Florida wants a masturbator sleeve. A sixty-five-year-old New York man calls in a DVD order for his wife: *Pound Cakes, Pussy Worship,* and *Black and White Volume 2.* A sixty-two-year-old California man orders a copy of the Sinclair Institute's Sensual Exploration series and *Great Sex Positions* for $65.75 and requests it be sent Express Mail so it will arrive by the weekend.

Nobody calls from New York City, San Francisco, Dallas, Chicago, Los Angeles. I have been wondering why, when I asked if I could listen in, managers eagerly agreed. Maybe this is why. I am listening to what media and politicians usually call "middle America" and listening to their voices demand what the sex industry is selling. If they are representative, then the mainstream really has shifted and the notion of community standards by which obscenity cases are supposed to be judged has shifted, too. Adam and Eve has an obvious interest in making this case.

Over the past decade, two famous obscenity trials—one in Ohio and one in Utah—demonstrated how far a community's perception of itself varied from private reality. During the case in Cincinnati, the local newspaper, the *Cincinnati Enquirer*, investigated Hamilton County's own community standards and found that Adam and Eve had sold twenty-six thousand X-rated videos to county residents in 2000. Adam and Eve had twenty-eight thousand different customers in the county. In January of 2001, 182,000 people living in the greater Cincinnati area visited an online porn site.

In 1996 two small video stores in Utah County, Utah, one of the most conservative counties in the United States and home to Brigham Young University, Mormonism's version of Notre Dame, were raided by sheriff's deputies after four thousand people signed a petition complaining that the stores were selling obscene materials.

Kay Bryson, the Utah County district attorney, called pornography one of the world's "misery-creating features" and "worthless." One of his assistants called porn "nothing more and nothing less than vile concoctions of scum, sleaze, and sludge." Bryson was sure the confiscated video titles used to accuse the owner of the stores were in no way an accepted part of the community standards of Utah County. "I know essentially what people in Utah County are all about."

At trial the defense attorney, a devout Mormon, revealed that Utah County residents ordered up nearly twenty thousand adult movies from one satellite TV provider, that the local Marriott sold about three thousand X-rated movies every year, and that the stores' owner rented or sold adult videos to about four thousand customers, a number equal to the number of petition signers. After a hung jury, Bryson insisted on trying the case again. The second trial ended in a quick acquittal in 1999, but the owner was bankrupt by then. Bryson was subsequently voted out of office after it was revealed that during an ugly divorce from his wife, a state legislator, he had used county-owned spy equipment to install a camera in a condominium she owned and where she was meeting a man who Kay insinuated was a paramour.

Phil Harvey had his own run-in with Utah. In 1986 Adam and Eve was raided by law enforcement officials from the U.S. government, the state of Utah, and the state of North Carolina as part of then Attorney General Edwin Meese's war on porn. Meese's campaign had proved effective at first, because twenty years ago most adult retailers were mom-and-pop operations or small-time businessmen who had neither the stomach nor the finances for a fight. By 1986, though, Adam and Eve was a multimillion-dollar business big enough to punch back.

The government figured it had an easy way to shut Harvey down by having the state of North Carolina prosecute him in nearby Alamance County. Bible Belt conservatives would be eager to convict, prosecutors thought. But they hadn't reckoned on Harvey's being considered a good neighbor and an important employer. Some of his employees had deep roots in the county. The jury also responded to Harvey's defense attorneys, who framed the case in terms of the government's trying to tell people what they could read or watch. It took the jury about five minutes to reach a not guilty verdict.

Then the Justice Department decided to file charges simultaneously in multiple districts around the country, cherry-picking the most conservative communities, including Utah. The idea was to make fighting the charges so prohibitively expensive that Harvey would have to give up and plead or lose his business altogether.

But Harvey, a cantankerous libertarian at heart, refused. The war between the government and Adam and Eve lasted eight years and cost Harvey $3 million, but in the end, after Harvey filed a civil suit against the government over its tactics, and a federal circuit court slapped the Justice Department for its behavior, saying, "We conclude that appellants satisfied their burden of showing that the indictment is the tainted fruit of a prosecutorial attempt to curtail PHE's future First Amendment protected speech," the Justice Department caved in return for a token face-saving guilty plea from Harvey to a minor mail offense in Alabama. He paid a fine. Meanwhile, Adam and Eve's sales grew at a rate of 20 percent per year over the period of the legal war.

Knowing that history, and the products they sell, you would think the people who work here would shun the conventions of respectability, but they are boring. Not in a bad way. They are all very nice and have given me a surprisingly open welcome considering they have no idea what I will say about them or their company. It's just that I was sort of hoping for dark personalities or women running around in thong bikinis. Something.

But Martin Smith grew up in Greenwich, Connecticut, the son of a partner in Pete Marwick Mitchell, then a big international accounting firm. He graduated from Choate prep school, then Vassar, and went to work for Procter & Gamble. He started a little Internet business. Then he came to PHE.

Mark Schoen, a native of Brooklyn, taught junior high school and coached hockey in New York until, almost by default, he began teaching sex education. He received a PhD and became an expert at creating sex education materials, including films.

Peggy Oettinger used to be a kindergarten teacher. She has three granddaughters.

Susan Montani worked for Ralph Lauren and a couple of cosmetics makers.

Katy Zvolerin, the director of public relations for Adam and Eve, is the daughter of an assistant high school principal and the secretary of the First Cumberland Presbyterian Church in Cleveland, Tennessee. She graduated from the University of Tennessee with a degree in journalism and PR. Now Katy writes press releases like this:

Adam & Eve Pictures is pleased to present exclusive contract star Austyn Moore in her naughtiest role yet! In Headmaster 2, all-American Austyn crosses the line! See her as a promiscuous schoolgirl who seduces teacher Tommy Gunn with her sweet lips on his cock. Spanking only makes her worse! Sister Roxanna Hall must do penance after pleasuring herself with a horny priest. She seeks forgiveness for the multiple orgasms she receives . . . and he blesses her with his own holy liquid!

The second night I am in town, I drive over to Montani's home, a big place surrounded by woods, for some dinner. Candida Royalle, a 1980s porn star turned director and producer, happens to be there with a couple from Holland who design Candida's line of Natural Contours vibrators, one of the biggest-selling items for Sinclair and Adam and Eve. Candida and I sit on Montani's couch and talk, taking time every few minutes to look at a drawing made by Montani's little girl, who runs upstairs excitedly, retrieves a new picture, and runs downstairs to show us. If it weren't for the fact that I had seen a few of Candida's movies in college—I remember one about a woman's prison and another one, called *Ultraflesh*, about an alien female coming to earth—I could not distinguish this gathering as being at all different from any other group of smart executive types figuring out marketing strategy. Later, we'll go out to Fuddruckers and have hamburgers.

Montani walks in and tells me about a recent PTA meeting at her daughter's school. "There were all these things you can sign up for and so I had to write down any special skills I had for possible job sharing and when you can come in and talk to the kids about what you do for a living. Well, there was a brand-new teacher and I was standing next to her and she handed me the clipboard and said, 'Can you please read down the list what the different things are so I can explain them?' When I got to the job share part, half the parents in that room fell out of their chairs." The thing was, Montani has told exactly two people at the school where she works. "So in the two years we have been at that school, half the room had discussed what I do for a living. It does make me feel odd sometimes."

Then she looks at me. "How about you?"

"What about me?"

"If you look around at our company, 90 percent of the people who work there, you could categorize them as a rebel. They have rebel characteristics. Just think of yourself. You are writing about this because you are a rebel somewhere and because it is a little bit taboo and you are a part of this cause."

I am? I generally don't like causes, but if I were part of the cause Montani is referring to, what cause is it exactly? I'm not sure I want to be enlisted into Montani's cause. I'm the guy who wouldn't jump in the deep end with two cute, naked girls.

I can't decide if I am a rebel, but I know Phil Harvey is. Like the others, though, you'd never know it by looking at him. He is a most unlikely-looking pornographer: thin, a little careworn, mostly bald. His narrow lips make him look as if he is in a permanent bad mood, but he has a wry sense of humor. He dresses like a haggard college professor, and for years Oettinger, who has been with PHE almost since its inception, has been trying to get him to buy a better car.

For me, the quintessential Harvey moment arrives when I drive to Adam and Eve's headquarters on my second day in town and pass Harvey as he walks along the side of the road picking up trash. Adam and Eve sponsors one of those clean road campaigns, and Harvey, who is sixty-eight years old and runs a company that earns over $100 million per year, takes his civic duty seriously. (A few months after my visit, the Hillsborough / Orange County Chamber of Commerce will name PHE business of the year, citing PHE's "foundation club" membership and "its good corporate citizenship and generous support of so many worthy causes in Orange County.")

Harvey is the son of a farm implement manufacturer in Illinois and a mother who descended from Chicago aristocracy. When he was twelve, the family moved to Connecticut. Harvey attended the elite Phillips Exeter Academy, then Harvard. He enrolled in the Peace Corps, served in the army instead, and then joined CARE. He spent five years in India feeding children and coming to the conclusion that ever more food from the West was not going to solve the hunger problem there. Not only did the charity serve to depress prices of local farm products, but Indians kept making more Indians and more mouths to feed. What India really needed, Harvey decided, was better family planning.

He enrolled in the School of Public Health at the University of North Carolina in Chapel Hill to study for a master's degree in family planning. There he met Dr. Tim Black, a British physician who had worked in Papua New Guinea. Together the two of them decided on a social marketing project to see if they could use free-market forces to promote and distribute condoms. At the time, federal law could be construed to make selling condoms by mail in the United States a crime. But they obtained permission from the university and Harvey made the project part of his thesis.

The two birth control entrepreneurs placed smart-alecky ads in college newspapers ("What Will You Get Her This Christmas . . . Pregnant??") and were a little surprised to discover that the project made a profit. They started a charitable organization called Population Services International (PSI) and funded it partly through the for-profit business they dubbed Population Planning Associates (PPA). Harvey and Black began adding other products to the PPA lineup, like books on contraception and a couple of nudie magazines, then other goods that might appeal to men, including ship-building kits and barbecue grills. But porn and lingerie and condoms were far more popular. Eventually, the partnership dissolved and PPA became Adam and Eve. PSI still exists. It branched out into other public health areas and is active in the third world. Ashley Judd serves on its board, as do other notables like Frank Carlucci, former chairman of the Carlyle Group, the private investment company that has minted money for George H. W. Bush, James Baker, and former British prime minister John Major, among others.

Harvey started a second charity, Washington, D.C.–based DKT International. It focuses exclusively on family planning and sexually transmitted diseases. He still serves on the DKT board. DKT receives grants from the U.S. government. ("That was what was so shocking to the feds when they came in," Oettinger told me, referring to the 1986 raid and subsequent prosecutions. "Over here they are trying to put him in jail, and over there they are giving him grants for his nonprofit work!") DKT also receives funds from the Bill and Melinda Gates Foundation, but in a very real way America's hunger for porn and sex toys finances contraception in Africa, Latin America, and Asia because PHE donates 25 percent of its profits to DKT.

Harvey has been through far too much to ever be the slightest bit apologetic about the way he has lived his life. I sit in his office—really, you'd think a guy making as much money as he does would get a decent office; this place is tiny, full of papers strewn everywhere, and the desk and the chair look like cheap rental stuff—and ask him about being an Ivy League do-gooder turned sex industry kingpin, and it quickly becomes clear that Harvey has never seen any point in being embarrassed. He is a defender of American liberty, a stance that jibes with his libertarian instincts and his support of the Cato Institute, the libertarian think tank (though he is a registered Democrat). He was never condemned by his family; his father actually owned a stake in the business during its early days. His mother chose to ignore it. "If I said to her, 'Gee, Mom, we are selling a lot of vibrators or sex videos,' she would have talked about something else."

The truth is, being in a controversial business is a kick, because it fosters a feeling of camaraderie, a "siege mentality. We all recognize we are doing something controversial and that our mothers and grandmothers might very well not approve, and everybody handles that in a different way, but we all have that in common."

All the good feelings come easier when the company is doing well, and lately it has been doing very well. PHE's growth slowed as it began to face what Harvey calls "fierce" competition from online retailers, but it has been able to bump sales by about 9 percent annually. "Over the past two or three years there has been a rapid acceleration in the demand for things that buzz. Overall we probably sell between $25 and $30 million worth of toys per year, a lot more than five years ago."

Sinclair has helped. "Sinclair's positioning in the marketplace removes some of the barriers a lot of people feel toward sexually explicit materials," he says, and then repeats the code phrase: "It is permission giving." For example, he says, Sinclair is able to place its ads in *Ladies' Home Journal* because the approach is softer than that of Adam and Eve, though these days, he tells me, "If you take the six hundred thousand to seven hundred thousand women who buy from Adam and Eve," it is not necessarily true that women need a softer approach anymore. "Women want more explicit these days."

After being in the business for thirty-five years, Harvey sees the sexual landscape changing more rapidly than ever. "There are now fifty thousand porn titles cranked out of Southern California every year. The national sexual dialogue has changed. Like the appetite for sex toys."

The company is finding itself having to sprint in order to keep up. For most of its existence, Adam and Eve sold only what

Harvey considered mainstream porn. In fact, he was chagrined during the conflict with the government to find that some S&M materials had found their way into his inventory. After that, he created an advisory board to screen out what it regarded as inappropriate or unhealthy depictions of sex.

"We still have the same standards with some interesting variations," he says. "Like tattoos. There was a time when we would not sell anything where the people were tattooed. Well, we'd be out of business now if we did that." In recent years, Adam and Eve has had to assert its power to tone down the work of porn producers and it is trying to figure out a new balance in depicting, say, fetish, which Harvey says "is much more common now."

"The last ten years have certainly seen much greater availability of some of the really bad stuff, violent stuff, some animal stuff. I am not sure why . . . We can sell bondage material if it is clearly consenting. But we have to try hard to explain that to directors." Earlier I had visited with an employee who filters porn titles. His discard box had more DVD packages in it than his "acceptable" box.

Harvey is extremely thoughtful on the subject of sexuality— he's a very smart guy in general—but he can't fully explain the surge of interest in, or acceptability of, his products. He has his theories, though.

Information is one. As more information about sex filters through society, people decide they want some of what they hear about. "If you have a woman who was told for twenty-five years, 'Just lie there; wait until he is finished,' well, she may develop a desire to have an orgasm once she discovers such things exist. Knowledge can precede desire."

Schoen, the educator, told me something similar. We are becoming more sophisticated about sex with more information, he said, and so we become more open to different varieties of it.

"Like espresso and lattes?" I asked.

"Yeah!" he said. "There's a coffee shop on every corner in the country now and so people want better coffee."

Pornography can help people discover: "'Oh, I did not know you could have sex that way, from behind or standing up or sixty-nine.' That could become a desire," Harvey says.

Too much knowledge is exactly what has alarmed many others. Back in the 1980s, when Adam and Eve was considering a move to Alamance County before it was prosecuted there, Harvey ran into strong opposition stirred by a local minister who told his congregation that such a move would pollute the community. "Would you feel your wife and children were safe?" he asked. It worked, and Harvey chose Hillsborough in Orange County. At the 1986 trial, the same minister stated that employees of such a company could never "be good citizens of our community" because they would be so corrupted by the influence of porn it would change them. The information would make them dangerous.

To Harvey, this smacks of a wish to maintain social control. "I think there are issues of power going in many, many ways. The crowd that is really afraid of this is afraid because it has to do with loss of control. Loss of control is a part of sex. It is one of the things most of us find is good about it." At first he seems to be referring to sexual power—we're talking about bondage—but he is also referring to something much more profound.

I have had enough years of Catholic education to recall St. Augustine's exhortations to keep one's mind disciplined and aimed at God from whom all good emanates. Destiny is in God's hands, not ours, and it is the sin of hubris to think otherwise.

But if sex is controlled by each person individually, church and state have lost an element of collective control. Pope Paul VI referred to this forty years ago when he issued *Humanae Vitae*, a document I had to study in school to learn church teaching on contraception and sex. "No member of the faithful could possibly deny that the Church is competent in her magisterium to interpret the natural moral law," he wrote. "It is in fact indisputable, as Our predecessors have many times declared, that Jesus Christ, when He communicated His divine power to Peter and the other Apostles and sent them to teach all nations His commandments, constituted them as the authentic guardians and interpreters of the whole moral law, not only, that is, of the law of the Gospel but also of the natural law. For the natural law, too, declares the will of God, and its faithful observance is necessary for men's eternal salvation."

The church literally controls your sex life. Moral order was established by God, Pope Paul wrote, and so husbands and wives "are not free to act as they choose in the service of transmitting life, as if it were wholly up to them to decide what is the right course to follow. On the contrary, they are bound to ensure that what they do corresponds to the will of God the Creator. The very nature of marriage and its use makes His will clear, while the constant teaching of the Church spells it out . . . Just as man does not have unlimited dominion over his body in general, so also, and with more particular reason, he has no such dominion over his specifically sexual faculties, for these are concerned by their very nature with the generation of life, of which God is the source."

Contraception, erotica, sex outside marriage—Harvey's reasons for being in business—challenge this authority, and the authority of the state, too, because the family unit is the keystone of the state. "Everything therefore in the modern means of social communication which arouses men's baser passions and encourages low moral standards, as well as every obscenity in the written word and every form of indecency on the stage and screen, should be condemned publicly and unanimously by all those who have at heart the advance of civilization and the safeguarding of the outstanding values of the human spirit. It is quite absurd to defend this kind of depravity in the name of art or culture or by pleading the liberty which may be allowed in this field by the public authorities."

Richard Nixon put it another way. "If an attitude of permissiveness were to be adopted regarding pornography, this would contribute to an atmosphere condoning anarchy in every other field—and would increase the threat to our social order as well as to our moral principles."

Interpreting "natural law" to make it a bedrock of human behavior is a core effort of neoconservatism just as it is for the Catholic church and other religions. Adherence to natural law (nobody really seems able to prove it exists) ensures social stability. Defiance of it invites chaos.

This is how Harvey explains the seeming contradiction that has sent me on the road, the question of how we can be an increasingly hypersexual culture even in the face of the supposed power of "moral values" crusades.

"So you have on one hand an increasing interest in sexual stimulation, whether it is pornography or vibrators and dildos, and on the other hand an increasing fear on the part of people who are really frightened by sex and their own sexuality who want to stop all that."

"Do you suppose," I ask him, "that the increased fear makes for louder protests?" Since people who watch porn or buy sexual devices for use in their own sex lives don't typically march with signs or petition the government, the field is left to those who oppose, no?

"I think it is possible. It is true, certainly possible, that what you call hypersexual, the increasing sexual stuff in our culture, is related to this issue of the far right, that Paris Hilton washing a car makes people who are afraid of sex more determined and more afraid and therefore more vocal. That seems to be a reasonable hypothesis: More sexual content in American lives makes some people more afraid and determined and energetic."

Perhaps, I think, they see a great unzipping. We are unzipping ourselves from restrictions imposed by society or religion or family, and we let loose: with practically an infinite number of ways to express desire, we are dashing toward some indeterminate future looking for an equally indeterminate happiness. But is sex doing the unzipping, or is something else unzipping sex?

I still can't help wondering about the influence of salesmanship. Could it be that all this "permission giving" is really driving the sexual culture, that we want more sex in our lives because Harvey's industry has sold us like Professor Harold Hill sold River City?

He gets his back up at "the idea that corporate America is some-how creating consumer slaves. That's nonsense." I haven't really suggested that corporate America is creating slaves to sex, neces-sarily, but I wonder if our sexual desires are anything like my own jones for a huge flat-screen TV with a Bose home-theater system even though I don't watch all that much TV and my old set works fine. I am also taken aback by his use of the phrase *corporate America.* I have never really thought of the sex industry the way I have thought of General Electric or Hewlett-Packard or the Union-Pacific Railroad. But of course it is part of corporate Amer-ica and has been for some time now, woven into the fabric of busi-ness in ways that go unacknowledged.

Obvious examples are easy to come by. Now that most travelers own cell phones and avoid the minibar, in-room hotel spending at the nation's largest lodging companies is powered by adult movie fees. Almost 40 percent of DIRECTV, one of the nation's largest satellite television services, is owned by Rupert Murdoch's giant media group, News Corp. It offers Hustler TV, Playboy TV, and four other adult services. Competitor Dish Network also carries adult channels. Cable companies like Cox, Time-Warner, and Comcast offer X-rated shows, too. Cerberus Capital Management, which bought Chrysler from Daimler-Benz in 2007, invested in the publisher of *Penthouse* magazine and helped keep it afloat in 2003 while former vice president Dan Quayle, a champion of "basic American values," now chairman of Cerberus, was a board member.

Supposing Harvey is correct, and that he simply opens doors by giving us permission, and that we can walk through the doors or not, I ask if he thinks we are any happier for doing so.

"Are we happier with this stuff than without it? Some people are and some people are not." Well, perhaps I have asked an obvious question so he has given me an obvious answer. "This is not the most important thing that defines happiness," he continues. His business is about fantasy. It is escape, a temporary thing.

"One of the reasons we almost always see large dicks in porn flicks is because people accept this as fantasy. If you wanted to make men feel good, you would have small dicks. I have suggested to some of our people here from time to time that there must be a niche market for small dicks, and they all say, 'Come on! They gotta be big!'"

We only achieve happiness when we have sense of accomplishment, Harvey says. "Only in overcoming obstacles of various kinds do we get any sense of fulfillment and satisfaction in life. A chess player does not get much satisfaction out of checkers."

Masturbation has always seemed a lot like checkers to me—fun but not very challenging.

Sexuality, Phil tells me, when it's good, can be a way of asserting or a "way of submitting oneself to the power of another person. That has strong psychological components, not just enhancing intimacy but ratifying a love between two people. The bond is important in life. Sex ratifies the bond."

When Harvey says this, I am struck by something Susan Montani and Candida Royalle said as we were talking in Montani's living room. Taboo is good, they said. "Doing something slightly taboo—don't you think when you do it, when you share that with a partner, it is like a special new link, a secretly shared thing?"

"Porn is not a huge taboo anymore," Candida said, "but it is still a taboo and that helps it retain its sexiness."

"So what happens," I asked, "when nothing is taboo?"

CHAPTER 2

What Would Jesus Do?

I Say Hallelujah as Christians Kiss the Missionary Position Good-bye

The new moralism in this country has been growing for the past two decades. The awakening is manifesting itself in the change in the national life-style.

—Jerry Falwell, 1986

L ike a lot of good Christian men, Joe Beam has wrestled with sex and been pinned to the mat. That was a while ago, when Joe was younger, but he still feels the pain of his defeat every day. So he has had the staff of the Four Points Sheraton in San Diego remove the TV from his hotel room. Joe likes TV. He'll catch *Boston Legal* anytime he can. But he'd rather miss a favorite program than expose himself to the seduction of the Adult Desires channel.

Joe Beam is a Christian preacher. He prefers terms like *teacher* or *educator*, but he's a preacher by training and inclination. Once his ministry was in an actual church, a Church of Christ, a group so conservative it seriously debates the propriety of music accompanying hymns and insists that Christians who join the Methodists or the Baptists, say, aren't really Christians at all because the Bible is the literal word of God and in the Bible there are no sects and those poor, misguided apostates are going to hell for sure.

Now, though, Beam runs an outfit based in Franklin, Tennessee, called Family Dynamics, part business, part personal mission, aiming to "build stronger marriages" through "interactive, highly effective faith-based marriage and family seminars." He spent his Friday night here presenting the first part of his Love, Sex, and Marriage lesson to a group organized by a local United Church of Christ congregation, an evangelical bunch who are not the same as the Church of Christ, though the distinction doesn't really matter to Joe. He says the same things to any conservative evangelical group who will have him. And last night, when he finished the talk on love, he did what he usually does when he's on the road. He went back to his room, called his wife, Alice, at home in Tennessee, read a little, went to bed.

No TV.

I have come to see Joe because he aims to help his fellow conservative Christians cope with the culture made possible—or capitalized on—by the likes of PHE and because he represents the other side of the contradiction I have been trying to explain to myself, the way we seem to be ever more lusty even while we are supposed to be ever more puritanical. The problem of how to cope with lust has tortured Christians for two thousand years, so I wonder if the estimated hundred million or so mostly conservative evangelical Christians in this country have come to grips with what Joe himself calls our "hypersexual" culture, and what strategy Joe will give them aside from condemning it. After all, if 50 percent of preachers are visiting porn sites, and 20 percent say they have been "addicted" to them, it stands to reason the congregants are struggling to navigate, too. Finally, I hear Joe Beam can make the Bible sexy. That's something I have to see.

This morning Joe is taking his time. He hasn't yet arrived in the large white tentlike structure the hotel has attached to the rear of

its building to accommodate a large group. But about two hundred church members have, and they are singing an old-timey
hymn.

There's not a friend like the lowly Jesus,
No, not one! No, not one!
None else could heal all our soul's diseases,
No, not one! No, not one!
Jesus knows all about our struggles,
He will guide till the day is done;
There's not a friend like the lowly Jesus,
No, not one! No, not one!
No friend like Him is so high and holy,
No, not one! No, not one!
And yet no friend is so meek and lowly,
No, not one! No, not one!
Jesus knows all about our struggles,
He will guide till the day is done.

And smiling. They are all smiling.

The song ends and Jeff Wadstrom, a local church poobah, walks
up to the elevated platform and stands behind a lectern. He greets
us and says he hopes we enjoyed Beam's talk on love last night.
"Now," he tells us, "the first talk today is going to be about sex."

"Wooo! Woo hooo!"

Men raise their arms. Wives laugh. Applause, applause. Wadstrom introduces a younger man, a newly married fellow, and asks
him to give an invocation. The newlywed bows his head, as do we
all, and addresses God, saying, "We are so grateful to be able to
talk about something that is so much a part of your plan and that's
the sex."

Ahh, yes. The sex. Joe always stresses that his seminar has three
elements: the love, the sex, the marriage. They are indivisible. But
nobody's kidding themselves. The congregation didn't pay Joe

Beam's fee of about $1,500 and his expenses to fly out to California to talk about love. Joe knows, and they know, that the sex is the main attraction.

We applaud again and Joe Beam walks onto the floor with a low, deliberate rumble. Joe is fifty-seven years old, a well-fed, silver-haired man with a schnoz and a couple of small handbags under his eyes that give his face a friendly elasticity. This morning he is dressed in khaki slacks, a red sweater vest, and brown tassled loafers. He looks like a retired country club golf pro who's spent some time in the clubhouse bar.

But his voice is straight out of the fundamentalist radio programs I used to catch as a kid in Ohio, late at night on AM radio stations, voices carried up north of the Mason-Dixon line by fickle astral projection. I thought they were very exotic back then, and now Joe's bourbon-rich basso profundo, the way he can make his voice ride the register up and down to evoke sadness, pity, shame, repentance, joy, and his gift of turning one-syllable words like *God* into three syllables make me nostalgic. But unlike those old-time preachers, Joe is not a fire-and-brimstone guy.

"Okay. Let's see how you follow directions. How many of you did not have sex last night like I told you to?"

Just a few people raise their hands and everybody laughs, except me because I'm feeling a little squirrelly about the idea of horny fundamentalists. This reveals my own prejudice to myself, the first hint that I am going to have to adjust my thinking about "Christian sex."

When the laughter begins to die, Joe stands up straight, squares his shoulders, and makes a pronouncement:

"Sex is the most wonderful gift God ever gave Christians."

He proclaims this like a thesis statement meant to banish any doubts in our minds that what we are about to hear is a legitimate topic for the virtuous. He's going to use real terms and talk about real life, he tells us, and we're all adults here, so nobody ought to be embarrassed by the words *penis* and *vagina* and *clitoris*. Frankness is vital. "I believe the devil works better in the darkness and God works better in the light."

Then, as if to strengthen his biblical authority to talk about the sex, he quotes the first letter of St. Paul the Apostle to the Corinthians:

> But since there is so much immorality, each man should have his own wife, and each woman her own husband. The husband should fulfill his marital duty to his wife, and likewise the wife to her husband. The wife's body does not belong to her alone but also to her husband. In the same way, the husband's body does not belong to him alone but also to his wife. Do not deprive each other except by mutual consent and for a time, so that you may devote yourselves to prayer. Then come together again so that Satan will not tempt you because of your lack of self-control.

Joe presents this little excerpt as an affirmation of God's desire for his people to lead rich sexual lives. "Sexual fulfillment is part of the marriage contract, biblically speaking," he declares. But the church has long ignored sex and that has led to great unhappiness. How can we expect a young woman who is told over and over, "Sex is bad, sex is bad," and then she gets married and hears, "Oh, you're married? Sex is good, sex is good," to adjust to her new status? "I feel like I'm sinning when I make love to my husband," he recalls women saying to him, and they want help.

Morris Gregg, a beefy sailor in the U.S. Navy, who's sitting next to me, is nodding furiously in agreement. He leans over to his wife, Deidra, with an "I told you so" grin on his face. Deidra puts the palm of her hand against his cheek and shoves it away, leaving him grinning and glancing sidelong at her.

Joe begins the sex portion of his seminars with this flurry of apologetics to inoculate himself against the charge of being lascivious. He believes he is tiptoeing along a fragile divide. He wants to tell us hot sex is God's will, but this hasn't exactly been the impression left by his fellow fundamentalists.

Former House of Representatives Majority Leader Tom Delay summed up the feeling of many fundamentalists when he declared that Christians in the United States were being assaulted by "our government, by the media, and throughout popular culture . . . For the last forty years, the anti-Christian Left in America has waged a sustained attack against faith in God, traditional moral norms, the rule of law, and the traditional marriage-based family."

James Dobson, head of Focus on the Family, one of the most powerful religious right lobbying groups in America, once told a conservative crowd that he wanted to turn America into the old *Andy Griffith Show*. "I want to go back to the days of Mayberry, with Sheriff Taylor and Opie and all of those good folks," he said.

So Dobson and many others have made sex a potent political issue. You wouldn't see Andy Taylor as the wise, kind Jesus figure shepherding his Mayberry flock of oddballs while advocating perversion. But perversion is everywhere in America. So Dobson has declared a "Great Civil War of Values," and you better pick sides because things aren't going so well for the good guys. "The traditionalists are being mauled," Dobson has said.

"Unfortunately, there are predators around your house that want to gain access to your sons and daughters. They will, if given an opportunity, twist, warp, and molest them. Indeed, they are tinkering with your locks today and seeking to break open the windows. Focus on the Family also stands ready to assist with the *defense* of your family. This is why our motto reads 'nurturing and defending families worldwide.' We care about both the inside and the outside of your home. All we need is your invitation to help. Let's work together to save the next generation.

"I'll leave you with this request for your financial participation . . ."

I mention Dobson because Joe has been a regular guest on

Dobson's radio program, and I'm trying to reconcile the man I see now with the Dobson rhetoric of war and the scary image of Ron Jeremy sneaking around the outside of my house. Joe Beam just doesn't seem like a cultural warrior. He has a personal philosophy that sounds pretty live-and-let-live. "I am quite convinced that when Jesus said, 'Love God and you love yourself,' and 'Love your fellow man as you love yourself,' on these two hang all. They might be the only two questions on judgment day. 'Did you love me? Did you love people?' Well, come on in.'" His AA meeting, he likes to say, is the best church he ever goes to. In fact, he wants no part of the politics of sex. He won't climb onto some red state barricade. He has his beliefs and they generally track Dobson's, but for Joe, sex is a personal issue, not a political one.

Joe Beam never imagined he would someday become a fundamentalist sex guru. Nothing about his life gave him even a hint. He was born in southern Alabama and raised in Augusta, Georgia. He attended Bible college, married Alice, had two daughters, and for fifteen years preached the gospel to Church of Christ congregations, a neat and tidy life blessed by God.

But when you walk a well-worn path, hardly having to think about what it is you are doing or where you are going, a serpent can trip you up. That's what happened to Joe when he was thirty-four and began to ask questions. Is God kind and good? And if he is, how can it be that his grace and mercy are bestowed only on Church of Christ believers and not on Catholics or Presbyterians? How has the church evolved into that? What does it mean if one of your daughters is mentally retarded for no apparent reason? Surely God's mercy has to be broader and more complex than he could ever have imagined.

So one day Joe Beam stood up in front of a Church of Christ gathering and said, "I'm submitting to you, my brothers and sisters, and I hope you'll prayerfully consider it, that any individual who's been baptized 'in the name of the Lord Jesus,' based on his faith, is a child of God. What I'm saying is there's a lot of people in this religious world who've submitted to baptism in the name of the Lord Jesus based on their faith who accomplished remission of sins whether they realized it or not."

Joe Beam did not feel like a heretic but he was called one, and the experience of being called one raised even more questions until one day he began to feel unhitched from the very thing on which he had constructed his life. Preaching no longer made sense. So he started building houses. He nearly went bankrupt.

You know where this is going, don't you? It's an old story in fundamentalism, especially among preachers. There is the defeated walk through the doors of a saloon, the women you find there, the divorce from your true love. One day you realize you are truly a fallen man. Joe spent three years in Satan's icy grip, a period he calls his "drinkin' and druggin'" phase. He became a regular at strip clubs, a pathetic figure telling jokes to the girls at night, working on a paving crew for a relative during the day, and aside from hell itself, there isn't anything quite as hot as laying asphalt during a southern summer. The drinkin' and druggin', the porn, the strippers. They all congealed into one giant sin until God finally figured Joe had had enough. One night he almost killed himself in a car and he could have killed other people, too, if not for God's guiding hand, and when he woke up in a hospital he did not even know where he was exactly until an old friend said, "What the hell are you doing?"

Joe Beam got mighty humble after that, crawled back to his wife, begged for forgiveness, and tried to make a new start. By some miracle, the grace of God, or maybe just because he was lucky enough to know a woman like Alice, she took him back and he became a different human being because he had just experienced the power and glory of redemption. When Joe Beam tells this story to somebody who asks him about the power of redemption, somebody who wants to know if maybe this is what his mission is all about, he thinks of Alice and tears up and his chin quivers, and Joe Beam is not even a crying sort of man.

This can seem like the Jimmy Swaggart moment, the Jim Bakker moment, the Ted Haggard moment, the tearful confession, the verbal prostration, the forgiveness and salvation. I won't blame you if you're skeptical, if you think Joe Beam's watery eyes are just a way of saying, "Look at me! I am you! God loves me! He'll do it for you, too, no matter what you've done. Pull back from the brink. There's a home for you here."

Listening to him, though, I have my doubts Joe Beam is any Jimmy Swaggart. Sure, he uses the shtick, but he also says he learned a few things out there in the wilderness of sin. The awful fact is, Joe *liked* some of the strippers. He *liked* bedding different people. He *liked* sex, and the view he got of sex outside that stained-glass tower sure was a lot more interesting than the view inside it.

He returned home to Alice understanding that sex, even sinful sex that made you feel guilty later, could be fun. As he and Alice worked on their reborn life together, they thought they might be able to help others avoid their pain by having that kind of sex in their marriages. He and Alice reasoned that Christians have been blocked. Whom can they turn to if they want to ask if they were sinning when a man stuck his finger in his wife's anus? Not Dr. Ruth. A lot of Christians, Joe knew, figured Dr. Ruth was just another sick unbeliever. No, there had to be somebody from the evangelical inside, somebody who would say, Heck no, my friend, you are not sinning and as a matter of fact here are a few tricks you can perform with that finger, and then they could enjoy the sweet wicked moment of having that forbidden door open before they drove home to said wife and said anus. That's what Joe wanted to give. So in 1994 Joe and Alice started Family Dynamics, partly to tell Christians that all the great sex, all the erotic excitement, he had outside his marriage, just about all the nasty, licentious temptation they saw outside their own marriages, can be, should be,

and must be available inside theirs. No need to leave the fundamentalist fold and go exploring.

So there he is launching into a mini-lecture on smooth muscle in
the penis, blood flow, and female lubrication. "For men, sex is a
reaction," he says. Then: "How long do you think it takes her to
get ready for sex?"

"Hour and a half!" a man shouts from the back.

"Hour and a half? Well, I can tell you won't get any sex today!"
We all laugh.

"See, this is what I hear from women all the time. They say, 'How
can I get my husband to quit going for the touchdown until'"—
Joe's voice drops dramatically—"'he's called a few plays?'"

More laughing. Deidra nudges Morris.

Men are blowing it, Joe says, because we don't fully appreciate
the sexual power of women. A woman can come, climb back down
onto a plateau of pleasure, then come again. Men take time to
recover. We've got a single-shot pistol. All this is standard sex
counseling, not much different from the stuff I've heard at sexology conventions or can read in any popular secular magazine or
my own column for that matter. The difference is that Joe tosses in
references to God and the Bible.

"Why can women be multiply orgasmic and men not? Well"—
he addresses the women—"I think God just likes you better!"

See, if men did it right, we could give women one orgasm after
another and he can prove it. God said so. It's right there in the
Bible, in the Song of Solomon: "My beloved is mine and I am his:
he feedeth among the lilies. Until the day break, and the shadows
flee away, turn, my beloved, and be thou like a roe or young hart
upon the mountains of Bether."

"What does that tell you about Solomon if he makes love to her
all night long, until the daybreak?" Joe waits a beat. "That he's the
king and doesn't have to go to work in the morning!"

General cracking up.

No, seriously, he asks us, what's going on here? None of us gets it.

" 'Feedeth among the lilies'? 'Like a roe or young hart'?"

"Oh," one man says, his face lighting up. "He's going down where the sun don't shine!"

Yes, Joe says. It's oral sex. Cunnilingus. The mountains of Bether are her pubic mound. Solomon is going down on his wife and making it last a long, long time. "I would cause thee to drink of spiced wine of the juice of my pomegranate"? Holy cow!

"If you do it right, it takes longer than half an hour," Joe scolds the men, "unless you go like this: *Slthfpthfslthpf.*" He slurps his tongue like an overheated Dalmatian. Deidra is staring at Morris.

Not only are oral sex and orgasms biblical, they can be important.

"Christians should be having great sex lives. We should be having better sex than anybody else!"

A few of us have gone wide-eyed. Others are excited, smiling wide grins that have nothing to do with salvation and the welcoming arms of Jesus. Not only has Beam talked about oral sex right out in the open, he approves. He's encouraging! This is the first time some of us, including me, have ever heard this message from a self-described man of God. The big room has gone buoyant with relief, enthusiasm, joy.

Joe builds on the swelling mood. You might be surprised, he says, how many commonly assumed sins aren't really sins at all! "You can have fun!"

"Amen!" somebody shouts.

This is the crux of Beam's message. The secular world has nothing to offer you that you cannot have within the sacred bonds of your marriage. Joe believes that "one of two things is happening in evangelical marriages. One or the other wants to do something they are not doing because they are scared God is going to zap them, so they live with this frustration, or they are doing it and feeling guilty about it. When someone who is considered to be a

Christian authority says, 'Hey, it's okay,' they have peace. They can enjoy it and not think they are going to die and go to hell in the middle of it. They assume they are wrong because they have been taught everything is bad. So they go outside their marriage to get it and say, 'Oral sex is pretty cool. I enjoyed the way that felt' and that's so frustrating to me. Why can't we get that kind of freedom inside marriage?"

We learn just how much freedom we can have in marriage when Joe tells us to turn to page 32 in our workbooks. He throws up a slide summarizing the page, a list of God's prohibitions. "A great deal of what the Bible teaches about sex comes in the form of prohibitions," the book states. "Don't let that make you think God is against sex. He made it! But he made it to be enjoyed in His design—not in any human aberration of that design."

I'm not really surprised when I read down the list. God is pretty firmly opposed to having sex with your mother. You can't have it with your father's new wife, either, though I once knew a kid who dreamed of doing exactly that because his dad's new wife was about thirty and very sexy, which was, of course, why she was his dad's new wife. No sex with stepsisters or sisters or the grandkids, your aunt, sisters-in-law, daughters, or granddaughters.

No homosexuality. In the Bible you get the death penalty. No shock there, but Joe seems very sensitive about this when he says it, almost apologetic. He's bound by the Bible, he insists. It's not a political choice or a prejudice. "If you are a literalist, you have to understand the Bible says you cannot do that." Then he moves on quickly as if walking on hot coals.

No adultery, fornication, rape, prostitution, or sex with animals or women having periods. Joe says that this particular law was created for Old Testament-era health reasons that no longer apply and so maybe you can have sex with a menstruating woman, but "others feel that it lists God's view of the sanctity of blood and should still be observed by Christians who respect God's feelings."

Even though Joe has given this seminar hundreds of times, he seems to struggle with two entries on the list. The first is from St. Paul the Apostle again, who told the Corinthians, "Do you not know that your body is a temple of the Holy Spirit, who is in you, whom you have received from God? You are not your own; you were bought at a price. Therefore honor your God with your body."

Well, he asks us, what does that mean? What could harm the body?

"Whips and chains?"

"Well, yes."

"Anal sex?" somebody asks.

Joe appears grateful for the segue from whips and chains. "Anal sex? Well, let's talk about that a minute. All the doctors have told me anal sex does irreparable harm to the anus. Remember, it's only wrong if it harms the body. Now the vagina can be stretched. It's made for that, for childbirth, and men, if you want to understand the effect childbirth has on the vagina, all you have to do is take a Ping-Pong ball and force it up your penis!"

The women seem to think this is very funny.

"Now, my belief system says you should not do anal sex because it harms the body, but you should check with your doctor about that. If it doesn't harm the body, then my argument falls apart." Joe leaves no doubt that he would prefer everybody under the tent stay out of each other's butts. As I look around, though, I see faces giving this some serious consideration.

Lust also appears to create a problem. Our workbooks read, "Jesus said it like this: 'You have heard that it was said, Do not commit adultery. But I tell you that anyone who looks at a woman lustfully has already committed adultery with her in his heart.'"

That seems straightforward enough until Joe looks at us and says, "Look at what's not up there. What would you expect to see?"

"Why isn't masturbation up there?" somebody asks.

Onan was struck down by God after "spilling his seed upon the ground," which would seem to be a rather definite sign of disapproval. But that's not what God was doing, Joe teaches us. God struck Onan down because Onan disobeyed God by not impregnating his dead brother's wife as God had commanded. There is nothing in the Bible that says you can't masturbate. "You cannot say this is a sin," he insists.

I'm not sure whether to feel relieved or to argue with the guy. My entire adolescence was shaped by my belief that wanking was a sin. The sinfulness didn't stop me, but I built an edifice of reactionary beliefs based on the evils of masturbation. If masturbation wasn't wrong at all, then I wasted a lot of schoolboy guilt and more complex rationalization of my behavior than Thomas Aquinas.

Just when I think he's gone far off the deep end, Joe pulls back with a caveat. Masturbation is only sinful if it involves lust for anybody other than your wife or husband. "If you masturbate thinking about somebody else, it's wrong."

I am soothed by the reintroduction of sin, but also fascinated that Joe has suggested such a conundrum. You can masturbate, but you can't think about anybody but your wife? What if you're twelve years old and don't have a wife and you can't help thinking about the Dallas Cowboy cheerleaders no matter how hard you try to think of St. Agatha having her breasts cut off? What if you do have a wife and your brain flashes on—I don't know—Jean Harlow in *The Public Enemy* or that Versace dress Elizabeth Hurley once wore? What if you start out thinking of your wife in the Versace dress, but she looks a little like Elizabeth Hurley?

As I sit listening to Joe, I begin silently debating him even as I grow fonder of him. He seems to be doing a lot of good preaching the gospel of hot sex in marriage. He gives up to thirty of these seminars per year (his organization also gives talks on other family-life topics) to roughly one hundred people at a time, so he makes a good living talking and selling his books, but he's not getting rich. I think he is utterly sincere. Still, it sure seems as if his take on the Bible and sex and the prohibitions depends an awful lot on that Song of Solomon.

I think this is a pretty big problem. Relying on scripture, and calling it infallible, is a trap and why, I think, sex and lust have presented such tormenting puzzles to Christians. The Bible is full of contradictions about sex. According to the book of Kings, Solomon had seven hundred wives and three hundred concubines, not exactly the lifestyle that fits Joe's worldview. And as for not hurting the body, St. Paul wrote, "I chastise my body to bring it into subjection," a favorite of some nuns I used to know who were experts at chastisement with a yardstick.

The fact is, some early Christian fathers were antisex. The very reading from Paul's letter to the Corinthians Joe uses to introduce the sex portion of his seminar begins, "Now concerning the things whereof ye wrote unto me: It is good for a man not to touch a woman." That's a pretty simple declaration. Paul understands that we all have baser natures, however, and so we can't all be celibate, like he is. So he grants the value of sex grudgingly. Marital sex is permitted as castor oil, bitter medicine we can take to avoid the much greater sin of fornication.

"I speak this by permission and not of commandment," Paul writes. "For I would that all men were even as I myself. But every man hath his proper gift of God, one after this manner and another after that. I say therefore to the unmarried and widows. It is good for them if they abide even as I. But if they cannot contain, let them marry: for it is better to marry than to burn."

According to Paul, "He that standeth steadfast in his heart, having no necessity, but hath power of his own will, and hath so decreed in his heart that he will keep his virgin, doeth well. So then he that giveth her in marriage doeth well: but he that giveth her not in marriage doeth better."

The early church fathers—Jerome, Ambrose, Augustine— looked at the same scripture Joe is using and preached virginity, the better to hasten the end of the world and call forth the Second Coming. They were suspicious of the erotic power of women, and the role of lust even in marriage, the very thing Joe is celebrating.

I'm on Joe's side when it comes to the value of lust and good sex, believe me. But as I sit and listen, I don't see how he can base this teaching on the Bible, and honestly, though it pains me to suggest it, I think Joe might be tying himself up in a knot of logic. I'm pretty sure Paul would not have been a fan of going down on your wife, no matter what the Song of Solomon says.

So I wonder if even fundamentalist Christians are having to accommodate, and if all the contradictions in the Bible could be one reason evangelicals long preferred to ignore the topic. Why would they even have to mention it? Every believer knew what was sinful and what was not, and pretty much everything was sinful unless official doctrine explicitly approved it. Actually it was assumed to be sinful because church leaders didn't address it. Sin was simply the default position. Masturbation wasn't just sinful, it was bad for you, a sign of perversion, a weak mind, a drain on manly reserves. Lord Baden-Powell, founder of the Boy Scouts, famously told his youthful acolytes in the first 1908 manual that a masturbating boy "quickly destroys both health and spirits; he becomes feeble in body and mind and often ends in a lunatic asylum."

All that changed around 1970. A few Christian leaders realized that pop culture had changed the dialogue. TV increasingly beamed hints of sex into the homes of America. *Playboy* was mainstream. Naked hippies mucked around at Woodstock. The church was no longer a refuge. Believers could see for themselves what the unbelievers were up to. Somebody had to say something.

In 1969 Charlie Shedd, a Presbyterian minister, wrote *The Stork Is Dead*, followed by two other books, *Letters to Philip* and *Letters to Karen.* They contained mostly unobjectionable advice to teenagers. But Shedd also called masturbation "a gift from God" and told the kids that even though sex before marriage was wrong, if you were going to do it, for crying out loud use a rubber.

Shedd created a furor. He was harshly criticized for legitimizing masturbation and premarital sex.

Then, in 1975, psychologist Clifford Penner was asked to give a lecture on "sexual adjustment in marriage" at his alma mater, the Fuller Theological Seminary in Pasadena, California. The wives of the seminarians—all the seminarians being men—needed help with the very problem Joe Beam has told us he sees all the time: If you think sex is bad all your life, how can you switch to thinking it's good on the day you marry?

Realizing he was going to speak to a group of women, Clifford asked his wife, Joyce, a trained nurse and an educator, to help. After their talk, a number of the seminarians' wives had their first orgasms. The Penners become popular speakers.

Just a year later, the *Los Angeles Times* ran a story on the Penners, headlined "Sex Revolution in Church Seen: Right to Pleasure Being Taught." That same year, Beverly and Tim LaHaye published *The Act of Marriage*. (LaHaye would go on to fame as one of the authors of a series of apocalyptic novels called Left Behind whose animating idea was that people who did not think like Tim LaHaye would miss the Rapture and be, well, left behind when everybody else ascends bodily into heaven.) *The Act of Marriage* was essentially a sex manual for Christians, which didn't just stress the duties but also talked about the fun.

A small wave of Christian sex books with titles like *A Celebration of Sex* by Douglas Rosenau, *Intended for Pleasure: Sex Technique and Sexual Fulfillment in Christian Marriage* by Ed Wheat, and perhaps the most famous, *The Total Woman* by Marabel Morgan, now best remembered for her suggestion that wives gift-wrap themselves in Saran Wrap to greet their husbands at the door, broke on the shore of evangelical America.

The Penners, however, were recognized within the fundamentalist world as the reigning experts because of their formal training. At first they were uncomfortable in the role, so they eventually took sexology courses at the Masters and Johnson Institute, just as

Joe is earning a graduate degree in sexology from the University of Sydney. They consulted for 1970s TV shows like *Mary Hartman, Mary Hartman,* and with producer Norman Lear. They conducted seminars in churches. They appeared on James Dobson's radio program.

They wrote books, too. In *The Gift of Sex,* the Penners include suggestions for how marrieds can have fun in bed.

> The man needs to be as active as the woman in creating new ways to tease and in preparing enjoyable surprises. One man came running out of his bathroom without any clothes on. He leaped over the bed on which his wife was lying, and then asked her to guess what Bible verse he was acting out. The verse was "Listen! My lover! Look! Here he comes, leaping across the mountains, bounding over the hills. My lover is like a gazelle." (Song of Solomon 2:8–9). They've had fun with that ever since.

They even include pencil drawings of sex positions featuring a couple that looks disturbingly like Rob and Laurie Petrie from the old *Dick Van Dyke Show,* drawings that led some to accuse the Penners of being pornographers.

Today, if you spend enough time on the Internet, you might conclude Christians think of little else but sex. Websites are devoted to sex techniques for Christians ("The male G-spot—how to find and utilize this little-known pleasure trigger to create mind-blowing pleasure for yourself"), sex toys for Christians, sexual counseling for Christians.

There are even sex therapy organizations for Christians, including one, the Institute for Sexual Wholeness, that boasts Douglas Rosenau and the Penners as staff members.

As Joe is doing, the Penners and the other Christian sex writers and advisers use philosophical and biblical justification. Like Joe, for example, the Penners say oral sex in marriage is fine. Everybody always asks them about it, they write, and in response, they cite the Song of Solomon again, arguing that it "speaks of total body involvement." "For some of us this freedom seems strange, unusual, and not part of the natural order, but the biblical model in the Song of Solomon seems to embrace such freedom."

A key question to ask, they suggest, is "What is natural" and therefore part of God's perfect plan? This is precisely the question American states asked when they wrote laws, like this one, in Maryland:

> Every person who is convicted of taking into his or her mouth the sexual organ of any other person or animal, or who shall be convicted of placing his or her sexual organ in the mouth of any other person or animal, or who shall be convicted of committing any other unnatural or perverted sexual practice with any other person or animal, shall be fined not more than one thousand dollars ($1,000.00), or be imprisoned in jail or in the house of correction or in the penitentiary for a period not exceeding ten years, or shall be both fined and imprisoned within the limits above prescribed in the discretion of the court.

The Penners, like Joe, argue that when it comes to married sex, "nothing is said directly about what is acceptable in our lovemaking activity. Hence what comes naturally must be the product of what we feel inside us."

That's a pretty big loophole. As long as one spouse does not feel violated, let the blow jobs begin. In fact, the Penners and a few other conservative Christian sex advisers were ahead of the government that claimed to be upholding Christian morality. It was not until 1990 that Maryland's law was found unconstitutional for heterosexual couples, a finding extended to homosexuals in 1998. Similar laws in twenty-four states were effectively repealed in 2003 by the Supreme Court decision in *Lawrence v. Texas*, which struck down Texas's antisodomy law over the vituperative objections of Justice Antonin Scalia and many of America's cadre of fundamentalist Christians.

That decision made anal sex legal, but the Penners don't approve of anal sex. They dismiss it in a paragraph arguing that it's dangerous. Unlike every other sex act they discuss, they cite no scripture.

Masturbation, though, is pesky. The Penners pump their hermeneutical muscles defending their view that masturbation is a natural gift from God. They cite the Song of Solomon again ("One night as I was sleeping, my heart awakened in a dream . . . My hands dripped with perfume, my fingers with lovely myrrh"), but the argument largely depends on refuting other Bible passages. And, as Joe has told us, there are criteria that must be met in order to assure that a jerk-off session doesn't veer into sin.

"The question is often asked," the Penners write, as if reading my mind, " 'is not all masturbational activity a lustful act?' " Like Joe, they say no if you're focused on your husband or wife or if, by some amazing act of willpower, you are not thinking about Halle Berry or any other human unless it's an "unidentifiable person" and you think only in "a peripheral, still-life way."

If you're a kid, the Penners leave the issue of what you can think about—except to say that porn is always bad—a little fuzzy. The head cheerleader at school might pass muster or she might not. This is mysterious. But in case anybody has any doubts about the rightness of their stance that masturbation without sinful lust is acceptable to God, they appeal to the lead general on the side of the Christians in the culture wars, James Dobson.

Dobson himself wrote a book, *Solid Answers*, in which he calls self-love "as close to being a universal behavior as is likely to occur." So we should not feel guilty; should not let it become obsessive (a relative term when it comes to teenage boys), lest it cause us to be hooked on porn; and should not slip into using it as a substitute for actual sex once we're allowed to have actual sex after marriage.

Dobson's endorsement of masturbation is now used as cover by other fundamentalists wrestling with demon lust. Dobson says it's okay, goes the argument. You can't criticize me.

"And as you already know, I quote in *Lust Free Living* one of the most notable Christians who has done the most positive work in these areas, Dr. James Dobson," writes Lowell Seashore, the founder of a group called Lust Free Living. Seashore is responding to an e-mail from a rival, Craig Gross, a founder of an antimasturbation, antiporn outfit called XXXchurch. Seashore argues that "m'n" (he treats the word *masturbation* in the abbreviated way the *New York Times* might treat *fuck* or *shit*), if properly scheduled like a colonoscopy, and if it's a rare event free of lustful thinking, is not a sin.

Gross doesn't buy it. "What is XXXchurch's stand on masturbation?" he writes on the organization's website.

> We have had literally thousands of emails about this particular issue. We have heard all the scenarios. "Well if I think about fruit while I'm masturbating, then that is not sin." Well isn't that clever. Or . . . "If I'm giving glory to the Lord while I'm doing it, then that can't be wrong." Hmmm. Why don't we just make that part of our Sunday morning services then? We have heard all the Pro-Masturbation Christian arguments and I wonder if these people are really dealing in reality. It's all very intellectual and quite scholarly, but we still don't get it. Sorry . . . You want to live a life that is honoring to God then start pleasing him and stop pleasing yourself. Stop making excuses and get some control over your life. Yes, it is tough. Yes, we know hormones are raging. However, God is calling us to holiness. Live an extraordinary life. Masturbation will leave you hanging every time!

Gross and his fellow XXXchurch members call their website the "#1 Christian Porn Site." They have become regular attendees at porn-industry meetings, where they hand out "Jesus Loves Porn Stars" Bibles and T-shirts that have become, naturally, hugely popular among porn stars. Unlike the buttoned-down earnestness of Lust Free Living, XXXchurch uses pop culture goofs that can make it seem like a goof itself. The line between spoof and real theology is so vanishingly thin at XXXchurch the whole organization is sometimes suspected of being satiric performance art. It has run a campaign called Save the Kittens based on an old ad parody declaring "Every time you masturbate, God kills a kitten." In 2007, Gross even mounted a debate tour, traveling by bus with none other than Ron Jeremy.

But whatever Gross's motives, young men and boys do visit the site looking for inspiration, tips on quitting masturbation, and mutual support.

"For lent, a couple friends and me decided to stop masturbating," one writes by way of introducing the text of a pamphlet for "Masturbation Anonymous." "It was kind of a joke at first but eventually we were really gearing into destroying masturbation in our lives. A friend of mine and I got a few ideas together on the bus one day and I eventually ended up writing a whole pamphlet on why masturbation is wrong . . . we were able to convince about twenty people to stop masturbating in my school for lent."

He describes the psychological horror of masturbation.

> After this ordeal I was ashamed of myself. Suddenly, I felt uncomfortable and guilty around girls. I could not get the idea out of my head that some how they knew that I had masturbated the night before . . . This may be why you feel disgusted with yourself, you cannot help but to imagine women you know naked offering you sexual favors, and you feel like it is unhealthy. As your morals slip you may start doing other unhealthy activities, or giving in to your sexual urges in "strange places . . ." Remain calm and tell yourself, "You don't own me masturbation! I'm taking my life back!"

The site also contains forums where young men and boys go for mutual aid in going cold turkey. Victory is declared if they have managed to be masturbation free for forty straight days, the length of time Jesus fasted and prayed in the desert.

> Posted: Sat., Jan. 13, 2007, 5:08 a.m. Post subject: 40+ day first attempt!
>
> Ok, well..here i go..its 12:06 AM and i just gave in..i'm tired of letting satan bully me around like that.. i wouldn't let any one at school do that! haha! so i'll post at the end of today which is..Saturday January 13th..this weekend will be pretty hard for me cuz i have nothing today plus an extra two days off on monday and tuesday! Pray for me!

But alas . . .

> Posted: Sat., Jan. 13, 2007, 9:26 p.m. Post subject:
>
> what the heck is rong with me..am i an addict? i couldn't last 13 hours!!...i want something i can just (mentally/spiritually) yell in satan's face, and put on little notecards and tape those all over the place, etc.

Joe doesn't waste time on the great masturbation debate or any other apparent paradox. He trims the scriptures down to fit his idea that better sex and more intimacy (as well as better communication and understanding) will make for stronger marriages. Lookit, he says, men have needs. Of the average married couple having sex, 35 percent are having sex twenty-four times per year or less. Every three days men get heavily eroticized and ready to mate, he tells us, because we're making scads of eager sperm during our three-day cycles.

"Why does the male body make millions of new sperm every three days?" Joe's voice drops to a low confessional. "Because not one of them will stop and ask for directions."

We're all laughing again. Complicating details forgotten. Time for lunch.

* * *

Though I never actually spoke to masturbation as if it were a person, I sympathize with the tormented boys writing into XXXchurch, and now feel a weird sense of relief. Despite my suspicions that Joe is molding Christian teaching, despite the fact I'm not even a fundamentalist Christian at all, that I do not think masturbation is a sin, or wrong, or even especially important, it is as if Joe Beam has lifted a weight I have been carting around since I was ten years old. So I find myself ignoring my doubts, and the fact that I never followed Joe's rules for self-pleasure. I am clinging to his benediction and hearing what I want to hear.

Like every other Catholic boy, I was tormented by masturbation. During one of St. Mary of the Assumption grade school's periodic outings to group penance, I found myself in a confessional with Father Schultz. Despite the square handkerchief that hung down behind the screen separating his face from mine, I knew he knew who I was. You just don't serve as an altar boy without the priests recognizing your voice. This was why I had previously failed, after several agonized internal debates, to confess to playing with my penis, but now I was determined to let it fly. Nobody had yet told me masturbation was a sin—I had only recently learned the word—but I had a feeling it was because it felt good and I felt naughty doing it and that was a pretty sure sign you were breaking a rule. I didn't figure whacking off was a mortal sin with a no-refund ticket to hell, but it had to be a pretty serious venial sin, and I reckoned you could rack up serious Purgatory time doing it, and so I wanted to make my soul right with God.

I said the word. Blurted it out, really, then held my breath. I thought Father Schultz might gasp or demand extra time to think over the gravity of my transgression and the appropriate punishment. Instead, he assigned five Hail Marys and three Our Fathers and elicited a promise from me to try to avoid my penis in the future.

Whoa! That's it? I thought. I had spent the past several months trying to gin up my courage to confess this horrible thing and Schultzy handed down five Hail Marys and three Our Fathers? I knew standard confessional prescriptions when I heard them; the other boys in my class and I always compared punishments. I must not be the only kid who'd done it. Maybe lots of people lead secret lives. Maybe a sexy parallel universe existed somewhere, like in California, or France.

Still, there was pleasure and there was denial of pleasure, and all you had to do was look at the lives of the saints to know which was better in the eyes of God, and so I continued to wrestle with my demon. Now Joe says forget it, or at least that is what I am hearing him say; I am choosing to ignore the caveats and enjoying a very real sense of relief that, as a nonbeliever, I cannot entirely explain.

I gather this is a common reaction. The rest of the audience, people who do believe in Joe's overall philosophy, are laughing and smiling as they mill around the tent during the break. They weren't unhappy before, and Joe's comedy has certainly contributed to the mood, but I also see a lot of relief. Some of them seem to be experiencing the giddiness you feel emerging safely on the other side after surviving some dangerous close call.

"My whole life I thought it was bad, or wrong, or not Christian," Maria Ochoa, fifty-two, tells me as her husband, Jose, nods his head vigorously.

"She understands it is not a sin like she thought," he chimes in. By that he means, not just having sex, but using new positions, "not just in bed" but having sex, well, elsewhere.

"I am very happy," Maria says, smiling as if she really is very happy. She is in menopause, she thinks, and after all these years "new doors are opening because of what I am learning today."

At least as much as Joe's lifting their burden of guilt or doubt, couples seem to be appreciating the sexology. "I am not accustomed to hearing a Christian speaker say the words *sex toy* or *vibrator*," Kym Blackburn, a newlywed here with her husband,

Matt, tells me. "I am learning things, like how the female can have orgasms and how it is possible to achieve a second one twenty seconds after the first. We will experiment with that!"

Morris Gregg says Deidra made him attend Joe's seminar. He didn't think he needed the instruction. He's been in the navy for a long time, and in the navy you see a lot of the world and get to know what's what when it comes to sex. He approved of her coming, though.

I get the impression from Morris that his wife has been much more sexually inhibited than he has been, that sin and sex, or at least the variations Morris has suggested, were intertwined in her mind. So Morris approves even if he has to spend a Saturday under a tent at a Sheraton. "It's normal and human," he says. Besides, if you don't get it from each other, you'll get it someplace else.

It's not that Deidra didn't want to have great sex, she did. But religion held her back until she found the United Church of Christ congregation, where she worships now, while Morris was off on a deployment. "I was raised Lutheran and some of these things were not mentioned. When I joined this church, I was 'Wow! These Christian ladies do these things? Wow, this is a great church!'"

All this ebullience about sex makes me suspicious of the church and even a little suspicious of Joe. I like his message and I like him, but I can't help wondering if loosening the sexual rules isn't a way to sell religion the way PHE sells products.

"I think our church has been trying to be more open about sex, to be real about it," one of the seminar organizers, Mary Wadstrom, told me earlier today. Now I am questioning the motivation.

One of the things I could always count on from the Catholic Church was that it was, and still is (officially, anyway), stubbornly unreal about sex. My own feelings about the Catholic Church are complicated, but at least its teachings are consistent. Sex is a necessary evil. Masturbation is wrong, oral sex is wrong, birth control is wrong, lust is weakness. This made us different from, say, the air-conditioned, cocktailing Episcopalians. But Joe is telling us we get to have all the fun of sex—as long as we are married and het-ero—with nary a worry, and Joe, like other Protestants, approves of birth control. He doesn't spend much time discussing it because his audiences have the same view and birth control simply isn't a point of controversy. He approves of birth control and oral sex and masturbation.

Joe tells lots of stories about Alice, his daughters, his friends, and often they begin with some version of "Now, my son-in-law, a fantastic wonderful Christian man . . ." or a friend, "a good Christian man." I sit in my chair and wonder what this makes me in Joe Beam's eyes. Joe seems like a decent guy. I don't believe everything he believes, but I like him. I wish he still drank, because I think I'd like to go out afterward, sit down, and have a scotch and talk. But I'm pretty sure I am not a good Christian man, according to Joe's definition, because I don't go to church and I grew up Catholic, which I know doesn't really count despite Joe's past ecumenical-ism, and I don't think you have to be married to have sex or even be heterosexual either. As he speaks, he talks a lot about "us" and "them" and "they," and I can't help thinking he is feeding his audience the dangerous notion that fundamentalist Christians are a persecuted minority in a sea of sexual depravity. But how is Joe's advice different from advice you would receive in the secular, non-fundamentalist, nonevangelical world? Sure, masturbation can get pretty complicated with Joe's caveat about lust. And there's the gay thing and the premarital sex thing, but otherwise there doesn't seem to be much difference between "them" and "us."

Later, Joe will tell me this is true. The us/them distinction is for the audience's comfort, not his. "We might have different values, but I think a great deal of commonality can be found between the secular world and the Christian world on sexuality. Because I am a fundamentalist Christian, I am going to believe that sex outside marriage is wrong. You say, 'But do you condemn those people?' I will teach them what I believe, but they are adults, and they make their own decisions. And I am not about to be in God's place and decide how God is going to handle things."

I wonder what Sister Huberta, my fourth-grade teacher, a woman who had taught some of our grandparents and who told us the most gruesome of the stories about saintly suffering in the face of temptation, would say about Joe.

When we return from lunch, Joe makes a show of standing at the front of the space, leafing through a stack of index cards on which we have written questions. He leafs and leafs, waiting for silence to fall as we take our seats, then waits a few moments before sighing heavily and saying, "I am looking at your questions, and let me say, you are a sick group of people!"

For just a quick beat, our faces go blank and then we look concerned. Hadn't Joe given us license to be frank? Have we overstepped? Has he lulled us into allowing our dark thoughts to rise through the surface so he can better aim the hammer of righteousness? The moment lasts no more than a second, but the uncertainty and communal fear of being found out is easily the most delicious moment of the day. And then we laugh. Joe is standing up there looking back at us, grinning, and we laugh like we mean it.

The questions aren't surprising. We want to know what to do about premature ejaculation, so Joe launches into a mini-lecture on the parts of the penis, and how a woman can pinch the tip and how a man—a man willing to work at it like an Olympic athlete in training—can use a muscle to stop his own ejaculation. If he masters it, such a man might even become multiply orgasmic himself.

"Can you give us techniques for oral sex?" Joe reads. And then he does, covering details like how a woman can place her tongue on the penis, why we men like it, why it's a bad idea to use lubricated condoms if our wives are going down on us.

He even endorses swallowing. We men can help, he says, by making our semen taste better. Load up on fruit juices or sugary foods. "You can say, 'I'm eating this cake for you, baby!'"

Morris Gregg, who looks like he has had a few pieces of cake in his life, opens his mouth in surprise, looks at me, sees my mouth is also wide open, and we mutely mime, Did he just say that?

"Now, if you put the penis into your mouth, the best angle is if you are in front of the male facing him," because this puts your tongue right under his frenulum, which is, Joe tells us, the penis sweet spot.

"Have you heard of the proverbial sixty-nine?" Some, but not most, stare back at Joe with empty faces, which gives him the opportunity to mimic the blank stare, go slack-jawed, and say, "Huh? Is that in Acts?"

"It's two people lying beside each other facing the genitalia . . . Now, I'm trying not to be too graphic here." Joe uses his arm as a not very accurate model and proceeds to demonstrate how to "create suction and warmth with your mouth and tongue here, and here." He points to parts of his arm, but I'm lost. Which is the elbow supposed to be? Wait, uh . . . Joe has moved on, using his hand as a vulva to explain how a man can lick a woman to orgasm.

Somebody has asked how we can create time for sex in a busy life. Joe launches into a scenario out of *Playboy* circa 1968, a piquant tableau featuring makeup and lingerie and high heels and a sexy greeting when we men come home.

"How do you think he's going to react to that?" Joe asks the women.

"Thank you, Lord!" shouts a man.

What about sex toys?

"Well, I usually get the question like this," he begins. "What does the Bible say about vibrators?"

Some of us laugh uncomfortably and I notice about half the couples hugging each other a little closer.

There is a long history of sex toys, he says. Why, around the turn of the last century doctors, the new psychologists and gyne-cologists, would masturbate women to relieve what they called "hysteria." Not surprisingly, a lot of women suffered from hysteria with some regularity and the doctors grew tired of using their hands. So they turned to mechanical and then electrical devices. "Can we use a vibrator? Sure you can, if you want to." Joe even endorses one, the Hitachi Magic Wand, partly because it's power-ful and partly because it doesn't look like a penis.

Joe knows many sex toys are illegal in his home state of Alabama, as they are in several other states. Section 13A-12-200.2 of the Alabama Criminal Code makes it "unlawful for any person to knowingly distribute, possess with intent to distribute, or offer or agree to distribute any . . . device designed or marketed as use-ful primarily for the stimulation of human genital organs for any thing of pecuniary value . . . Any person who violates this subsec-tion shall be guilty of a misdemeanor and, upon conviction, shall be punished by a fine of not more than ten thousand dollars ($10,000) and may also be imprisoned in the county jail or sen-tenced to hard labor for the county for not more than one year." You can't make such devices either. The ban, passed in 1998, was taken all the way to the U.S. Supreme Court in the spring of 2007, but the justices refused to hear the case, thus upholding existing law.

(This annoys Joe. He thinks they're "ridiculous laws. Stupid. Like oral sex laws were a way to cut back on homosexuality. 'If we do this, we can arrest homosexuals.' But it's difficult to legislate morality. I was born in the great state of Alabama and respect the great state of Alabama, but that law is ridiculous." When Joe says all this to me later, he pauses a moment. "I hope my career is not over now. I just do not wanna fight Dobson or the Falwells.")

Can we fantasize? About other people? somebody asks. "I am saying that is not good because now you've violated your relation-ship. Rather than fantasies, you should concentrate on giving your partner as much stimulation as possible. Concentrate on making love to your spouse. Look, if I were the devil, I would make sure she wound up fantasizing about other church couples."

This sparks a shouted question. "How about swinging?"

Swinging? This guy is asking about swinging? The very fact he thinks it's a question makes me wonder.

"I am telling you from a marital expert standpoint, it destroys your marriage," Joe says. "It destroys your sex life. But it is rampant in America. We are beginning to see those couples now in our New Beginnings seminars because one of them has fallen in love with somebody else. You know, I used to subscribe to *Playboy*. I got one every month. I remember I read an article, in the Playboy Advisor column, 'What do you think about us having other lovers?' and the *Playboy* writer said, 'It will destroy the relationship.' Even the heathens know that! Well, I shouldn't call them heathens. I don't know if he's a heathen or not. Let's say people who do not have our values."

Now that Joe has brought up *Playboy*, we want to ask him about porn. There's no mention of porn in the ten biblical prohibitions, somebody points out, to which Joe answers that yes, porn is not on the list, but you can't blame him because it's just not in the Bible and if you are going to be a book, chapter, and verse guy like he is, if you are going to take the Bible literally, well, you can't just go around making stuff up. Porn is bad, though. Very bad.

Hands shoot up. Joe has hit a rich vein. "Is all porn bad?" somebody asks, a little hopefully.

"See how many questions there are about porn? This is always among the top-five things I am asked by Christian audiences. Are we just wrong when we say porn is bad? It seems like we in the Christian community are the ones hung up on this."

This is a surprising admission because, yeah, it does seem like "the Christian community," by which Joe means fundamentalist evangelicals and Roman Catholics, mainly, are hung up on porn. On other areas of sexuality, he has used the word *abiblical* to say, Hey, it's not forbidden by the Bible, the Bible never mentions it, so, say, butt sex could be okay if it does no damage to the body. He's just said, though, that porn is also abiblical.

But Joe isn't only a Bible scholar. "So I wanna talk to you as a marriage expert. Let me tell you what it does to your marriage." He sighs in a great heave of sadness. "Yes, it will stimulate you. Looking at an aroused person is arousing. When I was drinkin' and druggin' those three years Alice and I were divorced, I went to strip clubs. Yes, I had no money, but I was hanging out in strip clubs. I'd get drinks by telling jokes. Now, Saturday afternoons are the very slow period and strippers would come by to talk to the sad guy. They called me the sad guy. And they told me stories. Well, I have watched them take in $300, $400 in an hour, but almost all of them were drug addicts or alcoholics and the reason why was that they felt so degraded. They generally think men are scum.

"My wife is fifty-seven. She does not look like she did at twenty-seven and never will again. If I get turned on by hard bodies, I am losing the ability to be turned on by Alice. But who suckled my children? Inevitably, it is a matter of time until the wife's self-esteem is destroyed. Get that stuff out of the house! Get the Showtimes and the Cinemax and all that stuff out of your house!"

"Umm . . . can we use instructional videos?" another man asks, a little quietly, perhaps thinking that Joe's arm, as nice an arm as it is, doesn't quite communicate the way a Sinclair video communicates.

"Get books. Get the books with line drawings. And play games with each other. Like 'First one who orgasms loses.' Really, you can do whatever you wanna do. Drop your inhibitions at the door of your own house."

The day is wearing on. Joe finally segues into the marriage portion of his seminar, a presentation mainly about communication skills and personality types. This lasts about an hour and feels a little perfunctory, or maybe it's just that the air of excitement has escaped the room.

Then Joe, who has spent much of his time striding back and forth across the floor in front of his audience, steps up onto the stage and grabs a stool. He walks it downstage and sits, with a deep exhale into his cordless microphone. If this were Vegas at two in the morning, there'd be a spotlight and a loosened bow tie and a drink in his hand.

Joe Beam was a broken man, he tells us. He worked as a pastor and hit his crisis, then tried building houses for a living and nearly went bankrupt. After he took that job with a relative's paving business, he nearly killed somebody while driving a paving machine across a new parking lot. The booze and the drugs grew out of that soil like weeds. Joe's voice is more deliberate, becoming quieter with each woeful step of his descent.

One night he found himself in an Atlanta strip club, he says, the sad guy, surrounded by disgusted women. He drank six beers that night. Took twenty Valium. There was a man he remembered back in Alabama, an attorney Joe himself had led to Jesus. Joe decided he had to see this man and so Joe left the strip club and started to drive. He made it all the way near to Birmingham before he crashed. In the hospital they said he overdosed; did he want to kill himself? And there he was with nobody to hold his hand.

"I never felt so alone."

Joe Beam's story fills the room. His audience is transfixed. Some are nodding along with his testimony.

He betrayed his wife. He betrayed his daughters, especially his angel, Joanna, who's mentally disabled, but Alice took him back. "We got married a second time. It was just the right thing to do. We did not love each other, but we learned how to be in love with each other and now she is my best friend. I pray every day, Lord, let me die first. I wanna get old with her and sit on the front porch. No matter how bad a marriage is, you do not wanna die alone.

"So if there is something in the way, the Xbox, a job, pornography, get rid of it. Make each other your focus. Please, please. You can do that.

"That's my time."

Joe Beam walks offstage and out the door.

CHAPTER 3

The Gonzo, Vibrating, Futurotic Pleasure Dome

I Go to Work in a Sex Xanadu

We are, after all, in the business of fantasy fulfillment.
—Fascinations Sales and Guest Care Manual, 2006

I have been accused of endangering small children. Not me personally, I suppose, me as the smallest of drones in the giant hive of the American sex industry. According to several concerned citizens quoted in the *Arizona Republic,* a Fascinations "romance superstore"—part of a chain of thirteen adult stores in Arizona, Colorado, and Oregon for which I am temporarily working—puts "kids in grave danger." Specifically, Edward de Santiago, one of the people quoted, was referring to a proposed Fascinations branch in Tolleson, Arizona, about two miles from where his daughters attend elementary school. He seemed pretty sure two miles were not enough miles to protect his girls from the danger of porn, sex toys, gag gifts, and cheap lingerie. So even though I am working in Tempe, much farther away from his daughters and their school, I have been branded.

Yet as far as I can tell, the only danger I present to society is rank incompetence at retail sales. I am sitting, a little panicked, in my new employee training session trying to avoid looking like an imbecile and failing. My five fellow newbies are not betraying the slightest hint of confusion, but I'm completely lost. I have a college degree my colleagues lack, about twenty more years of life experience, and I can read Chaucer in Middle English, none of which qualifies me in any way for my new job as a "romance consultant." (Or any other job, for that matter.) So I am writing notes furiously as Trista Windels rattles off store polices, procedures, and statistics, all of which I am supposed to remember and begin using tomorrow.

Trista is a pretty, waifish nineteen-year-old with long, straight blond hair and eyes of such a deep emerald green that people unconsciously find themselves staring at them. Trista survives mainly on Red Bull and cigarettes, apparently absorbing from the air whatever nutrients her body requires, which she knows isn't exactly the most healthful strategy "but, whatever." She isn't into makeup, though she does wear coverup for the occasional blemishes that still pop out of her teenage skin.

She grew up in Detroit Lakes, Minnesota, not far from the South Dakota border. About seventy-five hundred people live in Detroit Lakes, but the town seems bigger because in summer the place swells with tourists who stay at a few lodges and resorts along the shore of Lake Detroit. Besides servicing visitors, people around there farm, mostly. Corn. Soybeans. Cows. Trista spent part of her childhood growing up on a dairy farm but didn't like it much. She worked at a tanning salon for a while, then gave manicures, then worked as an aid in the Alzheimer's ward of a nursing home. She used to wash dead bodies. When she graduated from high school, she planned to go to a community college to earn a degree as a licensed practical nurse, but when her boyfriend moved to Phoenix, Trista figured that even though he was the only person she knew in the entire state of Arizona, and she had no idea of what she would do for a living, moving there wasn't going to be any worse than changing soiled sheets and preparing dead bodies.

It is about seven thirty at night and Jennifer, Marlena, Kyle, Kira, and Ashley—the other members of my training class—and I are gathered with Trista in the back storeroom surrounded by porn DVDs, leather body harnesses, and penis-shaped dildos proportioned to satisfy the fifty-foot woman from *Attack of the 50 Foot Woman*. This is distracting enough, but Trista's Red Bull and nicotine–propelled stream of instructional language keeps me at least three bullet points behind on our corporate handouts.

"G.U.E.S.T." she says. "Who knows what G.U.E.S.T. means?"

Wait, wait, what page is that?

"Greet, Understand, Educate, Suggestive Sell, Thanks," Kira says.

Before I can finish writing the acronym, Trista moves on. What comes after "Greet"? *U*? What's the *U* stand for again? "Can you go back?" I plead. "To the G.U.E.S.T. part?"

"Brian," Trista says with exaggerated patience, "it's in the handout in your packet. Have you read your handout?"

I have not read my handout. I was supposed to read my handout earlier today, to be thoroughly familiar with my handout, but I slacked off in a nearby taco shop. "I haven't had a chance yet," I say. Trista raises a scolding eyebrow.

At least I grasp the main idea. The store is dedicated to customer service, and through some magic technique no doubt gleaned from a sales consulting guru, part of my job is to bump sales by communing with shoppers about their sex lives. This will allow me to sell additional items by suggesting products to match my patron's particular sexual menu or, better yet, expand the menu. The idea is making me queasy. It's one thing to sit in my office far removed from readers and write a column in which I quote experts doling out advice, but quite another for me to go mano a mano over a penis pump with somebody who may be much bigger than I am. Am I really expected to "find out if there is a specific fantasy that he is trying to realize" when a male shopper is thinking of buying a love doll? The booklet suggests I "help that customer complete their fantasy by suggesting additional items like matching bra and panties." I am not a shy person, but I do not want to have a discussion with a guy about why his new vibrating Aria Giovanni "love goddess" with vagina, ass, nipples, and mouth, should be outfitted with a nice lace demi underwire. Nor do I aspire to suggest all the good uses for Sphincterine Ass-tringent, a product promising to give your ass a "fresh minty flavor."

The nature of the merchandise also complicates my longtime phobia of the term *company policy.* The last time I worked in anything remotely resembling retail sales, I manned a Standard Oil station on Memorial Drive in Lancaster, working the 10:00 p.m. to 6:00 a.m. shift. You wouldn't think there would be much challenge in sitting all night behind bulletproof glass, speaking through an intercom, and turning pumps on and off with a keyboard, but I quickly became overwhelmed. I liked my blue gas station shirt with the attached name tag because its rugged bravo cachet appealed to girls, but I turned it in after a drunken guy ignored my repeated warnings about exact change and then handed me a twenty for five bucks' worth of gas. When I kept the twenty he ranted from the other side of my protective window, and I picked up the phone to mime calling the police.

"I'll go!" he screamed, pointing a trembling finger at my nose. "But I'll be back." I told my manager that being threatened by guys with bellies full of beer at three in the morning was my reason for leaving, but really, it was my inability to follow company policies regarding the cash register, organizing the credit card slips, and figuring out the drop safe. I am flashing on that experience right now and not liking it. Back then, I didn't even have to try to "sell" anything while complying with company policy. People either needed gas or they didn't.

Nobody really needs Sphincterine. At least I don't think so, and I seriously doubt I will be able to pitch the need for a minty-fresh ass with a straight face. Add all the injunctions Trista is giving us now about the corporate structure, our pay rates, our uniforms, our break periods, and time clocks, and I am becoming embarrassed by the mere anticipation of my failure as a romance consultant.

This whiny nervousness is not what I expected when I formulated the half-baked idea of working here. While much of the fundamentalist community may be debating the pros and cons of masturbation with the diligence of medieval scholastics, it seems to me that much of the rest of America is no longer worried if self-pleasure, or any other sexual activity between consenting adults, will land them in hell. Judging by the mail I receive, my reticence about discussing the nitty-gritty of sex with my potential customers makes me a fogy. Could that be true? What sort of person consumes the products Edward de Santiago believes put his daughters in danger? Are these the people James Dobson thinks are creeping around our houses right now? Are they worthy of the government crackdowns social conservative voters and political pressure groups advocate?

I have chosen this Fascinations store because it is big, a sexy Costco, if on a somewhat smaller scale. Middle America, I have been told by members of the industry, is flocking to such stores. Fascinations is one of several growing chains billing themselves as a new kind of adult establishment, offering comfort to the bourgeoisie. No more skeevy guys sitting behind messy counters smoking and reading back issues of *Mature Nymphos* magazine, no more peep booths with dim lighting and sticky floors, no more parking two blocks away on the bad side of town out of fear somebody will see your car out front. Fascinations's local rival, Castle Megastore, a chain with seventeen outlets in Arizona, Washington, Alaska, Oregon, and New Mexico, spent over $500,000 in 2007 upgrading its own facilities to make them more couple and female friendly. At the store where I am working, the parking lot is large and well lit and at the moment it is hosting several SUVs, a Volvo, a beat-up Chevy, and a few Toyotas.

But I am not thinking about this big picture now, I am trying to avoid humiliating myself in front of my fellow trainees. At twenty-five, Jennifer is the oldest. She is single. She had a baby seven and a half weeks ago, but I would never have known if she hadn't told me, because she is thin and rangy with black hair hanging in stringy curls down her back, a couple of tattoos, a pack of cigarettes at the ready, and a sandpaper demeanor that suggests the American lottery of fate has directed her to an adult store. She's not happy about it, and she's not unhappy about it. There are worse places to work, and who knows, it could be fun.

Marlena has just turned twenty-five. She applied for the sales position here as a second job to make a little extra money. Kyle is twenty-three and recently arrived from Alaska. He's pudgy and opened-faced with the buzzed blond haircut of a high-school varsity baseball player. Kira is a pretty, heavyset girl from Yuma. Like Kyle, she's new to Phoenix, just looking to land a job in her new city. Ashley is twenty, overweight, and dresses like a goth long-haul trucker with black combat boots, a black flattop haircut, some facial piercings, and eye makeup suitable for the Grand Ole Opry before it went pop. I am the only nonsmoker.

And then there is Trista, who is explaining that we'll be given two sales goals, one for every shift we work and one for the entire day. These will be posted in the break room. If a shift makes its sales goal, 2 percent of that shift's total sales will be divided among employees as a bonus in addition to our $8 per hour wage.

But there are rules. No facial piercings that show, please. No strange piercings at all unless you can cover them up somehow. If you do have a facial piercing, like Ashley's eyebrow ring, you'll have to wear a clear, plastic "keeper" during working hours. Cover your tattoos. Wear your uniform at all times, including the official maroon polo shirt, khaki or black pants or skirt, brown or black shoes. Name tags at all times. We are professional consultants.

For some of my new coworkers, working in a sex shop represents a step back from edginess and into the pastel embrace of corporate image.

No matter what you might have thought before you walked in here, Trista tells us, our clientele are not lonely middle-aged perverts. The customers are women, mostly. Only a third are men. Most are in committed relationships. Forty percent are college educated. These people do not want to be served by punked-out goofballs or scary guys with sketchy hygiene. They want young, fresh-faced, eager sexual educators, which, by the way, is what you will become in addition to your romance consulting. You will have to learn all about the toys because two-thirds of the customers buy them. Lubes, oils, lotions come next, but do not forget the DVD sales and rentals. By item volume, as opposed to dollar value, porn is a big part of the business.

The one sure way to get yourself fired, Trista says, is to fail to check customer identification when someone walks through the door. Every person must show a driver's license or some other official ID to prove he or she is at least eighteen years old.

Trista gives us a quick overview of the store's products. There are about 8,000 items in all, over half of which are DVDs. Customers can choose from 1,354 different sex toys. Until this moment I had no idea 1,354 sex toys existed and I have no idea how one would use 1,354 sex toys. The most expensive toy is a mysterious item called a violet wand, at $449 with attachments. The store also stocks lots of joke items—drinking straws shaped like penises are always popular at bachelorette parties—naughty greeting cards, books on sex, skin magazines for all persuasions, Japanese porn manga, lingerie, and costumes.

"This place is crazy at Halloween," Trista says. "Every girl wants to be slutty at Halloween. It's like it's okay then. There will be lines out the store waiting for dressing rooms."

She directs us to our employee packets and the twenty-page "Introduction to Products." "Customers place a great deal of trust in your suggestions," it says, a frightening thought if true. I glance through the booklet's lists of product benefits. Almost every item promises to enhance sex in some way or other, but even the store sounds skeptical about some, like Tighten Up Shrink Crème, which is supposed to "provide the sensation of a tighter than normal vagina." The description smacks of bet hedging to me.

Then Trista escorts us on a field trip through the store. We start in the dungeon room, a small section devoted to riding crops, whips, padlocks, nipple clamps, and other devices used in bondage, domination, and sadomasochism (BDSM). A love swing hangs from the ceiling and I think back to Kathy Brummitt and the Sinclair love swing video.

"Does anybody actually buy these?" I ask.

"Oh, sure," Trista says. "Not many people buy the violet wand because it's so expensive, but some do." She opens a glass case and takes out a small brown handheld device resembling an electric screwdriver. A glass tube terminating in a pancaked disc juts from the wand's tip. Trista plugs the wand into an outlet, turns it on, and right away we hear a whirring sound. The glass tube glows neon purple. Trista holds it half an inch above her forearm and sparks fly from the glass tube to her skin. She demands we all try it, so we'll know what we're selling, and it feels like being hit with needles of static electricity.

I suspect the violet wand is here mainly for show, to burnish the store's credibility among the BDSM set. I have no way of knowing that before my walkabout through American sex is over, I'll be seeing much more of the violet wand.

When we leave the BDSM dungeon, Trista talks enthusiastically about the porn DVDs, or, as we are trained to call them, "the adult titles."

"The new titles go here," she says, resting her hand on a small display shelf at the end of a row of bins stuffed with thousands of them.

"Oh, that's awesome," Jennifer says, laughing, when she spots one new title. "*The Da Vinci Load*!"

"Okay, over here are the BDSM DVDs. They generally do not have sex in them," says Trista, who, I am about to learn, has a very restrictive definition of sex. "I did not know that, and then I rented one and was scared out of my mind . . . Over here, there's squirting. I never knew what squirting was until I started working here," she says, referring to female ejaculation. "My boyfriend's favorite porn star is Teagan Presley. My favorite porn star is Cytherea because I'm really into squirting and she is, like, the squirting queen! I prefer gonzo and wall-to-wall" DVDs, she says, describing videos free of plots or characterization. "Oh, and I really like Belladonna," she says, holding up a DVD titled *My Ass Is Haunted.* "These here are oral mainly. They don't have any sex either, or almost no sex, just oral. Foreplay."

The magazine rack is peppered with titles I've never heard of: *Bizarre, Taboo, Tight, 18-Year-Old Hotties, Just 18, Leg World, Mature, D-Cup.* An entire comic book series revolves around mother–son, grandfather–granddaughter, brother–sister incest. I could spend days reading titles from the book section to learn how to do everything from bukkake to extreme bondage.

During our review of the love dolls, there is some serious discussion about a material called CyberSkin and one known as Futurotic, ultrarealistic, high-tech compounds that are meant to more closely duplicate the feel of real human flesh. Trista removes a CyberSkin product from its box and all five of us reach out to fondle and squeeze the molded ass of porn star Chasey Lain.

"Um," one of the young women asks, "how do you, um, clean a doll?"

"Well," Trista explains without hesitating, "a lot of guys do not ejaculate in the hole."

Some of us aren't so sure. We feel the need for discussion. What strategies should we recommend to any man who says he will indeed be spilling his seed into the rubbery depths? Some of these dolls are pricey, and a guy is going to want more than one love-making session for his money. At least this is the general consensus of the class members. The doll will have to be cleaned. We have taken Trista's oath to customer service seriously and we want to provide a good answer to any man who asks.

"Swabs?" suggests Ashley.

"You could squirt it with a hose," Kyle offers.

We pitch one suggestion after another until Trista finally says, "Like, okay, whatever," a rhetorical trump card that silences the class. We move on.

The next section contains small missiles of rubber and silicone, most of which Trista describes with some variation of "and this thing goes in your butt." She holds up a leather harness belt with a steel ring meant to be worn over the pubic bone and demonstrates how one of the large dildos fits through the ring to give the wearer a strap-on penis. "A lot of guys like it when their girlfriends wear 'em." Trista explains. "They like it in the butt."

In dongs and dildos, scores of outsized replicas of disconnected penises hang from hooks like hunting trophies. A few of these have porn-star endorsements, too, and when Jennifer sees one molded from a guy named Julian, she recognizes the name right away.

"Oh, he's hot."

As we walk, Trista exhorts us to keep an eye on the gay and transgendered toys and magazines. Many straight men, or men pretending to be straight, are shy about their interest in homosexuality, to say nothing of being comfortable enough to walk up to a cash register manned by a fresh-faced young woman, so they steal these. Don't pressure anybody. Get a price range, talk about the qualities of each item, listen carefully. Try a compliment. Say, "Wow, I love those shoes. Where'd you get them?" Create a conversation so a customer will relax and realize there is nothing scary or odd or shameful about shopping here. It's all perfectly normal. Everybody does it. Just like a trip to Toys "R" Us.

* * *

In 1945, at the very end of World War II, Beate Uhse, a twenty-seven-year-old German woman trained as a pilot, fled Berlin in a Luftwaffe plane. She settled in allied occupied territory and the next year reinvented herself as a sex educator and entrepreneur. In 1962 she opened what is thought to be the world's first sex shop, the Institute for Marital Hygiene, a name chosen to deflect accusations of prurient appeal. Dildos, condoms, and educational literature were health aids, therapeutic for people who needed therapy.

The appearance of sex shops took longer in the United States and depended on a confluence of events within the overall sexual revolution. Most important, in 1965 the United States Supreme Court, in *Griswold v. Connecticut*, found that a Connecticut law forbidding the provision of contraceptive information, techniques, or treatment to married couples was unconstitutional. Griswold effectively overturned, at least for married people, the nearly one-hundred-year-old federal Comstock law, named for Anthony Comstock (who, coincidentally, was born in Connecticut), a Christian antiobscenity crusader who believed talk of contraception fomented lust.

The first sex shops were really "adult bookstores" selling skin magazines. Sometimes a headshop would stock cheap vibrators and dildos along with the blacklight posters, roach clips, and bongs. But slowly, court decisions and the growth in numbers and kinds of sex-related products gave potential shop owners both the right to open and the merchandise to sell. In 1970 what is thought to be the first porn movie (aside from stag films) released in the United States, *Mona* (about a virgin who apparently thinks oral sex doesn't count), made a brief appearance, followed by others, most notably porn's first big hit, *Deep Throat*, in 1973. American counterparts to Beate Uhse's store began peppering the landscape, often near new adult movie theaters. But the liberalizing court cases left one regulatory caveat: zoning. Cities were free to regulate stores by ghettoizing them into low-rent parts of towns. Sex shop owners responded by living down to the reputation. They played up sleaze and skipped any effort to appeal to customers with niceties like decor or service. Sex sold itself. What more did anybody need? All you had to do was throw up a few purple lights, paint the windows black, hang the goods from the wall, and charge three times what the stuff was worth.

Feminism changed the paradigm. In 1973, about the time the fundamentalist Christian community was trying to come to terms with the sexual revolution, Betty Dodson, who had earlier mounted exhibitions of erotic art, founded women's sexual consciousness-raising groups where attendees were invited to admire their own genitals. In 1974 she self-published a book called *Liberating Masturbation: A Meditation on Self-Love.* That same year, Dodson acolyte Dell Williams opened a shop called Eve's Garden in New York.

In 1975 Joani Blank, a thirty-seven-year-old San Francisco activist and sex therapist, founded a publishing company, Down There Press, to publish a book she wrote called *The Playbook for Women About Sex.* The male version followed the next year, and in 1977 Blank opened a tiny retail store in the city's Mission District called Good Vibrations. The idea of the store was to give women an alternative to unsavory sex shops and to provide them with reliable information about sex and sexual pleasure. Sales gradually expanded and the store opened two more branches, another one in San Francisco and one across the bay in Berkeley.

Blank, who was more missionary and activist than businesswoman, wanted to spread the word that bright, clean sex shops with friendly, knowledgeable staff could fill an important need in the lives of women and, by extension, the men and other women—there has always been a strong lesbian component to the Good Vibrations story—who loved them. So she started an apprenticeship program for would-be store owners. Two women,

Kim Airs from Boston and Claire Cavanah from Seattle, enrolled. Cavanah subsequently founded the Seattle version of Good Vibrations, Toys in Babeland (now, simply Babeland).

Kim Airs, a former administrative assistant and lab manager at Harvard University who once worked as a high-end escort at night and was an enthusiastic sexual experimenter, had long been frustrated that the only way she could obtain sex toys was by venturing into Boston's infamous Combat Zone. She wasn't ashamed of sex, wasn't embarrassed by sex, and didn't see why she had to take a risk to buy a sex toy. Upon leaving the Good Vibrations program, Kim tried to find space in Boston and in Cambridge for a store of her own, but rents were too high in safe areas, or landlords refused her because of the nature of the business. Finally, she found space in nearby Brookline and opened her own shop, Grand Opening! in 1993. She was thirty-five.

Now sex shops have gone completely mainstream. Phil Harvey's Adam and Eve outfit has been franchising stores all over the country, with about twenty-five stores so far. They look a lot like Fascinations—boxy and brightly lit. Larry Flynt's Hustler Hollywood stores have opened a dozen branches. Priscilla's, another big-box chain with dozens of stores, has spread beyond its Kansas City base to much of the rest of the Midwest and all the way to Las Vegas. When a few Penthouse Boutiques opened on the East Coast, complete with marble floors and chandeliers, some town fathers objected, but the less predictable reaction came from denizens of the old-style dank. They compared the new stores to Starbucks. All the character, they complained, was being washed out of sin. Sex was being homogenized.

People do not feel much like buying penis-shaped drinking straws before lunch on a Wednesday. I started my first full shift half an hour ago and haven't had a customer yet, and I'm keeping my fingers crossed the trend continues. If the place gets busy, somebody might actually need help, and I'll be alone and unaided, adrift in an eleven-thousand-square-foot sea of sex. Here I am in my maroon polo shirt, my name tag hanging down my chest, looking the part. Yet I am practically hiding behind a row of phallic candles. The whole idea of a modern adult superstore is to seduce new consumers by presenting a friendly face and using words like *romance*. These big stores are repackaging sex, trying to sell it with a smile and a fine "Howdy-ho, neighbor!" Most of the products are exactly the same as those in the old, dark sex shops, even if there are more of them and more variety. But the lights are bright, the store is immaculately clean, and we romance consultants are peppy and bright-eyed in our uniforms. Well, everybody else is. I'm having trouble getting into the spirit and I'm not sure why. Moral guilt? No. I don't feel any moral guilt. I don't think I'm harming Mr. de Santiago's children.

Still, I'm uncomfortable and a little ashamed of being uncomfortable. To tell you the truth, I just don't want to have the conversations I am anticipating. Sex shops have always represented sad statements of failure to me. A man can't attract a woman, so he buys a love doll or three hours of other people fucking so he can stroke his way to some impoverished version of satisfaction like Garp's poor wrestling coach. "You wanker!" "You jerk-off!" That's how we used to insult each other. You weak, pathetic symbol of withered manhood—Lord Baden-Powell's nightmare vision of the chronic masturbator come to life. And a woman? Well, she hasn't got a man, so she buys an imitation of a man and hides it in her lingerie drawer for lonely nights after the Rocky Road is eaten and the sad movie has ended. "I think someone in this house should be having sex with something that doesn't require batteries," the wayward daughter says to the defeated single mother in Ron Howard's movie *Parenthood.* Or she's got a lump of a man, a man she sees across the couch and secretly despises for his failures, and turns to her vibrator, bought under cover of night in a furtive dash into a sex shop, for escape.

This is silly. These scenarios are not true, at least not always. Many happy couples enjoy using sex toys, watching porn, and playing dress-up. And why should anyone feel shame if they aren't part of a happy couple? They shouldn't, of course. Everyone is entitled to a little blissful release. Buying a dildo or a love doll ought to be easier, not tougher. But I am unable to fully divorce this rational thought from decades of perception that a sex shop represents failure. Despite the nearly oppressive effort to pretend selling sex is exactly like selling Frisbees or decorator sinks or night repair antiwrinkle cream, and that the salve for whatever need is bringing customers into the store is to be found on these aisles, that we are performing a valuable public service, I think what has me spooked, so unexpectedly spooked, is participating however peripherally in someone else's embarrassment.

On the other hand, it could be I'm just making excuses for being a ninny. Either way, I don't feel like a "romance consultant." So I am hunched over and wary, pretending to read a candle label as the day's first customer walks through the door.

She is a sturdy woman with brown hair and a confident ease. Her name, I am about to learn, is Jennifer and she is twenty-eight. Two others have come with her, a man and a woman. I gather they are married. The three of them wander around the store, smiling, mostly at the merchandise. They make a stop at the Love Bar, the long wall of vibrators and the equally long, clear display shelf on which demonstration models are placed like small vases on plastic platforms. Typically, you can't handle the vibrators in a sex store, but these days the big stores have them displayed and battery equipped so you know exactly what each one offers.

Jennifer requests in a firm, assertive voice that I join her at the Love Bar. She wants some help. I look up, manage a thin smile, and join the trio. The wife is holding a vibrator shaped like a penis straddled by a rabbit. Trista informed us in training that these are "personality" vibes. Some have dolphins, some butterflies, and some, like this lepus version of Strangelovian Slim Pickens, have rabbits.

"Is this the one from *Sex and the City*?" the wife asks me.

I know this! This is a question I can answer because Trista, bless her, talked about it. "A lot of women will come in and say, 'I want the toy Charlotte had,'" she said.

"Really?" I asked.

"Oh, yeah. It's huge. Everybody wants the *Sex and the City* vibrator."

In the context of the Jimmy Choo shoes, the Fendi handbags, the Cosmopolitan-drenched lunches, *Sex and the City* turned sex toys from a feminist statement, or a cause for embarrassment, into aspirational objects.

Marty Tucker, founder of Topco Sales, one of the world's largest sex toy manufacturers, couldn't be happier about it. Back in 1969, Marty was working for McDonnell Douglas as a metallurgical engineer and dreaming of rocket science. "I wanted to be Marty von Braun," he told me when I visited with him. But once America reached the moon, winning the space race declared by John F. Kennedy, the big increases in funding that characterized NASA's budgets through the 1960s began to slow. Marty realized that working for a contractor like McDonnell Douglas might mean improving on the last generation of rockets, but that there probably would not be any great leaps for a while. He was ambitious and eager and unwilling to wait. So Marty bought himself a small manufacturing company that made rubber creatures like snakes. Disney was an early customer.

In 1973, after he invested some money with a friend in the entertainment licensing business, he branched out to create rubber toys based on TV, movie, and comic-book characters. He also made a few dildos; the technology wasn't any different, really, and, he recalled, sex toys were "a good way to go to make money."

A few manufacturers were already in the sex toy market. But when the VCR entered homes in the late 1970s, and brought porn with it, companies began making sex toys on an industrial scale. Marty Tucker's Topco Sales, now headquartered in a huge building near the Ronald Reagan Freeway in Chatsworth, California, was one early pioneer in this industrialization of sex. He created sex toys like a cock ring designed to prevent male premature ejaculation, and a latex-sheathed vibrator with soft foam inside to make it seem more like an actual penis instead of a hard plastic stick of dynamite.

Though he had not intended to become a sex toy titan, the business was impossible to resist. The profit margins were huge. You could import components (or the whole toy) from Asia, use unskilled labor here to assemble them, and for a few cents make a vibrator you could wholesale for $10 and sell at retail for $20.

Quality was irrelevant because customers would buy whatever they could get. "You just knocked them out however you could," Marty told me. Most sex toys were junk. To avoid scrutiny by the Food and Drug Administration and other governmental agencies like state antiobscenity squads, manufacturers couldn't say that a vibrating dildo was meant to give a woman an orgasm; they had to call it a "novelty," meaning that it isn't really supposed to be used for anything. Wink, wink. Heck, down in the Bible Belt, Marty said, they used to call dildos and vibrators "cake toppers" and sell them as novelty cake decorations. So there was no higher authority to field consumer complaints—in the unlikely event somebody would fess up to needing a sex toy and actually make one—than the unshaven lout behind the dimly lit counter at Midnight Blue Adult Books.

By 1977 Marty Tucker was getting rich. Unbeknownst to him, one of the licensing deals he had bought into was for a comic-book character he had never heard of, the Incredible Hulk. CBS had just launched a TV series starring Bill Bixby and Lou Ferrigno as the two versions of the title character, and Marty found himself selling thousands of rubbery Hulk dolls to stores like Kmart and increasing numbers of sex toys to mom-and-pop sex shops.

In the thirty years since, five companies (Topco, Doc Johnson, Nasstoys, Pipedream Products, and California Exotic Novelties), all American, have dominated the worldwide sex toy market, though this is beginning to change. All five are privately held, and accurate sales or profit figures are virtually impossible to obtain. Estimates of annual sales vary wildly, from about $1.5 billion to $5 billion. (One big five CEO, Nick Orlandino of Pipedream Products, an erstwhile maker of dope paraphernalia, said he expected $120 million worth of retail sales for his goods in 2006 and that the company's sales had been growing 40 to 60 percent per year until about 2004, when new entrepreneurs, inspired by *Sex and the City*, realized just how much money there was in orgasms and began glutting the market. "Growth is explosive. We were rated one of the fastest growing companies in L.A. County [by the *Los Angeles Business Journal*]. We were up there with Trader Joe's and the Cheesecake Factory, you know?") Whatever the number is, suffice to say it's a lot of money and Topco is generally considered one of the two biggest, partly because it sells products to companies outside the sex industry. It makes a small piece for Microsoft's Xbox, for example.

Marty was sixty-seven years old when we met. He's short, slender, and fit looking, and on that day he dressed in a black rugby shirt and khaki pants. Glasses were one of the few concessions to his age, though he was a little discombobulated, having spent the day before flying back from China, where he has a home near Topco's Chinese manufacturing facility in Shenzhen. There he employs fifteen hundred people in a corporate campus of several buildings. (About five hundred people work in Chatsworth.)

Marty had the bearing of a man who enjoys life, and why not? He was married to a younger Chinese woman, and the sex business, he said, "is a really fun industry." He was never embarrassed about it. When his daughter was five years old, a little boy asked what her father did. "My daddy makes souvenir weenies," she answered.

"We never pushed it in their faces, but if a product was on the kitchen table we didn't try to hide it. I have a five-year-old nephew, Chris. We made an adorable product, a picture of a woman with cleavage for a computer mouse pad. It has two bumps in the shape of breasts and with our four-color printing they look like breasts. You rest your arm in her cleavage, right? Well, Chris puts his hand in there and smiles the biggest smile. It's instinct."

Topco hasn't even had any legal troubles, he told me. The closest call in all these years wasn't about a sex toy. A woman's cat ate part of an Incredible Hulk figure and the cat died. She threatened to sue.

Still, Topco's chief chemist, the Technical Director of Drugs and Cosmetics, told me that the company is harassed by the federal government. "We have had over fifteen visits from them for plant conditions, manufacturing conditions. But I don't lose," he said defiantly. "Not to the government. FDA, DEA, FBI, immigration—they all have a file on us."

I asked him how a chemist comes to be the technical director of drugs and cosmetics for a sex toy maker and he said he was hired away from a contract pharmaceutical and cosmetics manufacturer that serviced big-name labels like Estée Lauder. Topco wanted a drug license because it manufactures sexual lubricants and products like penis desensitizers that have to be registered with the FDA, and it wanted to make a pubic hair shave lotion. If it was going to expand, it needed somebody familiar with good manufacturing practices in the cosmetics industry.

His parents thought his new job "was funny as hell." And despite holding a divinity degree from the University of Northern Iowa, and having once considered becoming a Lutheran minister before going to graduate school, and still attending church regularly, he didn't regard working in the adult industry any different from working for any other contract lab. This job had some extra perks, too, like free sex toys and company orders to test out all the new products. "We have a lot of enthusiastic people here!" he said.

Topco takes pains to seem like any other industrial outfit, and maybe it is. Topco's holding company, Vast Resources, Inc., sounds like an oil driller or a gold-mining company. Basic Solutions, Inc., the mainstream side of the cosmetics and health products business, has goods on the shelves of major retailers all over the country. Sure, the chemist told me, they tried to keep a wall between Basic Solutions, maker of Nature's Dew feminine lubrication, and Topco, manufacturer of the Carmen Luvana Doggy Style Cyberskin Vibrating Pussy & Ass. But let's face it, that wall is more and more like a screen because "the adult field is really coming into its own." Johnson & Johnson is in the adult industry now. It makes a warming "massage" lotion that's really a stimulating sex lube and is advertised on TV. Basic Solutions makes a private-label sex lube that's in the second-largest drugstore chain in the country. Women have created a great boom in the whole industry. They watched *Sex and the City* and they wanted products and not just the crummy junk. They want quality now. In the old days, he said, "the guy in the raincoat was buying it," so quality was irrelevant, but no more.

The market is about high performance. Women demand "a longer ride with a sweeter slide, and we can give it to them."

Thirty-six-year-old Justina Walford, the director of public relations for Topco, took me on a tour of the plant and offices. When I told her I suspected the hyperrealistic porn-star genitals sold in stores were just created out of some guy's imagination with the help of a computer design program, she laughed and walked me into a closet-sized room adjacent to the factory. A large massage table and equipment used to take molds sat on the floor. The wall was decorated with photographs of Aimee Sweet, one of Topco's endorsers, kneeling on the table with her butt in the air while several artists slathered a gooey compound on her rear and vulva. In another series, she is sitting on the table while the guys smooth the stuff over her breasts. These molds were used to re-create Aimee Sweet's assets, which were then used by thousands of men all over the world. I reckoned that if I were Aimee Sweet this would be a very heady thing.

In the factory, a few dozen workers, mostly Hispanic immigrants, mostly women, tore into boxes from China and removed one giant penis after another and dozens of leather "slappers" used for spanking. As they gossiped in Spanish, or listened to bouncy ranchera music playing through headphones attached to CD players, they cleaned each one, packaged it in individual plastic cases, and reboxed it for shipment to distributers.

The art department reflected the industry's realization that women increasingly control the sex toy business. Graphic designers working on computers were creating new package labeling for a line called Grrl Toyz, a play for the generation influenced by hip-hop, "riot grrl" rock, and female athletes. Previously, much of the packaging was supposed to appeal to men, with photographs of naked models, often with their legs spread wide, even if the toy, like a vibrator, was meant for women. Now the men and women in the art department were drawing cartoon women who were thin, attractive, and dressed as in-charge go-getters. The toys themselves were pink and blue and orange.

"We are trying to tone down the language, too," Justina said. "Among younger people this is all totally normal. Hey, for my generation, a third date in a sex shop is not all that unusual."

The next day I visited the Adult Novelty Expo trade show sponsored by the industry trade publication *Adult Video News* at the Sheraton Universal Hotel adjacent to the Universal Studios lot. There were 136 exhibitors selling everything from PVC bedsheets to audio CDs telling sexy bedtime stories. Hundreds of store buyers milled through the booths looking for new merchandise. Topco's display was movie studio worthy, an enormous operational retro soda fountain with a guy making sodas and malts and Topco

CEO Scott Tucker, Marty's son, chatting up a rush of retailers. Most of the merchandise on display was gleeful, celebratory, with rite-of-passage names evoking big-girl bicycles and training bras. One popular toy was called My First Butt Plug.

Topco makes My First Butt Plug under the Hustler brand. It has such deals for other labels, too, like Adam and Eve, Penthouse, and the first sex retailer of all, Beate Uhse.

When I spoke with Marty back at the factory, I had made a comment: "Looks to me that you have a license to print money."

"We do," he said. As I sat down at the counter to my free soda, I knew why he couldn't repress his smile.

As I am working in Tempe, Arizona, a man named Asher "Jerry" Sullivan is trying to open the Cafe Risque adult supercenter just outside Waldo, Florida. "Supercenter" is a tad grandiose. The building, a former bar, is made of cinder block, and Waldo, situated north of Gainesville, not far from the Georgia border, is tiny. But any size is too big for some of the town's residents. While being remodeled into a store, it has been heavily protested by local church groups. According to reporter Tiffany Pakkala writing in the *Gainesville Sun* newspaper, approximately 150 people picketed in April 2006. A sign read "Americans for Morality."

At the same time, five bikini-clad women danced nearby in a truck with a Cafe Risque logo on the side. Guys in cars drove by. They honked and waved.

Construction continued until one night when a forty-one-year-old man using a combination of swamp water, yeast, rotten eggs, and detergent sabotaged the building. State officials called the attack domestic terrorism. The fire department wore hazmat suits.

In Knoxville, Tennessee, a twenty-year-old Bible student set fire to the Town and Country Bookstore, motivated, he claimed, by a desire to serve God. He was dressed as a ninja.

Other opposition to stores like mine is more organized. Morality in Media, for example, an organization founded by a Catholic priest, has been lobbying and advocating to close up the adult industry for decades. In 1983 it met with President Ronald Reagan and takes credit for convincing Reagan to launch the new antiporn drive that ensnared Adam and Eve.

Clearly, such efforts haven't worked, but people keep trying. Actor Stephen Baldwin, star of movies like *The Sex Monster* ("What would happen if your wife said yes to a ménage à trois . . . and loved it!") and *Mercy* ("Venture into a world of deadly sexual pleasures"), has sworn to single-handedly prevent the opening of the Nyack Video Store outside of New York City. Baldwin, who says he is now a born-again Christian, has promised to shame workers building the store, and future customers, by photographing their license plates, tracing the numbers to their names and addresses, and then publishing the information in the local paper.

But Baldwin has latched on to a dubious strategy. Many of my customers don't seem to care if anybody knows they shop in an adult store. Apparently I have worried for no good reason at all. Far from being embarrassed, the patrons are actually pleased with themselves for investing in a little slice of life.

Jennifer, for example, whose friend asked me about the rabbit vibrator, was in town visiting. She asked her friends if they wouldn't mind coming along to Fascinations so she could stock up on sex equipment because where Jennifer lives, in Logan, Utah, there's just one tiny adult store.

"It's a pretty Mormon area," she explained.

"Are you Mormon?"

"I used to be, but I converted to Catholicism. My husband's a Methodist. He's back in Utah, serving as a marine recruiter."

Jennifer used to be a marine, too, which somehow didn't surprise me. She was part of a helicopter flight crew flying off the USS *Bataan.* In Afghanistan she became the first female door gunner to see combat. So, no, she's not afraid anybody will see her buy a sex toy. She and her husband used to visit a store outside Camp

Lejeune in North Carolina where everybody knows everybody, and those stores were sleazier than this one. She'd happily shop in Logan if there were any selection. Hell, she and her friends back at Camp Lejeune used to talk about which toys worked and which didn't. I'm pretty sure Stephen Baldwin wouldn't get very far intimidating Jennifer about anything.

Now another woman, about thirty-two, shouts, "Can you help me?" She strides across the store, holding a long purple vibrator as if it is the Olympic torch.

"Hi," I say, my body momentarily seizing. An awkward beat elapses. "I see you've got the Slimline G there."

Trista informed us that the Slimline G—a Topco product, by the way—is a popular vibrator because it is both inexpensive and bent at one end to stimulate the G-spot, an area inside the vagina that, say believers, can produce strong orgasms. All my female trainee buddies claimed they had G-spots, loved having G-spots, made good use of their G-spots—more detail than I wanted to know, but sharing goes with the sex store territory.

"That one's designed to hit your G-spot." I tuck my arms behind my back, lean forward slightly and knit my brow, trying to appear professorial. "Are you interested in G-spot stimulation?"

"Maybe."

"Well, we have several vibrators you might find helpful." We walk along the Love Bar, picking up a few models so she can try them out on the palm of her hand. I look to see if she's blushing. She's not. I might be.

"Shopping during a lunch break?" I ask, partly to change the subject from her G-spot and partly to find out why there's a guy trailing one step behind us. Yes, she says. She and this fellow are software developers at a nearby company.

"You guys dating?"

No, they are not dating. They are not married. He's just a work buddy.

"I came with her to give my two cents," he says.

"Gee. Close friends," I say.

"Oh, I know a lot of people who come in here," she replies offhandedly. "It doesn't bother me." Family members, a few friends. They all know she shops here. What's the big deal?

"A place like this is clean, it's well lit; this is not a sleazy atmosphere," he observes. "And you know everybody does this stuff, it's just that some people try to hide it."

Next, Sarah, a twenty-three-year-old receptionist, tells me she likes shopping in adult stores like Fascinations because although some mall stores, like Spencer Gifts, have started carrying a limited supply of sex toys, "there are little kids in the same store and that makes me uncomfortable." She is happy to tell me that she has a vibrator at home. Sometimes she uses it with her boyfriends, sometimes not. She and her girlfriends talk about what gadgets work best. They complain about how much they cost. "People my age are just much more comfortable talking about this stuff than maybe people were in the past," she says.

"I am proud of my vibrators and the trips I make to Fascinations!" Kimberly Pikna-Nyhof tells me. Kimberly, thirty-two, a business consultant, compares her new sex toys with the Easy-Bake ovens of childhood. "You know how when you are young, and get a new toy, you are excited to play with it and show it off? As an adult it's the same thing."

Not everyone is quite as open as Kimberly, but those who aren't think they should be able to be. They aren't shy or embarrassed; they just don't want any blowback from people who think sex shops, and the people in them, are deviant. Jonas, for example, is a twenty-one-year-old mechanic for the sheriff's department and he's studying to become a deputy. He owns a couple of vibrators already because when he sprang one on his girlfriend a few months ago, she sort of freaked out at first but then thought it was a blast. "She just exploded in a very good way and from that time on, she's been, like, 'Let's try a couple of others.'"

Being the accommodating chap he is, Jonas is looking for new gadgets. Nothing wrong in that, is there? No. Hell, no. But there's that hoped-for career with the sheriff's department and so he thinks discretion is in order. He brought along his buddy, Ryan, who has decided a little backup in the bedroom could come in handy.

"You guys doing a little male bonding over dildos?" I ask.

"We've known each other for a long time," Ryan says.

"We were raised in a predominantly religious community just outside Orem, Utah, where the rules about sex were very strict," Justin explains. "It was a Mormon community. That could be why some guys would be afraid of it, not sure if it was good or bad or weird. People can be afraid of change."

Don't get the wrong idea, he volunteers. He's not some liberal. Quite the opposite. "I always vote Republican."

"I'm a school-board official," another customer, a middle-aged woman, tells me when I use Trista's sales strategy of making conversation to ask what she does for a living. "That's funny, huh?"

We are sitting at a table in the middle of the store where I have just demonstrated the Hitachi Magic Wand, the powerful, plug-in vibrator Joe Beam recommends. ("Whoa!" she said, watching her hand jiggle as she held it. I'd love to sell her one of these babies, but she had that granny-behind-the-wheel-of-a-Ferrari look on her face in reaction to all that horsepower.) If somebody were to know she shops at a place like Fascinations, no matter how clean and shiny it is, she could be seen as something less than upstanding, or worse, a danger to the community. Sex disturbs people and that's too bad. Personally, she thinks buying sex toys is healthy. She owns a few and even asks her nineteen-year-old son to return items for her because that's a good way for him to learn a little more about sex, you know, "in case he's curious."

I say that at nineteen there is a good chance he's curious and she confesses another motive, too. Returning something to this store is a chore because it is located far from her home and she'd rather he make the trip. There is a Fascinations branch closer to her own neighborhood, but it has been picketed and she doesn't want any-body to see her walking in and then make a fuss at the next school-board meeting.

At this a friend of hers, another woman, volunteers that her "kids are not affected by this store at all. They don't even know what it is." Then she adds, "And I'm a Republican!"

Funny how people seem to blurt this out. Nobody has said, "And I'm a Democrat!" Surely I must have waited on Democrats.

"What are you?" I ask the school-board lady.

"I'm a Democrat."

There. But she doesn't wield her political party affiliation like a talisman to ward off any implication that she is immoral or loves her children less because she is sitting with a Hitachi in her hand.

Like the aspiring deputy and the school-board member, a male–female firefighter couple would rather not be outed as dildo or porn purchasers, but boy does it make them angry that they feel they have to hide it. He is a wounded veteran, for Chrissakes, who grew up in a Pentecostal church in Kingman, so he knows what that's all about, but when he went in the army his life changed.

"From that point on it was free game. It opened my mind, exposed me to all sorts of different beliefs all over the country, all over the world."

"It is way enlightening to go to Amsterdam," his girlfriend pipes in.

"Yeah," he says. "We're supposed to be a free country, but just go over there and they're allowed to do so much more!"

I'm not exactly sure what they are allowed to do in Amsterdam that we are not allowed to do in the United States except smoke hash and advertise hookers in brothel windows, but I guess he's referring to the general attitude. Maybe you can do it here, but people expect you to feel bad about it.

"There's a museum there," she says excitedly. "It's an erotic museum!"

They look at each other and grin at the word *erotic*. I am standing two feet away, but I can see their pupils dilating. I wonder if I ought to leave them alone. Then he looks at me. "We are extremely sexual together." No kidding. Is there a company procedure for dealing with couples in rut? I should have studied my packet.

His girlfriend is older than he is and though she always figured she was sexually adventurous, she was tame compared to him and his friends. There's a world of difference. At parties with his buddies, somebody will slip a porn DVD into a player and it will run as background entertainment. "His generation are like, 'Hey, just let me lead my life,'" she says.

Their sex life has become one big experiment. "I will see something and say, 'Oh, let's give that a shot,'" she explains. "It's a big thing for us. We don't draw lines. Well, we did draw one line. Anything that hurts. We have talked about other people, but that depends on how strong we are in our relationship. If we did bring somebody else into bed, it would be like they were a toy."

"Yeah," he says, "we'd treat 'em like a toy."

It's just too damn bad, what with all that American hero BS that "we're in the public eye and so we have to be completely upstanding," she says. They're kind of tired of the whole hero shtick, actually. Being a paragon is a burden. Back at the firehouse, brother, that's where you get the real story about America's heroes. "We get back to the house and it gets pretty bad" with the sex talk and the jokes and the porn. "Like, there's this poster at work? An old-style nurse with a cap, kneeling, and Uncle Sam's hands on the side of her head, and it says, 'Take one for America.' But we have those things behind closed doors so when the public comes in that is not what they see."

I mention something liberal and sensitive about sexual harassment and she laughs at me.

"Hey," he announces, "maybe I am going to hell, but I'll be driving the bus!"

The other customers are equally defiant, if less colorful. They don't think they should have to apologize to anybody or feel the slightest sense of shame. "This should not be part of any political discussion," the school-board lady's Republican friend says. "This is about personal choices. I separate the two. Some politician should not be able to ban this. This is the basis of America! Personal choice!"

Arizona is a conservative state, but it also has a strong libertarian streak. I wonder if that explains what I am hearing. This is the state, after all, where you can find accountants and housewives and pizza delivery drivers walking around with guns on their hips because the state says any law-abiding grown-up can be Wyatt Earp. The Fascinations in Tucson had a policy of not allowing armed people to enter, fearing, I suppose, a heated discussion over Chasey Lain's ass could erupt into a shooting match. But local shoppers demanded their Second Amendment right to weaponized porn browsing and Fascinations rescinded its no-guns policy. Now, shoppers and employees are free to wander the dildo aisle with deadlier strap-ons.

Sex shops may seem like an unlikely place for a battle over liberty, but that's how mainstream they have become. My store (I think of it as my store), located in a typical spot for the new breed of adult outlets, looks like a smaller version of Wal-Mart, a comparison easy to make since there is a Wal-Mart Supercenter just down the street. There are also gas stations, a dry cleaner, a GE Consumer Credit office, fast-food shops like Quiznos, a Mongolian grill, a Baja Fresh, the offices of home builder T. W. Lewis. The whole street is one long, stuccoed, consumer-cured slice of cheese melting in the brilliant Arizona sun.

Near the end of my first shift, as I am leaving the gift section, I look across the store and see a fellow employee having a serious conversation with a man in a business suit holding a sex toy in his hand. She is half his age, but his head is bowed low, and he is listening the way you might to your doctor who has just prescribed Lipitor and is explaining why you really need to get your cholesterol down and what foods to avoid, and how you can prevent your heart from seizing up if you really go through with your idea of buying a mountain bike.

Another employee, who earlier today showed off the twin rows of piercings down her back through which she can run a ribbon so her spine looks like a laced corset, is talking to a woman about fifty years old. They are shopping for DVDs. My colleague is explaining the term *gonzo*.

Two women in their twenties walk up to me holding a Clone-A-Willy kit, a system for molding a penis into one's very own customized vibrator. A steal at $49.99.

"Does this really work?" they ask.

I have no idea whatsoever if it really works. But I have decided to stop being so reticent. I am working in a sex store. Nobody else seems to be giving their own presence here any more thought than they would in the Wal-Mart. Nobody is embarrassed. Hardly. People are here to buy: they have the cash, we have the merchandise—that's capitalism.

"Yeah, it works!" I say with as much enthusiasm as I can muster, reading the label as I speak and thinking back to my day with Marty Tucker at Topco Sales and my visit to the hallowed ground where Aimee Sweet's sweetness was duplicated. "You mix the powder with water to make the molding stuff. Then you get him hard and spread it over his penis. You've got to make sure you keep him hard, though." I look up at the girl who first asked and say, "That shouldn't be too tough for you," and they both giggle. "Once it's dry you take it off, pour in the liquid rubber stuff, let it sit, and you'll have two of him."

They laugh again, thank me, and go stand in line for the cashier. Though I have had lots of conversations with customers, this is my first sale. Now I am a romance consultant.

Trista was naive once. When she first started working here a year ago, the manager and the other romance consultants made fun because she had never heard of a G-spot or had an orgasm or used a sex toy. The heavy Minnesota accent probably didn't help either. And she had only been out of high school for two months, so naturally she was shy, as I have been, about talking to customers. (Though I am a grown man who writes a sex column, so I'm still working on my own excuse.) Somebody would approach her and she would answer questions as she had been trained to do, but then she would become self-aware and think, Oh my God! I am talking to this person about vibrators! and begin stuttering. Finally, she picked up a copy of *The Good Vibrations Guide to Sex* and read it front to back, which is really saying something because Trista isn't much of a reader. Her boyfriend, Eric, is the reader.

As far as Trista knows, folks don't talk about sex in Detroit Lakes, a town that still boasts about the fact that rocker Bobby Vee got married there in 1963 to a local girl. Well, that's not entirely true; Trista knows people talk about sex everywhere. Her own mother had tried to have a birds-and-bees sit-down with her daughter, but Trista thought the idea was freaky. "No, Mom! Shut up! I don't care! I don't care." Way, way too weird to talk to your mom about that stuff.

What Trista means is that there was not a lot of conversation about sex beyond the basic in-and-out fact of it. "When you had sex with somebody from Detroit Lakes it was just plain sex like everybody else has, unless you had it with somebody from Fargo who knows something."

I'm not sure on what Trista is basing this conclusion, but her neighbors in Detroit Lakes probably have not read *The Good Vibrations Guide*. "If you say you own a vibrator, they are, like, 'Oh my God! Are you kidding me!' and they'd be laughing because sex"—by which Trista means sex as she has come to know sex through working in a romance superstore—"is so, like, down low there."

Trista was not entirely ignorant of the subject when she came to work here. She had experienced sex. Exactly which time was her first is open to debate. Maybe it was a thirty-second encounter in the closet of a friend's house, but that time she barely knew what happened. They had gone into the closet at the instigation of other boys and girls, zippers were unzipped, and she just sort of ended up doing it, but as soon as he stuck that thing in, she shoved him off and said, "Go away, go away," because nobody told her that sex hurts. So does that count?

The second time Trista had sex was a little better, but the boy still didn't come or anything. The third time it was better still. Really, though, Trista's sex life began last year when she moved to Phoenix. That's when the world opened up.

Soon after she arrived, she and Eric were driving by the store and he suggested she get a job here. He told her it was a lingerie store and maybe he thought it was just a lingerie store, but Trista thinks he tricked her. Okay, not really. I mean, twenty feet into the store you see sex toys, so she knew she wasn't applying in any Victoria's Secret. Still, she likes to tell the story this way because otherwise it sounds like she came all the way to Phoenix to sell dildos and porn.

Trista had seen porn back in Minnesota. Sometimes a friend would slip a DVD into the player and run it when parents were away, but she thought porn was crazy. Even after she was hired, she vowed she would never watch a blue movie, never use a toy. Why would she even want to? After her fifth day of training, though, a manager gave her a handful of DVDs from the various genres and suggested she take them home and watch so she knew what she was selling. At first she felt dirty. She couldn't watch them. But she and Eric persevered. Same thing with sex toys.

Now Trista can hardly believe her metamorphosis. "This job has opened me up completely!" she tells me. The girl who once blushed and stammered when speaking to customers casually details how she rented movies with G-spot play in them, took home the Slimline G, "and made Eric watch. I said, 'Do this! Try it! Do this,' and it worked! It was a different sensation. For a while

I wanted to just do that because before it was just plain sex like everybody else has." Even if Trista isn't sure what she wants to be, she does know she would rather not be like everybody else.

As much as she enjoyed the G-spot breakthrough, though, squirting has become her forte. Trista always thought it was unfair men could ejaculate and be done and "feel like you accomplished something." When she saw teen porn idols like Cytherea squirting, it was a revelation. Squirting on cue is not easy, though. "It hurt like hell for a while," but once she got the hang of it, she became a squirting missionary, evangelizing female customers at every opportunity. "I wish everyone could watch squirting DVDs to know what it is and try it."

That's the thing about working in a store like Fascinations. You learn so much about human sexuality. When she went back to Detroit Lakes for a visit and told her friends where she works, "they were like, 'Sweet!' Can you get us porn? I'm like, 'Yeah,' and that's all they care about. They think this store is just movies like a Blockbuster with porn." The store is so much more. It has helped her to grow. She knows how to please Eric now, and he knows how to please her. Sex doesn't have to be normal and boring. It can be Red Bulled. "That makes life more enjoyable."

Working here has dramatically changed her life for better and for worse, she says. The better is easy to list; she's just done it. The worse isn't. The truth is, Trista would like to find another job. She thought about selling cell phones in a mall.

"I wish I would have worked here, learned all this stuff, and then quit. I watch porn now, and it's not enjoyable after a year straight."

She doesn't have any close friends in Arizona. Eric has a few, but they talk about stuff that doesn't interest her. Mostly, she works and then goes home to Eric and they play some porn. "My boyfriend thinks more of it. I watch porn all the time, too, but I critique it like a movie. A lot of times we watch it and have sex at the same time. He likes that, but it's also, like, he says, 'Do we have to watch porn every time we have sex?'"

The sex toys also worried her for a little while. At first, she only used a vibrator when Eric wasn't around, but then she would use it as foreplay and "then it got to where I'd have to use it, and then have sex. Eric was, like, 'God, could you just put it away? Am I not good enough?' There for a while I was kind of scared."

She can talk to any customer about any sexual subject you could ever imagine, yet "I almost wish I was more naive."

"You know," she says, looking at me, "there is a lot to think about there. I never really thought about it."

By my second shift I begin to hit my stride. Whiling away the time during a slow period, I picked up a tester bottle of sex lube from Germany called Pjur Eros. I drizzled two drops onto my fingertips, rubbed them together, and as if I had just dropped acid, began hallucinating about sex. It felt that good. The stuff is also absurdly expensive at $41 for a small bottle, so I figured that I had found a product I could fully endorse while increasing my dollar volume to boot. Since the wall o' lubes is on the way toward the front door and the checkout line, my strategy is to snag customers after they have visited other parts of the store and make a pitch for this one product to enhance whatever else they've bought. I'm roaming, too, netting customers who seem to be wandering without any particular purpose and walking them over to the lubes to try my favorite.

Oh, and I have also begun referring to myself as the store's lubrication specialist, as in "Hello, I'm Brian, the Fascinations lubrication specialist." I am résumé plumping. Sue me.

My plan works surprisingly well. The Topco chemist was right: women are looking for a longer ride and a sweeter slide. Men, too, for that matter. Sometimes I grab them by the arm and say with near-religious fervor, "No kidding, you have to come over and try this!" When they rub their two fingertips together as I did, their eyes get the same glassy look. True, some balk at the price, and no matter how much I argue that this one bottle will last months, making it more cost effective in the long run, they refuse. There is no reasoning with some people.

That's when I pull out my secret weapon: "But this will work even in water!" I smirk and leer mischievously, a look I intend to communicate, "Huh? Know what I'm saying? Huh? Phoenix has a million swimming pools by my unscientific estimate. This place practically runs on chlorine. Having sex on the pool float, or in the spa, drinking a glass of wine, I mean, come on, man, do I have to spell it out? I'm a romance consultant. I am a professional. Just trust me." This converts a few of the reluctant and boosts my batting average to about .300. Not bad for a rookie.

As I contribute to the store's daily totals, I begin to feel a closer kinship with my coworkers. We talk a lot during slow periods. Christine tells me about a time a couple of weeks ago when she sold a strap-on to a concerned mom whose son had been born without the normal complement of male equipment. "That way he could hang out with his friends and not feel strange," thanks to his new bulge.

Shona is about to quit for a higher-paying job but is sorry to be leaving her regular customers—the female transsexual who comes in all the time, the man who had spent years fighting the feeling he was supposed to be a woman, the married couples looking to stoke new flames. "I feel like I can help them work out some things in the bedroom, make them closer so they can have more intimate moments, more kissy-I-love-you moments."

Every customer has a story.

Assistant manager Nikki Gavin tells me about growing up in Mississippi, how she was active in her church group, and how she learned how to have anal sex with her boyfriend when she attended a sex toy party back home. She married the boyfriend and they live here now. She works in the store and he goes to graduate school for a degree in religion. He hopes to provide wisdom and guidance to people one day, and in her way, she is already doing the same. "I am happy to talk about what I do, good sex techniques. Eighty percent of my conversations with friends turn to sex. I know this confuses people. I don't smoke, I drink only occasionally. I do not do drugs."

My coworkers could be working at other retail jobs, but they say they are proud of helping people. Many customers won't talk to their doctors about sex, or see therapists, but they'll walk through the doors of a store and tell their most intimate secrets to a twenty-one-year-old romance consultant.

A woman about sixty rushes into the store on one of my day shifts and heads straight for the dildos made of Pyrex glass. I've been trying to sell some of these since I started working here, because at a hundred bucks, they are one of the more expensive items.

I start a small sales pitch, but I needn't bother. "Yes, yes, these are great," she tells me as I struggle with the keys to the case in which they are kept. "They last forever if you don't drop them on the tile of the kitchen floor." Seems she fumbled hers after warming it up in the microwave. I don't imagine she tells this story to her bridge club.

I wait on a mother and daughter shopping for their son/brother's birthday party. He'll be twenty. They've decided porn and a couple of sex toys are exactly what a twenty-year-old man would want. "What's on these DVDs?" the mother asks me as we stand by the bins.

"Lots of sex." I half expect her to recoil.

"Well, duh! But what kind?"

I do my best to explain wall to wall, gonzo, couples, interracial, mature, BDSM, anal, fetish, Japanese, alternative, retro, gay, cream pie, voyeur.

"What do you think he would like?" the mother asks the daughter.

"How should I know, Mom! Ones with girls."

I pick out three DVDs at random and hand them to the mother, saying, "These. He'll love these."

People come in harried, sometimes, like the young couple rushing to get home after having a meal out. I am showing them a butterfly-shaped strap-on vibrator (Joani Blank invented the first one) when their cell phone rings. "Is Brendan in his pajamas yet?" the husband says. "Okay, we'll be home in about fifteen minutes."

"Babysitter. Look, this'll be fine." And off they run, leaving me to wonder about the emergency vibrator purchase.

One or two regular customers make a habit of visiting the store late, near closing time so they can jabber with the employees. Artie comes in about three nights a week. One night we stand around the porn bins and he leafs through the DVDs, rattling off more porn trivia than I had ever hoped to know. Artie coaches baseball and looks the part with his athletic shorts and T-shirt. He's about thirty, short and square with black hair shaped in a military-style cut, and he really does have an astounding mind for porn. Artie can tell you, if you want to know, what video featured Janine's first girl-girl scene, when Tera Patrick made her first movie and who directed it, when Devon first went anal and with whom. He owns over two hundred DVDs. Currently he is working on placing every one of his DVD covers in plastic slips so he can assemble them in three-ring binders.

"You know, Artie," I say, "it's possible you are getting a little carried away."

"I was just thinking about that today. I guess this is my fetish," he answers as if everybody has a fetish, has a right to have a fetish, and this may as well be his.

On those late shifts, groups of couples sometimes come in after eating and drinking at nearby restaurants. Something about tequila seems to convince a lot of people that a naughty excursion is a wonderful idea. I come close to selling a love swing to a woman who is part of one such group. She eyes it as I lean back in it, looks at her husband, eyes me, and starts laughing a little too loudly.

"Interested?" I ask.

"Oh, I would never!"

"Tonight she almost had enough to drink," her husband whispers to me. She is just one tequila shooter away. They'll be back.

Another woman seems interested in the vibrators. "Isn't this the one from *Sex and the City*?" she asks, holding the rabbit vibe.

But she can't buy, she says. She coaches kids in a sport. If a few of the parents ever found out she was even in this store, they would ask questions she would rather not answer.

I don't think she has to worry. I don't think the school-board member or the aspiring deputy or the firefighters have to worry either.

Take Good Vibrations. Joani Blank is no longer a part of the operation. For a long time it managed as a co-op, a few hippie women and lesbians and sex activists fighting a good fight. It's a regular California corporation now, the Ben & Jerry's of sex toys and porn with a values statement that says, "Sexual pleasure is an important part of all of our lives . . . everyone should be able to live the sex life that's right for them. We take it as our mission to respond to all forms of sexual shame and support people as they discover their authentic sexual selves."

Good Vibrations used to be more Birkenstocks than Ferragamo, but new bus ads show a well-dressed suburban woman swishing a signature Good Vibrations shopping bag. The marketing director used to work for Restoration Hardware. The new merchandising manager was formerly at Pottery Barn.

About eight months from now, the *Arizona Republic* is going to ask the mayor of Tolleson, the nearby town where Mr. de Santiago accused the store of endangering his kids, how the city feels about the presence of a romance superstore. Adolfo Gamez will declare himself a fan.

The store will have made donations all over town, become "a model for others to follow." "As controversial as they were when they came in, you don't hear a lot [of negativity] anymore." Hizzoner will claim he's not actually been in the store but he's, you know, "heard" the store is very nice and that it sure seems to do a lot of business.

"They've been nothing but good for us."

CHAPTER 4

From the Bedroom to the Bank

I Caddy for a Sex Toy Sales Titan

> I see a definite spiritual revival that is touching the standards of conduct of the entire society, which has gone too far toward sexual freedom.
>
> —Pat Robertson, 1986

Six days before I arrive in Kansas the Shawnee County District Attorney has indicted adult stores in Topeka with multiple counts of promoting obscenity. The indictments resulted from a campaign called Prairie Wind by a group of fundamentalist Christian ministers. They used a Kansas law mandating a grand jury be impaneled whenever enough petition signers want something investigated. With the collective mass of their followers, the ministers reached the minimum number of signers; the jury set to work, and soon arrived at the indictments.

Something similar had already happened in Wichita, where Operation Southwind, another project of conservative churches, forced the convening of a grand jury in 2005. But Southwind ended somewhat disappointingly for the ministers there, because, though the petition called for his office to investigate just about every adult store in the city, the local district attorney handed down only one indictment, against a Priscilla's:

> The grand jury charges:
> That in the County of Sedgwick, and State of Kansas, and on or about the 9th day of September, 2005, A.D., one KELLOG GIFT SHOP, INC. d/b/a PRISCILLA'S and ROBERT FLOYD did then and there unlawfully or recklessly possess obscene materials, to-wit: a DVD entitled "Sucking Cock Is Good for Your Health" a/k/a "Sucking Dick Is Good for Your Health" with the intent to sell, lend, or deliver said obscene material.

There is no mention in the indictment of whether or not sucking cock really *is* good for your health.

The fundamentalist constituency was not satisfied by a single indictment over a single DVD making a dubious health claim. It became even more disgruntled as the trial date receded into the far future thanks to procedural maneuverings.

The indictment yield was paltry, apparently, because the state's obscenity statute had earlier been ruled unconstitutional for being so broad it could be interpreted as criminalizing sex. So the ministers persuaded the state legislature to change the law. The new law was passed in July, the Topeka indictments handed down in August. In his statement announcing the indictments, Shawnee County DA Robert Hecht summarized the rule changes:

> The statute criminalizes selling, giving, delivering, or distributing obscene material which is material, taken as a whole, [that] appeals to prurient interest, which means material, applying contemporary community standards, [that] would be found to have patently offensive representations or descriptions of ultimate sexual acts, normal or perverted, actual or simulated, including sexual intercourse or sodomy or mas-

turbation, excretory functions, sadomasochistic abuse or lewd
exhibition of the genitals and which lacks serious literary,
educational, artistic, political, or scientific value. Obscene
devices, by statute, are defined as dildos, artificial vaginas
designed or marketed for the stimulation of human genital
organs and not for the purpose of medical or psychological
therapy.

Of course, this was exactly what I had been doing in Tempe,
Arizona, assiduously promoting obscenity by trying my level best
to sell vibrators, dildos, and porn where genitals were most lewdly
displayed. When the grand jury was convened, it found the same
thing was happening right there in Topeka.

Phillip Cosby, the Kansas City–area director of the National
Coalition to Protect Children and Families, an organization
devoted to moving "the people of God to embrace, live out, pre-
serve and advance the biblical truth of sexuality," hailed the
change in the state's obscenity laws and the Topeka indictments.
(His biblical truth, apparently, is somewhat different from Joe
Beam's or the Penners'.) He rallied his troops, telling the faithful
of Wichita, "I predict your current obscenity trial against Priscilla's porn outlet will soon stop treading water in pretrial contin-
uances and be moving forward." He then told his Topeka
followers that Hecht was chomping at the bit to get some grand
jury indictments. "The scriptures, the Federal and Kansas law[s]
agree," he told his followers statewide. "Obscenity is illegal and
immoral and should be exposed for the danger it is . . . the only
variable is our resolve. If not you, Who? If not now, When? If not
here, Where? I am only a phone call away to help. STAY STRONG!"

The indictments and the organized campaigns against adult
stores are just the sorts of things that would seem to prove the
people of the Heartland, my former peeps in the fly-over states,
the states annoyed by the liberalism and arrogance of the coasts,
were firmly opposed to American sexuality as practiced by the

people I have met so far. But the press release from Robert Hecht hardly seemed that of a DA eager to launch a small war on "obscenity":

> Our citizens, speaking through their representative legislature, have decided that obscenity, and obscene material or devices, should be, and are, outside the reasonable protection of the First Amendment and should be prohibited. Clearly, where to draw the line, and how to so define the material is not easy which is why, in my opinion, such charges should not be brought only by a District Attorney exercising his/her discretion, but by a Grand Jury as the bulwark between government and citizens and the best expression of community standards and values.

Call me cynical, but to my mind, this required very little insight to gloss. "Our citizens" (a group of religious zealots), "speaking through their representative legislature" (state politicians who would never want to be seen opposing a "morals" law), "have decided that obscenity, and obscene material or devices, should be, and are, outside the reasonable protection of the First Amendment and should be prohibited." (When this gets overturned by the Supreme Court, don't blame me.) "Clearly where to draw the line and how to so define the material is not easy" (why don't you just let me prosecute crooks?), "which is why, in my opinion, such charges should not be brought only by a District Attorney exercising his/her discretion but by a Grand Jury as the bulwark between government and citizens and the best expression of community standards and values." (Like Pilate, I wash my hands.)

Maybe Hecht really was eager to start prosecuting, but if he was, and if he was sincere in that release, he worried me. I've never trusted a jury of my fellow citizens to tell me what is legal to say or write or what art I can create, and what isn't.

In 1973 Supreme Court Justice William O. Douglas wrote:

"To many the Song of Solomon is obscene. I do not think we, the judges, were ever given the constitutional power to make definitions of obscenity. If it is to be defined, let the people debate and decide by a constitutional amendment what they want to ban as obscene and what standards they want the legislatures and the courts to apply. Perhaps the people will decide that the path towards a mature, integrated society requires that all ideas competing for acceptance must have no censor. Perhaps they will decide otherwise. Whatever the choice, the courts will have some guidelines. Now we have none except our own predilections."

Douglas lost that battle, *Miller v. California,* which upheld a California obscenity law by a reasoning that has proved so unworkable in real life that California is now the porn capital of the world. From what I have seen so far on this journey around America, though, Douglas has been vindicated. As he suggested, many Americans have decided. They like sex toys, especially sex toys "marketed for the stimulation of human genital organs." The more stimulation, the better, thanks. A lot of people seem to like porn, too.

Still, maybe it's different in the Heartland.

Missouri and Kansas have many signs making sure you never forget that you are, in fact, in the Heartland. You start seeing them soon after leaving the Kansas City airport, located on the Missouri side of the Missouri River: Heartland Propane, Heartland Presbyterian Center, Heartland Barbecue, Heartland Humane Society, the American Heartland Theater.

I am headed to Shawnee, Kansas, a place that was once a pioneer outpost, then a small manufacturing and agricultural town. Now it is part of the suburb-o-plex of Kansas City. I am driving to Brooke Reinertsen's place. She and her husband, Tracy, and their children live in a new subdivision on the western edge of town, beyond the Applebee's and the Boston Market and International House of Pancakes and the T.G.I. Friday's.

Brooke's neighborhood is brand new. Some of the lots, carved out of what used to be farmland, are flat spots of dirt waiting for a building. Some of the houses are empty, ready for their first occupant. The Reinertsens live in one of these brand-new houses, and when I pull up to it late in the afternoon, the place looks grand with antebellum touches like soaring rooflines and columns. An enormous carnival-colored play center dominates the backyard. An equally enormous Cadillac Escalade fills the front driveway.

I ring the doorbell and a boy in a peewee football uniform answers. He is Brooke's stepson on his way to practice. When I walk into a small foyer with marble-tiled floors, a male voice, Tracy's, tells me to come on into the living room. Tracy is sitting on the couch watching the PGA Championship on a big, flat-screen TV. We make our introductions and Tracy says, "You're really doing this, huh?"

"I sure am."

"Oh, man."

Tracy is about thirty-five, a good-looking guy with short dark hair. He's wearing sweat socks. He looks like the kind of guy who might object to another man he has never met accompanying his wife to a party, but instead he is sympathizing because the party I am attending tonight with Brooke is a special kind of party. Brooke is a Passion Consultant (everyone in America being a consultant—are there no more salesmen?). During tonight's event Brooke will sell sex toys, lotions, and lubes to a house full of women. Tracy has no desire to be within ten miles of such a gathering. He foresees my testosterone draining away into a puddle on some woman's kitchen floor. I'm not too sure of the wisdom of the idea myself. Eventually, I did warm up to romance consulting at Fascinations, but I have been trying to convince Brooke to let me become one of the very few men to sell Passion Parties products, in the Heartland, mind you, while prodding women to tell me about their own sex lives. Now, thanks to the Kansas legislature, there is the added worry of committing a crime. I doubt I'll be arrested, but at least one woman in Texas has been. Cops in Burleson charged a Passion Consultant there with obscenity. After a court fight, the charges were dropped.

"She'll be down in a minute," Tracy says. "You want a beer?"

"No, thanks," I say. And then, looking at the big screen TV, "Who's leading now?"

We talk about a relative unknown golfer named Chris Riley and speculate how long it will take before he collapses and Tiger Woods does what Tiger Woods always does. Standings, though, are really beside the point. Tracy is helping me man up before my first party, a form of inoculation, I guess.

Passion Parties is a Las Vegas–based multilevel marketing home party company organized along the same basic line as Tupperware, Avon, and Mary Kay Cosmetics. Brooke is a leading light in the network. Tracy sells construction materials and makes a decent living at it, but Brooke, who has just turned thirty, makes hefty coin, over $100,000 per year. She and her "downline," the women she has brought into the Passion Parties fold, will sell well over $1 million worth of adult joy, mainly in the states of Kansas and Missouri. This may be the Heartland, but some people in the buckle of the Bible Belt must have an appetite for the devices the Kansas legislature has declared obscene.

Brooke's shoes clack onto the marble tile in the foyer. She seems frazzled, a little out of breath. Beads of perspiration are rising on her forehead. It is a hot afternoon, and Brooke is rushing to be on time for the party, but the house is air-conditioned. The real problem is that she gave birth to a little girl seven months ago and the pregnancy played havoc with her body. She gained weight she is struggling to lose, and her hormones have gone completely haywire. But even with the extra weight Brooke has a pretty, uncomplicated moon face surrounded by blond hair she has tied up off the back of her neck in an effort to stay cool. She's wearing business attire with a long-sleeved blouse, which isn't helping with her overheating, and low heels.

"I feel sort of underdressed," I say after our hellos, referring to my jeans and buttoned shirt. Exactly what does one wear to a suburban sex toy party?

"No, no, that's okay," Brooke says pleasantly. "Everybody else will be casual, too. I try to wear business attire to project a professional image."

The image is very important to Brooke because she wants to communicate how much fun a woman can have with the products she sells, without veering into sleaziness. Like wearing a maroon shirt and khaki pants and a name tag at Fascinations, wearing business attire says, "I'm not one of the creepy people and so neither are you." More "permission giving," as the folks back at Phil Harvey's place would say.

Tracy has already loaded Brooke's bags of samples into the back of the Escalade, so Brooke urges us to hurry because we have a long drive to make. We're headed for Missouri. Brooke and I hustle to the Escalade, ascend into it, and drive off into the early Kansas evening.

Tonight Brooke is presenting in a small town on the other side of the river, Grain Valley, Missouri, another farm community turned Kansas City suburb. Brooke thinks the trip will take longer than it does and she hates being late, but I wish she'd slow down a little. A Cadillac Escalade is a cruise ship of a vehicle. Brooke is driving it like a ground-hugging Formula 1 machine even while searching for the correct off-ramp in downtown Kansas City to hit Interstate 70. The headline will read:

RUBBER PENIS PYRE, SEX LUBE
IMMOLATES ESCALADE OCCUPANTS

I try making small talk meant to relax Brooke, but she's pretty serious when it comes to her business and won't be distracted.

Brooke has done hundreds of these parties since she started three years ago, but she operates like a strict sea captain with no lolly-gagging permitted. If it weren't for the bags of gear in the back, I could see her as a driven attorney, a hedge-fund manager, or a head nurse.

Brooke grew up in a nominally Christian household in Topeka, but church was not a big part of her childhood. She's not a church-goer now. Many of her customers are, though, and she's perfectly comfortable with whatever anybody else wants to believe. Some-times people who would like to join her downline tell her they're worried about what fellow church members might say if they found out the woman in the pew across the aisle had started sell-ing lotions and toys and oral sex how-to books. One prospect told Brooke she would love to be a Passion Parties lady, but she was the daughter of a preacher. Brooke told her about the parties she's done for a church-affiliated Christian book club.

When Brooke was a student at Kansas State out in Manhattan, west of Topeka where she grew up, she majored in family studies and thought about being an educator. As a senior project, she developed a program to teach parents how to speak to their chil-dren about sex, sex ed in Kansas schools being pretty ineffective, she thought, because it was all about abstinence and Brooke didn't think telling a teenager not to have sex meant they really wouldn't.

After graduation, she went to work for the state of Kansas as a child abuse investigator. Then she and Tracy married, and she became a mother to Tracy's son. Soon she had one of her own and found the day-care bills barely kept pace with her social worker salary. Finally she decided to stay home, but living comfortably is difficult on one salary when you have a young, growing family. Financial pressure and Brooke's inherent ambition led her to explore ways to make a little money and get out of the house. "I was looking for something to do and my sister-in-law, who lives in Baltimore, called me and said she had just seen these women on TV who make all this money doing something called Passion

Parties." She researched the company online, made contact with a local representative, and trailed along to observe a party.

"I had no idea what it really was," Brooke recalled one afternoon while we were driving to another party at a somewhat less death-defying pace. "I was freaking out. I totally didn't know what I was expecting, but it was something I could see myself doing. That week I jumped in and it pretty much took off."

Brooke buys her samples from Passion Parties and orders the products she sells to individuals from the national organization. She pockets the markup. Plus, Brooke gets 5 percent of sales from every woman in her downline. When she reaches certain sales levels, she becomes eligible for car allowances, bonuses, trips. Still, she thinks she has not entirely left her social work behind.

"I sell lots of people their first vibrator. Last weekend a woman—married for twenty-three years and never had a toy—told me she was getting divorced. I can't recall if she had orgasms before or not, but she never had a toy and she was married for twenty-three-years." Brooke shook her head in mystified regret. "She was close to fifty and she told me, 'I do not know where my clitoris is. I am so embarrassed by that.' I was like, 'No, that is very common.'

"Women are just not getting that education and all of a sudden they are supposed to grow up and get married and enjoy it and they don't even know where their clitoris is! Now you do get some women who saw the rabbit vibe on *Sex and the City*, lots of them, usually the more advanced ones. Things like *Sex and the City* and *Real Sex* on HBO opened it up and made it all right to talk about sex. And Oprah. It makes it all right to say, 'I want a Rabbit Pearl, too.' Women are looking for you to tell them, 'It's okay. Everyone else is doing it.' They want to know they are not the only one."

Fortunately, Grain Valley is hard by I-70 and the trip is freeway all the way. So we arrive at the turnoff twenty minutes before

Brooke had estimated. Her hands around the steering wheel visibly relax and we take our time on the town's surface streets, a good thing as it happens, because there is so much new construction, so many new pocket subdivisions, each one looking exactly like the one before, we can't tell just where we are. Some of the lanes aren't even marked. Brooke does spot the street sign for the road where Julie Bunton, our hostess this evening, lives with her husband, two children, and a cat. But we can't find Julie's house because all the houses look alike and there is no congregation of cars to say "Party here!"

Brooke's a little worried about that. Why aren't there any cars? Will it be a small crowd? "Usually there are at least twenty people," she says as we crawl up and down the street, looking through the windshield. Sales are better with more people, not just because there are more prospects, but because once a critical mass is achieved, the flying sex talk creates more sex talk and the room heats up. People run off the resulting energy and become brave.

At last, we spot the house numbers on the Bunton place. Brooke parks and pushes a button to open the rear hatch. I jump out and gallantly grab for a big greenish roller contraption.

"Watch out, it's kinda heavy," Brooke says belatedly. I have nearly dislocated my shoulder. It must weigh well over a hundred pounds. The second bag is lighter but still hefty. "How much stuff do you have in these things?" I ask.

"You'll see when I set up inside, but it all gets very heavy."

The Buntons' home is a tidy, squared-away place, with a tiny front yard covered in grass, a line of stepping-stones leading to the front doorstep, and a wooden American flag screwed onto the wood panel siding by the entrance. A Kansas City Chiefs helmet is etched into a stone near the door. A few women have indeed arrived, though it's not yet a full house. Folding chairs are set up in the living room, which opens up into the kitchen. A small chocolate fondue fountain is burbling on the kitchen counter guarded by two liter-sized bottles of wine. A platter with cut vegetables splayed over it and a cream-filled dipping cup in its center sits on the kitchen table along with a bowl of potato chips and a pan of brownies. There's even some thawed shrimp and cocktail sauce.

Brooke begins setting up her display on a velvet cloth draped over little platforms of varying elevations. She arranges a few bottles and jars, then asks Julie where she can set up the "office." At these parties, all ordering is done in private so no one will feel embarrassed by having to shout out an order in front of everybody else. Meanwhile, I hover around the shrimp.

A couple more women arrive and Julie greets them.

"Who's he?" one says, pointing at me.

Until now, as far as guests knew, I was just a guy helping haul Brooke's gear, but now she decides this is as good a time as any to let them know why I am here. Given the prissy "office" arrangement and the reputation of the Heartland audience, I've been a little concerned women will either walk out or want me to walk out.

"This is Brian, everybody. He's a writer. He's working with me for a few days."

"You gonna be writing about us?" somebody says.

I've still got a shrimp in my mouth. Well, okay, two. Look, I'm hungry, and anyway, I don't have a speech prepared.

"Uh-huh," is all I can manage.

No matter. With a little assist from Brooke, who provides a detail here and there, they fill in my story on their own, while I smile mutely and dab at the corners of my mouth with a napkin. The women do a very good job of guessing why I am standing in Julie Bunton's dining area holding a plastic glass of wine and chewing on shrimp because they are media savvy and fully aware of their Heartland status. Reporters and writers have been running around the Heartland for a few years now, conducting anthropology. Mainly those efforts aimed to explain why Heartland folks (always "folks") are so different from people in New York City or Los Angeles (never "folks"). So they infer I am here to find out what people in small towns think about sex and why women go to "sex parties" and if they're hicks the way they think they are so often portrayed. When Brooke says, "He's from California," somebody back in the living room says, "We have sex here, too!" and then everybody laughs. Except for the hicks part— I don't think they are hicks—they've got it basically correct and I haven't had to say a thing. I pick up another shrimp.

Brooke finishes setting up her little display, and I keep waiting for one of the women to voice some objection to my presence. It never comes. More women arrive and somebody says, "Hey, this guy is going to make us famous for sex toys!"

Nobody is going to ask me to walk out.

"Do you all know each other?" I finally ask.

"Well, that's my mom," a young woman says, pointing to another woman, about forty, sitting in front of the fireplace hearth.

"And that's my mom," says another, indicating a woman sitting in a recliner next to where I am standing on the threshold between the kitchen area and the living room. "My aunt's over there."

"These here are my cousins."

"We're sisters."

One woman turns out to be a grandmother to another woman in the room.

"Are you really her mother?" I ask the woman sitting in the recliner.

"I really am."

"You aren't skittish about this?" I ask the mom.

"Not at all. My daughters are more uncomfortable with me being here than I am with them being here."

A few more women arrive, and Brooke says, "Okay. We may as well get started."

She had warned me that she tends to bull her way through her sales pitches. She likes to pass around the sample products in order to start conversations and giggling, and the resulting noise can fill a room. That's okay, she had told me, because people are having fun and when they have fun, they buy, but she has to keep going or else the party would last all night. By the time Brooke begins her presentation, standing in front of the display she has created, the volume is already high. But Brooke launches into a rapid-fire prologue about Passion Parties and how women can make extra money doing something that's so much fun by joining her network. Then, like Trista at Fascinations, Brooke tells the women that selling Passion Parties products is as much public service as it is business—stronger marriages, healthier lives, greater intimacy, journey of self-discovery.

She distributes long order forms with nearly 150 items listed in columns. Julie retrieves Dr. Seuss books from the kids' room so the women can use them as lap desks when writing their orders for the Mini Tongue vibrator.

"The first product I want to show you is our Luxurious Bath and Shower Gel with pheromones," Brooke says, speaking over several conversations. Brooke always starts out with products like bath gels and salt scrubs, deferring the more explicit appurtenances for the second half of the show. She says this is a way to organize the pitch around the senses, starting with smell first, then taste, then touch, but really, it's just a lot less intimidating for all concerned if you kick off with bath gel and perfume instead of the nine-inch-long Chocolate Thriller with the "lifelike veins."

Brooke pushes the irresistible attraction power of pheromones and quickly moves on to Bedazzle perfume, and then a body gel with glitter mixed right into the gel to accentuate cleavage, and finally a honey-flavored body powder "you can put in three places, and then tell your partner you put it in four and have fun as you keep him guessing." Partner. Not husband or lover. Not everybody here is married or straight.

Brooke's script is carved deeply into her brain. Even as her eyes dart around the room to alight on this woman or that one, they aren't really focused. She could be thinking about her newborn daughter, or why the navigation system in the Escalade went on the fritz, or how hot she feels even though the house isn't really that hot. The spiel just keeps coming, hardly pausing even for a shouted question. After she talks about each product, she starts it circulating around the room and the women smell it or feel it or taste it and talk about it among themselves. Brooke knows that is where the real selling happens.

Taste that strawberry massage lotion! Every woman dabs a little on an arm and dutifully tastes. "To really be great lovers we need to activate all five of our senses . . . this is Silky Sheets, you can spray it between the sheets to give them a silky feeling, smells great too and really dries up that wet spot . . . Okay, ladies, rub a little of the Fireworks warming gel on your arm, ready? Now rub, lick, blow. Rub, lick, blow. You can practically breathe your partner to orgasm with this . . . Tasty Tease comes in strawberry, piña colada, and mint, will also inhibit the gag reflex, here's another gel, hot and tingly, also makes your lips fuller, called Nipple Nibblers, this is our number one product, Pure Satisfaction a clitoral gel to stimulate your clit and make it fat and juicy makes orgasms stronger, harder, longer and gives you lots more of them! Use it in the morning to get going for the day the price is just $39.50 and that's less than $.05 per orgasm! I'm going to put this jar in the bathroom so during the break I want each of you to go in there and rub some on and feel just what this does for you."

Just before the end of Part I of her sales presentation, Brooke slows down and pulls out a rubbery tube and a long, phallic-shaped bottle of lubrication. "Now, ladies, this is Gigi." She squirts a load of lube from the bottle into Gigi, and then slowly slides and twists Gigi up and down the bottle. "This is going to make your job a lot easier," she says, sounding like a roving vacuum-cleaner salesman who has just tossed a handful of topsoil on the carpet.

Pairs of interrogating eyes look at me, though I fail to notice, at first. I'm still standing on the threshold between dining area and living room, leaning up against a wall. I am entranced by Brooke's technique, and absentmindedly rolling the word *Gigi* around in

my head like Maurice Chevalier walking through a sunny Paris
park. I think I might be smiling. Brooke gives Gigi one or two
more slow, sliding twists around the bottle, then stops and looks
at me, too.

"When I took the porn class, it became the difference between
what I was and what I am now," Anne, one of the guests, tells me
during a break in Brooke's spiel. Anne is thirty-two, slightly older
than some of the women—Julie Bunton is only twenty-five—and
single, "which makes me an old maid around here."

By "porn class," she means a course taught at the University of
Kansas in Lawrence by a professor of social welfare named Dennis
Dailey. Anne traces her sexual liberation from small-town thinking to the porn class. Actually, the course was on human sexuality
in everyday life, but Dailey showed a few explicit educational
films and photographs in the class so students knew exactly what
was up with human sexuality in everyday life. Naturally, they
dubbed it the porn class and kept it constantly oversubscribed.
When a few state politicians heard about the class—which had
been going on for years—they tried to shut it down, insisting the
videos were antithetical to Kansas values, encouraged sexual
deviancy, and contributed to the degradation of the conservative
sexual morals of the American college student. In 2004 one used
the contretemps over the porn class to create a campaign statement: "Some Kansas professors are using your tax money to turn
their classrooms into red-light districts." She won the election.

What really peeved certain politicians, though, was not the
nature of the imagery used in class but the thinking it might spur
in the minds of kids, many of them from small towns. "Their
minds are being formed, their morals are being formed," fumed
state senator Kay O'Connor to the Associated Press. "We don't
need this kind of information."

Anne is sitting on Julie Bunton's couch, next to her younger sister, when she tells me about the porn class, and the deeper she gets into the story, the angrier she becomes. She took the course back in 1995 so she was not affected by the subsequent controversy, but she remembers how the course changed her life.

"Being your sexual self in the Midwest, you are under scrutiny. Taking that class gave me a level of personal freedom." Anne grew up Southern Baptist, in a family of Southern Baptists who meant it, and back when the Dailey thing was in the papers, she attended a barbecue with other family members. They railed against her old professor and his porn.

"For the first time in my life I stood up to them and said, 'That isn't true, knock it off! He has a regimen in class. It is a class about learning about yourself. It's not pornographic!' They shut up after that. It was the first time I checked them." She says "first time in my life I stood up to them" with pride, leaving little doubt that standing up to her relatives was a long time coming.

Nobody ever talked about sex in her family. "Hell, no! No no no no no." She and her sister like to joke that their parents had sex four times and they know that for sure because there are four kids to show for it. She still never talks about her own sex life within her family. "I'm a virgin, you know," Anne says, winking. "Actually, I really was a virgin until I was twenty."

"No! Really?" her sister, sitting next to her on the couch, asks.

"Yep."

Ever since the porn class, she has been sexually evolving. Don't get the wrong idea about Anne, though. She chooses her words carefully, so I understand that this postcollege personal freedom she speaks of was mostly in her head, a way of thinking. She didn't start her own double-penetration DVD collection or pick up random men in bars. She doesn't like porn, not because she objects to it, but because she is just not interested in it. Rather, "I became willing to at least learn about sexuality. Sex ed in school was a joke. I don't even remember anything about it; it was pointless and a waste of time." Again, she wants me to know that willingness to learn doesn't mean she'll do everything she learns about, but she has been presented with a wider sexual menu than she imagined, and once in a while she'll explore it.

Masturbating, for example, "is a stress reliever." Sometimes, with her work as a legal analyst for a major Kansas City law firm, "I have all the stress in the world. If you want a utilitarian excuse, that's it."

I haven't asked for a utilitarian excuse, or any excuse at all. Anne is talking to herself.

Then she surprises me by telling me about another rebellious act in a region dominated by Baptists. Anne converted to Catholicism. Always the former altar boy, I can't resist pointing out the sin of masturbation and premarital sex. "Well, I take birth control, too. Now that I am Catholic, I feel freer to express myself sexually than when I was Southern Baptist. I feel more freedom as a Catholic."

I am positive nobody has ever told me the Catholic Church sexually freed them.

I must look surprised, because Anne says, "Yes, really. I know Catholics are all about procreative sex, and I am all about birth control and family planning and responsibility." Anne decides on her own sexual course without reference to God's law, neither the Baptist version nor the Catholic one. She works from her own compass. "What criteria do I use? There are no real criteria. I cannot answer that question. I know where my lines are."

"Based on morality? Some other foundation?"

"It is based on my comfort zones, what I am comfortable with physically and emotionally. That is a difficult thing to put my finger on, though."

Anne pities women who haven't taken her leap into a new way of looking at sex. "They do not allow themselves to get to that place. They would be unclean, not wholesome, and it's not because they cannot, it's because they won't. Growing up in this area, it would be bad."

Brave talk, but Anne commutes to Kansas City, passing a Priscilla's store every day. "I am curious, but I never would go in. I worry about social acceptability and how my reputation would be viewed."

I think Anne is related in some way to an older woman, Kathy Pierson. I could be wrong about this. I haven't quite figured out who is related to whom and how, because there are cousins and sisters and mothers and an aunt sitting around here someplace, and there's been a couple of divorces to complicate matters. But I do know Kathy, forty-four, is the mother of two of the women here and I gather a relative by marriage to some others, though exactly how she fits into what is becoming a crowded family tree is lost on me. Anyway, Kathy says she fully understands Anne's journey because she has been making it herself.

She married into a big, extended local family with deep roots in the area when she was just nineteen. She felt swallowed up. The Southern Baptist dogma was tough to take, too. "It was God's way or no way, but I was sheltered and that's all I knew."

She was reborn at thirty-four when she divorced. The world suddenly seemed so big. Here she was, supposedly a mature woman with two children of her own, yet still so naive. From now on, she vowed, the only boundaries she would obey would be her own. The first time she had sex with a man after her divorce, it was like the first time she had ever had sex. She'd experienced orgasms with her ex, mainly when he gave her oral sex, but they felt more like a mechanical reaction. She was too filled with anger to enjoy them. Better if he hadn't touched her at all. The first time with somebody new, though, was like gliding off a tall building.

With so much catching up to do, Kathy became a voracious student. She had a lot of male buddies in the U.S. Department of Agriculture office where she worked in Kansas City, and she would ask them all kinds of questions. After they told her men masturbate at least once a week, she went out on a date with a man and said, "So, is it true men masturbate at least once a week?" and he dropped his fork. Lately she has been trying to ease off the questions. Porn helps. She learns a lot from porn, though she doesn't see much of it.

Kathy also enjoys her vibrators. Masturbating with a vibrator "takes the edge off." Once, her two daughters found one of Kathy's vibrators. "They got mad at me and said, 'You're just a sex freak!'" Now they are sitting across the room, scanning Brooke's list of goods.

What Kathy really wants is a relationship. She doesn't have many dates despite being tall and attractive with a strong jaw and light-colored hair. Honestly, she often feels lonely. She cries into her pillow at night, but there's no use in whining because she's got two daughters to send through college, and at the moment that mission is more important than men or sex.

Kathy is forty-four, Anne thirty-two. Younger women at Julie's party tell me an entirely different story, as if an asteroid had hit the earth soon after Anne went to college and changed everything. They don't say anything about rebellion; they are matter-of-fact.

Melissa married at seventeen. She's twenty-eight now, making her only four years younger than Anne. She is also a churchgoing Southern Baptist who enjoys watching porn with her husband and shopping at Priscilla's over in Blue Springs. Tonight she's got her eye on one of the cock rings Brooke has brought, the one with a little sleeve to accommodate a bullet vibrator. Her husband can push his scrotum and penis through that thing so the vibrator bullet hits her clitoris just right when she's on top. She likes that.

Another woman, a local teacher, also in her twenties, shops at Priscilla's, too, but not the one in Blue Springs. She and her husband drive over to Lee's Summit to reduce the chances she'll run into one of her students' parents, though, come to think of it, how could they complain? "What are they doing there? That's the way I look at it." She and her husband like to experiment with sex and porn. Some things work, some don't. Lately they've been taking "baby steps" with anal sex because after five years, you know, things start to repeat and you need to keep 'em fresh.

"Times have changed," she says. "I'm not sure why. Things are just more openly discussed, more freely accepted. I think it is a shift in our thinking, the whole society."

I find Kathy Pierson's eighteen-year-old daughter coming down Julie Bunton's stairs, so I wheedle her to sit with me on the landing. She is very pretty, thin, with the best of Kathy's features. We talk a little about what it's like to come to one of these things with your mom, whom you once accused of being a sex freak, and she admits that it can be a little strange. But without any prodding from me, she recalls the day her mother looked at her and said, "You're having sex!" and her daughter responded, "How did you know?" and Kathy said, "I can tell from the look on your face." The great thing about her mom, though, is that she didn't panic.

"She is liberal that way. We can talk about it. Like, she knows my best friend, and her mom has no idea she's having sex and my friend hates that because she can't talk to her mom and so she talks to me and my mom."

She's religious, she says, a Baptist, so I ask if she ever feels guilty about having sex with her boyfriend. She looks surprised, as if she has never thought about guilt, as if by asking the question I have revealed myself to be hopeless. Don't I get it?

"Get what?"

"The Internet."

You don't learn about sex from school. Maybe a little from an older sister, and certainly nothing from church. No, dude, it's the Internet. When she has questions about sex, she just goes online and it's all there. Her church may be the place to learn about matters of the spirit or God, and her school may be the place to learn about geometry and the Entente Cordiale, but the Internet is a more reliable and honest sex academy than her church or her school, and it is a place where people don't go to hell for having sex. It has killed sex guilt. "I bet I am more educated even than some women in their thirties. Things are way different now."

She did not need a college course like Anne's because she really isn't a citizen—or a captive of—her small town the way I was a citizen of mine and Anne and Kathy were citizens of theirs. Her small town isn't nearly as small as it used to be, for one thing. It's filling with anonymous-looking tracts occupied with anonymous people, salmon far out of their home waters. More important, she does not have to leave to go away. She can project her mind through seventy different channels of cable TV and sojourn in the digital realm via the Internet, becoming part of the global pop culture mind without the slightest sense of being displaced.

"We have always been twenty-five years behind the rest of the country," Anne told me a few minutes ago, "but now we are catching up."

I'm into my second vodka and orange juice slushie but still not feeling anything other than an urge to pee. Brooke has set up her presentation and gotten partway through the first half. Eight women are sitting roughly in a circle on a couch and some chairs in a tiny living room of a town house in Kearney, Missouri. They are listening to Brooke's rat-a-tat-tat. I am now convinced that Brooke, who has been a very sweet guide and mentor, doesn't actually hear what she says anymore, because if she did, there would be a terrible mental cost to giving this same talk three times per week.

The women here are cops, mostly, or employees of a local police department, and so, from nowhere, it occurs to somebody to say, "Hey, I wonder if this could be considered 'conduct unbecoming an officer.'" After a few giggles, and jokes about conduct that might *really* be unbecoming an officer, another cop says, "You know, maybe it would be!"

Hmmm. On the one hand, we're in a private house on our time, says a third. "Yeah, but on the other, this guy's here."

Being "this guy," I feel I should put their minds at ease. I also don't want to be kicked out into the middle of a development of town houses in Kearney, Missouri. "You know, you are not actually doing much of anything," I say. "You're shopping."

True enough, they reply, but . . . supervisor . . . public image of the police . . . "Some of us work with kids in schools," one says, "and you know how there is all this hysteria over kids and sex and porn." Nobody is looking at porn, and Brooke doesn't sell any porn, but some people out there might not get the distinction. "They think they are a perfect community and holier than thou," one explains. But the kids, they hardly need protecting from information.

"Do you know what a 'queef' is?" one asks.

"No, what's a 'queef'?"

"A pussy fart. I learned that one a couple of months ago from a seventh-grader. He heard it on Howard Stern."

Color me educated. The queef story reminds one of the cops about a recent incident.

"We had a disturbance call over a 'dirty Sanchez'!" The cops all burst into laughter. "A guy . . ." She can't finish the story.

Hahahha hahah ohmygod . . . hahaha.

"No, really?" another one asks. "A dirty Sanchez?"

Head nodding, gut grabbing.

Everyone is laughing except a woman who isn't a cop.

"What's a dirty Sanchez?" she asks.

This is too much. Hahahahahahahahahahaha.

I consider explaining a dirty Sanchez as a way to restore my credibility after proving I know less sex slang than a seventh-grader. But I'm not so sure I should be the one to tell her a dirty Sanchez is a smear of shit placed on the upper lip of a person receiving anal sex by a person performing anal sex. Actually, it's mostly a jokey urban legend spread by the Internet, especially a wildly popular porn site called Bangbus on which a "bus driver" named Dirty Sanchez picks up women to have sex on the bus. Luckily another cop who has managed to stop laughing long enough explains it to her.

"Some guy," says the woman who brought it up, "reached around and gave a dirty Sanchez to his girlfriend, and she hit him. He had heard about it and thought he'd try it! Started a big fight."

Hahahahahahaha.

The Internet convinced the guy a dirty Sanchez was a hep sex move. "How stupid can you get?" Yeah, you'd be surprised at what goes down around here, some of the crazy-ass shit people do.

The police officers describe a town living publicly on one plane and privately on an entirely different one. They live the dichotomy themselves. Every one of them watches porn, almost always with their husband or boyfriend. Every one of them uses sex toys. None of them thinks they are especially liberal, either politically or morally, but they all experiment with sex.

"My doctor told me no more food products anymore! No more bananas!"

"That's something I learned in tantric," another says, referring to the way her lover massages between her toes.

When Brooke talks up the Tasty Tease gag inhibitor cream, another cop is dismissive. "Shoot, practice'll teach ya you don't have to gag!"

"I pulled one of those cock rings out, and he said, 'Honey, I don't think that's gonna fit!'"

"If he were that big," another says, referring to a large cock ring, "you'd never have to worry about flying solo!"

The department held a sexual harassment course recently, but the women here didn't see the need for it. "Shoot, I already know how to sexually harass! Why do I have to take a class?" Hahahahahaha.

The woman who isn't a cop tells me she's actually very conservative. "It was two years before he saw me naked," she tells me of her husband. "I was raised very strict Southern Baptist. No dancing, no cars, no kissing. I still prefer country over rock. My mother told me you get pregnant from French kissing. My father said 'Honey, just do not do anything below the waist.' That was my sex talk."

Though she told her son during her much more inclusive sex talk with him that his father was the only man with whom she has ever had sex, that isn't true. There was a fiancé when she was very young, so along with her husband, that makes two. The fiancé was a tender, considerate lover, but even so, "I wish I could say it was only one man."

Unlike the other women in the room, she doesn't consider herself especially experimental, though her husband has talked her into oral sex and they are working on anal now, and she has been enjoying it all, so it's a good thing all this learning came during middle age. "If I had known in high school what I know now, I probably would have been a huge slut!"

She has never had a threesome, has seen porn but doesn't really like it, and won't go into an adult store—there's one not far away snugged between a McDonald's and a Popeyes Chicken & Biscuits place. She sends her husband. But she also says she doesn't care if anybody else has threesomes, or is gay, or consumes porn, or does whatever else they want to as long as everybody else is a grown-up and agreeable and they aren't pushing her to do it, too.

All these women say they are religious to varying degrees, go to church, are patriotic (the son of one cop is serving in Iraq), and take their jobs as police officers very seriously, despite all the kidding around. This is red state territory. Western Missouri is about as crimson as you can get. Could it be, I wonder, that the noise created by a few fundamentalist preachers, amplified by media, has created a convenient, if mythical, story line?

I don't have any way to know if the women I am meeting at these sex toy parties share attitudes with a majority, or a tiny minority, though if their attitudes are shared by a minority, I don't think it's tiny. I do think, because every one of them has said so, that they are not vocal about their personal lives and what they see as a right to their own sexual habits. They like having access to porn and sex toys. They see nothing wrong with either. But they are not exactly signing petitions or marching, not because they feel in any way guilty or shameful, but because they think what they do is nobody's business. They are content to allow the community to think one way about itself while behaving in another.

In 1962, when Pat Davis was seventeen years old and about to be married, her mother sat her down and said, "You know, there will be things he will expect." This was her sex education. When Pat told me this story at the Adult Novelty Expo, the day after my tour of Topco Sales, I was incredulous. I heard the same story from Joe Beam as he recounted the mother–daughter talks of women he has counseled. In fact, I've heard this story a few times over the years, usually told as a bit of apocrypha. But Pat insisted it was absolutely true. So let's say it is and that it also happens to fit nicely into the explanation she gives for why her mission as president and CEO of Passion Parties is so vital to women everywhere. She's not just selling sex toys, she argues; she is selling female sexual liberation and a slice of happy satisfaction.

Pat was born in Memphis, raised in Arkansas, and spent over thirty years living in Virginia and attending conservative Methodist churches. Many women she knew led constrained sexual lives. She has gotten rich trying to unconstrain them. If Passion Parties were a traditional business it would be about as big as PHE. All the representatives combined sell about $100 million worth of oils, lotions, and battery-operated love to retail customers every year and Pat has a couple of pretty nice houses—one near the ocean in Del Mar, California, and one in Las Vegas—to show for it.

When we met, Pat had just come from touring some of the displays on the show floor. There were a lot of new products to explore and she, with Joanne Harvey, her director of operations and finance, was trying to decide which new gewgaws, lotions, lubes, and devices ought to be added to the Passion Parties approved list. Manufacturers were happy to see them coming. Every Passion Consultant like Brooke, and there are hundreds of them all over the country and in Canada, was a miniature retail store. The entire network moved a lot of merchandise.

Pat portrays herself as an outsider to the sex industry. Unlike Marty Tucker, she coyly objects to being included in the same business category as, say, Wicked Pictures or *Hustler.* She prefers slogans like "We empower women from the bedroom to the bank."

But this was not a mission she sought. Pat was a veteran in the world of multilevel marketing. Like Brooke, she started out selling to make a little extra money and along the way sold vitamins and cosmetics and health products. Then she formed her own consulting company to teach her successful techniques to others.

One day, a friend called and said a new company needed a little advice, but it was a different sort of company. Pat shrugged and said, "How different can it be? What kind of vitamin is it? What lotion or potion? Couldn't be that different."

Well, Pat met with the president "and then went into a meeting where they turned off the lights, and held up a purple thing, the newest, latest, vibrating, light-up thing. They were passing it around and saying, 'Ooh, doesn't it feel real?' and I was like, 'Alrighty then!' I had never had one, never touched one, never used one."

She consulted for the company for three years. "Finally, I caught what they were doing and realized it was more than a toy," Pat recalled. While it may be true that Pat converted to the religion of female pleasure and empowerment, she had also been around the multilevel marketing game long enough to know a hot idea when she saw it, and by the time *Sex and the City* hit HBO, Pat realized how much the sexual conversation in America had changed. Suburban and small-town women were ready, if they could just get over the perceived ickyness of the products. "That is when I called Joanne"—with whom she had sold cosmetics at one time—"and said, 'I think I have my hands on a gold mine, a diamond in the rough. They have a beautiful mission doing a lot of good things, but what can we do to market it so it would be acceptable to people?' " The key, she said, was to play down the ooh-la-la and play up the health, joy, and satisfaction to which Americans are entitled.

Pat bought the company, hired Joanne, declared herself a soldier in the cause of sex toys for women, and set about winning over the Heartland. In her hard-nosed business way, she was doing for small-town and suburban women what Joani Blank and her successors had done for urban women, but Pat was doing it on a massive nationwide scale and without a political agenda.

Though she prefers not to be considered part of the adult industry, she cannot escape the association. Banks have turned down Passion Parties business. Some shippers won't handle the product. A payment processor abruptly announced it would no longer work the Passion Parties account after years without a peep. "One day I got an e-mail from their abuse department saying they do not deal in pornography," Joanne told me. "I e-mailed them back and said neither do we!" One consultant used to hold meetings at a pizza place in Anaheim, California, but was booted out by the manager when he found out what the product was. "We don't want your kind in here," he said.

"She has a lovely family! They go to church!" Joanne said, and I am reminded of my customers at Fascinations who said, "And I'm a Republican!"

Consultants in the state of Alabama are offered two different kits, one with vibrators and dildos and one without in order to accommodate state law, though most seem to take the all-inclusive deal. Really, Pat kept telling me, Passion Parties is about the romance, not the sex. "Sixty percent of our product line is lotions and potions, only 40 percent needs batteries, and not all that is phallic." Then she pointed out again how the business is a boon to female self-determination. Sherry Turner down in Bruce, Mississippi, near Tupelo, used to work in a textile plant trying to support herself and her kids. Then Sherry became a Passion Consultant hoping to supplement her income and within a few years she and her downline were moving over $5 million in merchandise every year.

Well, yes, but Bedazzle or Silky Sheets are not why women gather in living rooms. Without the vibes and dildos and how-to-have-sex books Passion Parties is just another network marketer selling moisturizer. With the batteries, you can buy stuff that will get you off. That is why the company is eleven times bigger than when Pat Davis took over, not because it sells scented creams.

Pat Davis is part of the adult industry, so much so her success has spawned imitators. Topco started a home party division of its own, as has Adam and Eve. Passion Parties already had its own competitors on the traditional multilevel marketing model, like a Cincinnati-based company called Pure Romance. Pure Romance got an endorsement from Jessica Simpson, a good Christian girl who said she was a virgin when she got married.

Before our last party together, the one where Brooke has promised I will finally get my chance to sell something, I take a day to drive around Shawnee and points west.

You have to squint a little to picture the Shawnee of just two decades ago. The old downtown has been made almost completely redundant by concrete traffic arteries lined with big-box chain stores, and the interstates. The First Baptist Church anchors the main street, Johnson Drive, and the Fine Arts movie theater, a Deco-inspired building that doesn't show movies anymore, sits in the center. A few blocks to the north, the town fathers have re-created the pioneer village with a stable and cabins and general store. There are a few houses from the early 1900s on nearby streets. A side street off Johnson Drive is named for Chief Blue Jacket, a defeated Shawnee. You have to drive pretty slowly to catch all this, but nobody really wants you to drive slowly.

I pick U.S. 24, a secondary road that roughly parallels I-70, for the drive west. On the outskirts of Shawnee, I pass the National Agriculture Hall of Fame next door to the Kansas Speedway out in Bonner Springs. After that, the landscape opens up and the only radio station I can receive that doesn't play country music features rock oldies, a category that depresses me because "oldies" refers to songs I listened to in high school.

Near the tiny town of Tonganoxie, I make a U-turn into the gravel and dirt parking lot of the Paradise Saloon Gentleman's Club, a strip bar. There's another car in the lot, but the place isn't open yet.

Lawrence looks exactly how I imagined it would look, a small, brick college town, not exactly the center of a "red-light district."

After I pass by Topeka, I find myself in the middle of farms growing soy and corn. In the distance, a freight train runs straight through the corn, only the tops of its cars showing above the tassels. Clouds are building on the horizon.

I blame the scenery for why I failed to slow down when I entered the village of Rossville. I am looking at what there is, the neat aluminum-sided houses, the rusty spur of a railroad track, a big wooden building I take for a grange, when the red lights flash in my rearview mirror. Damn! I know better. State highways may say 50 or 55 mph, but as soon as you see anything that looks like human settlement, you slow down because even tiny towns need to resod the ball field and there's no better way to finance the project than by snagging a stranger who doesn't see the sign saying 25 MPH.

I pull over to the side of road, directly across from a general store, and reach into my pocket for my California license. The cop is going to love that license. He walks to my window and says what all cops say, and I say what all drivers say—didn't see the sign, very sorry, boy, how stupid of me—and when he sees my license he asks me what I'm doing in Kansas.

I am tempted to say that I'm in Kansas to ask a bunch of women about sex and go to sex toy parties, but that probably won't go over well.

"I'm a writer. I'm working in the area for a few days."

"Oh yeah, whatcha writing about?"

"Well, actually, I am writing about women who go to these things called Passion Parties."

"Sure. We got one of those women here."

We chat about how nice I think Kansas is, which is true, by the way, and he lets me off with a warning and gives me directions to I-70. I pull into the general store's dirt lot, back up, head the other direction, and immediately see the sign PASSION PARTIES BY BRIDGET.

Later I call Bridget Remer. Her grandfather owned the store in Rossville, she tells me. She was raised there and in the village just east on U.S. 24, Silver Lake. Now she teaches junior high in Topeka during the day and presents Passion Parties at night. She sells over $50,000 worth of merchandise per year. Not only is she not worried about the new state law, she says she's had "clients" from the DA's office, state senators, "some pretty high up clients if you know what I am saying, and no one has ever said, 'Hey.' But I do have a gal on my team, a consultant, who was a secretary for a lawyer. She shot me an e-mail after the indictments of the stores saying, 'Fair warning. You might be the next one they are coming after.' I was, like, 'Well, bring it on.'"

"What do we have to do out here in the country, especially in small towns, but hang around bonfires and drink Bud? If people can get together and learn a little about human sexuality in a safe environment, that's good."

"You know," I say, "I keep hearing about all the fighting over sex, but it seems to me that people around here are pretty much live-and-let-live."

"That's a fair assessment," she answers. "My mom played the organ in St. Stanislaus Catholic Church and I said to her, 'Mom, I am doing this business,' and she said, 'Could you not sell baskets or something?' I said, 'No, Mom, this is what I need to do.' My grandfather ran the store in Rossville, where you got stopped. I said to Grandpa, I said, 'I am gonna start this business' and he leaned forward—he was seventy-nine or eighty—and I said, 'I am going to be selling adult toys.' He smiled and said, 'I owned a variety store in St. Mary's [the next town west on U.S. 24], and people would drive all the way down from Topeka to look into my naughty box.' That's what he called it, his 'naughty box.' From then on I knew it was okay with Grandpa."

She excused herself. It was getting toward evening, the light was fading, and the kids wanted to play some softball with her out in the yard.

That night, Brooke and I drive back into Missouri, far out into the countryside. The Escalade cruises down narrow asphalt roads as Brooke looks for the right house, but the houses are tough to see because they are spread so far apart, up long gravel driveways, set back in the trees. The hostess for tonight's party, Tanya Willoughby, told Brooke to look for balloons tied to a mailbox, but we haven't seen any yet and the landscape is more woods than houses now.

Finally, just about dusk, we see some balloons over a rise in the road. A small pickup truck parked in the front yard at the bottom of the gravel drive has a FOR SALE sign in the driver's window. Brooke pulls in and we climb the hill toward the Willoughbys' place, a small ranch-style house that may be a converted doublewide mobile home. I open the SUV's door as two men approach. One is Matt, Tanya's husband, wearing a baseball cap and a white T-shirt and holding a beer can in his hand.

Matt looks me up and down, shakes his head, and asks if I want a beer. He and his buddy are going somewhere—I don't catch where—in the friend's truck and maybe I'd rather come along than attend one of these "wiener parties"?

"I think you're crazy," he says when I say thanks but no thanks.

Brooke and I carry her bags into a small living room. Portraits of two of Tanya's brothers, one in Marine Corps dress blues and one in National Guard combat fatigues, sit on a small bookcase. A copy of the Open Bible, a study Bible, sits on the coffee table in front of a couch along with a *Bambi 2* DVD.

Most of the women who are coming are already here. They are gathered in the kitchen eating snacks, including a gooey butter cake so sweet it makes my teeth hurt. One woman is wearing an old sateen track suit. Another a one-shouldered black T-shirt with "Baby Girl" scripted across the chest. A third is wearing a green and yellow John Deere logo T-shirt that says, "Been there. Cut that."

These women are skittish to the point of fright. Nobody tries to talk with me, though I make a point to say hello to a few of them. It's as if I have a zone of contagion around me; as I move in any direction in the cramped kitchen / living room, women move away. I had expected this before but became lulled by the easy way other women have spoken to me about their lives. So now I'm surprised.

Brooke sets up as usual; then Tanya directs her to a small bedroom down a narrow hall. The "office" will go in here, on a card table. Tanya is pregnant. This will be the baby's room and she and Matt have been working on it. A ladder rests against a wall, half-finished Winnie-the-Pooh wallpaper border dangles loosely, a few cans of Similac sit at the bottom of an empty closet.

I am already regretting that Brooke picked this party to let me sell. I don't sense much goodwill, and I seriously doubt any of the women will be interested in the Pyrex dildo Brooke has selected for me to present. It is one of her most expensive items. This is going to be a tough room.

Brooke is already perspiring heavily, and soon after she begins the spiel, she looks almost panicked. There is no boisterous conversation, no giggling, no shouted questions. She is a stand-up comic dying on stage. Finally I decide to interrupt.

"Excuse me, Brooke. Can I ask everybody if they are very uncomfortable with me in the room? Does anybody want to ask me any questions?"

"I have a thirteen-year-old stepson!" says a woman, who is herself about twenty-three.

"I'm not sure what you mean."

"I don't want him knowing I'm here! What if his mother finds out?"

"What about the people at church?" asks another.

"Okay, what about the people at church?"

"They'll know!"

"Do you think you are doing anything wrong?"

"No."

Like the first party I attended, some of the people in the room are related to each other either by blood or marriage.

"You've got family here, right?" Heads nod. "So who are you hiding from?"

Well, it turns out they are hiding from "others" mostly, an ill-defined group they assume will be condemning. They see themselves as a vanguard and are not very comfortable in the role.

After some reassurance from me, Brooke starts again. Gradually, the room warms up. At the break, the women go into the bathroom one by one to rub Pure Satisfaction on their clitorises and the mood brightens more.

"Whoa! That stuff is comin' home with me!" one says.

"I'm gonna use it when I have a toy between my legs," says another.

"You ain't put any on, have you, Brian?"

"No, uh . . ."

"Come on. Fair is fair. Come on. You get in there and put some on your dingle."

Everyone thinks this is very funny.

So I go into the bathroom, lower my pants, put some Pure Satisfaction on my fingertip, and rub a little on my dingle. A tingly feeling like menthol makes me conscious of my dingle, but that's about it. Maybe you have to own a clitoris.

As my dingle and I mingle during the break, the talk turns to the Internet. "Ricki and I are total MySpace whores!" one woman says, naming a co-hostess of the party. Ricki confirms that, yes, she is a MySpace whore, made so much easier now that high-speed access has come to the area. They spend hours on MySpace messaging each other and cruising to see what else, and who else, is online and what they are doing.

Somebody is getting married soon, and of course they have to plan a bachelorette party. But where to go for the big night out? Shaft, a gay nightclub in St. Joseph, emerges as the clear favorite. "I like it there. The gay guys know how to dance, they're fun, and they don't try to pick you up."

During the second half of the party, as Brooke hauls out the dildos and vibrators, everyone is relaxed and open. "My husband drives me crazy with that thing!" one says when Brooke displays a long phallic vibrator. They play with the vibrators and laugh about the ways they can use them.

"And now Brian wants to show you a special item."

I stand in the back of the room holding a nubby glass penis. I tell them I sold one of these to a woman in Arizona who liked hers so much she had to buy a new one as soon as she broke her old one. I talk about the nubs. I say it is worth the extra money. You can warm it up in hot water or cool it down in cold water. You can stick it in the dishwasher. I keep talking because every face is blank. I don't know if it's me, my maleness, or the pricey item, but nothing works. I smile weakly.

"Okay, and now Brooke has some more to show you." I hand her the glass dingle and slink away to the back of the room.

A few minutes later, Brooke has finished. She retires to her "office" and one by one, women arrive, sit under the Winnie-the-Pooh wallpaper, and pick out items.

Matt arrives home early, but Tanya quickly banishes him before he crosses the threshold of the front door. The women are busy buying their own satisfaction. Why doesn't he go downstairs and watch TV? "The remote's down there," she says, as if the remote control is tempting bait.

Meanwhile, I sit out on the front stoop with one of the older women. She's been to a few of these parties, she tells me. Most of the women in her family have toys, which is wonderful because things used to be so buttoned up around here. Southern Baptists had such a grip on everyone's lives, including hers, that nobody ever talked about sex and especially how to make sex feel good. Her own mother and father hardly seemed to show each other any affection. Despite all that, she wasn't a virgin when she married at eighteen. Then one day, she realized nobody had to live their lives like that. Her husband, thank goodness, he was open and tender and loving. She just got lucky. They enjoy their experiments, the bondage, the anal, the girl-girl-boy, the boy-boy-girl . . .

"Wait. Whoa. Threesomes?" Massive bugs from the surrounding woods have started strafing the light by the door, so I wonder if I've heard her correctly.

"Oh yeah. Sure. Of course, I get competitive in everything, including sex, and so I got a little competitive then, too. I want to win, though I'm not sure what it was I was supposed to be winning. So I didn't really care for it." She's glad she tried it, though. That's how you survive thirty years of marriage. You try new things.

"I can't imagine going through life unsatisfied," she says. "I sure don't want that for my kids."

"So sex is very important to you?"

"Sex is important. Oh yeah. It is another way of being satisfied and happy. I cannot imagine not having sex."

On the Adult Novelty Expo's second day, I met up with Kim Airs, the woman who had been tutored at Good Vibrations and had gone on to create Grand Opening! Kim ushered me around, introducing me to various corporate executives, with an excited enthusiasm. "Oh wait, you gotta meet these people!" she'd say, and off we would run. After years of feeling radically at odds with the rest of America when it came to sex, Kim now felt the warm and fuzzy welcoming embrace of acceptance.

"Just look at Amazon.com," she said. "You can buy sex toys on Amazon. How cool is that?"

But the biggest, most exciting growth, Kim told me, was at the high end. Cheap sex toys sold by the likes of Passion Parties were once all you could get, but now everyone in the know wants to go upscale. One northern California metallurgist was making vibrators out of titanium for $600 apiece. "Over here, though, you gotta meet these guys," Kim said, as she and I half trotted to a booth. "These guys are getting sex toys into department stores!"

She was right. JimmyJane had crossed over. The products weren't sold in most adult stores like Fascinations, and they weren't sold by home party outfits. JimmyJane had succeeded in making sex toys into fashion accessories.

The company was started by an industrial designer named Ethan Imboden. As company legend has it, Imboden attended a dinner party with chic friends in San Francisco who moaned about tacky vibrators. They were so pedestrian and inelegant. Sure, maybe it was cool to have a rabbit vibe during the *Sex and the City* era, but now somebody ought to bring some real sophistication to sex with a stylish, quality product. Just as Pat Davis realized a new market was ripe for exploiting, Imboden realized a market represented by his friends was ripe for upgrading. Since he had done design work for clients like Herman Miller, Nike, and Motorola, he knew this was a market he could supply.

Shannon McClenaghan, the president of JimmyJane, handed me the signature product. At first I thought it was a tube for a nice Cuban panatela. It was plated in gold, and the motor was removable, so when you sent your bags through X-ray for that trip to Heathrow, security wouldn't ask you any embarrassing questions about a hollow tube. It costs $350. Other models were made of stainless steel or platinum plate ($460).

To be sure JimmyJane's vibrators got to the right people, Imboden attracted a team from far outside the sex industry. They were mostly people whose radar had been finely tuned to find the next big cultural thing, and sex, they knew, was it. Shannon was a San Francisco attorney who had worked on consumer projects for Apple and Home Depot. The VP of sales had worked for Barney's, the chichi New York department store. Another came from the Whitney Museum.

The line launched in 2005 and the design world, the self-consciously hip, peed themselves with excitement. Editorial features ran in *W, Elle, Nylon, Esquire, GQ, Arena, Marie Claire.* The vibes were included in the schwag bags for attendees at the Golden Globe movie and TV awards show. Kate Moss was seen buying the gold version in New York. In no time, you could buy JimmyJane vibrators at ultracool temples of consumerism like Fred Segal in Beverly Hills, the gift shop of the Delano Hotel in Miami, Harvey Nichols in London. Sonia Rykiel in Paris and Henri Bendel in New York snapped them up, too. JimmyJane vibrators were immortalized in sculpture at Miami ArtBasel, the international modern art week for the jet set. Chrome Hearts, the jewelry and accessories brand made famous by the Rolling Stones, Lenny Kravitz, and Karl Lagerfeld, offered JimmyJane vibrators at their pricey stores. JimmyJane even attracted Silicon Valley venture capital. They didn't want it advertised, but Tim Draper, the founder and managing partner of Draper Fisher Jurvetson, funder of Hotmail, Baidu, and Skype, and Phil Schlein, a VC who spent eleven years as the president and CEO of Macy's California, became JimmyJane backers. JimmyJane succeeded in adding glamour gloss to masturbation, the ultimate lowbrow pursuit.

Walking around the Adult Novelty Expo with Kim, I began to believe the lock the big-five makers once had on the adult industry was being quickly eroded. It wasn't just the JimmyJane people—there were dozens of agile, small-time sex entrepreneurs creating any number of products from sex furniture to Web-based dildos made to be operated remotely by somebody at the other end of a computer. The big five had thrived in the days when America was undercover about sex, but if committed Southern Baptists were shopping for Tasty Tease, those days were gone. People weren't shy anymore. You no longer needed a mafia connection to move a product into a town, you needed an Internet connection. Phil Harvey was right about the adult industry being just another part of corporate America, and the fate of individual companies would now be driven by the same rules that govern Starbucks and Microsoft and Delta Airlines.

As I exited the expo, I passed the Nasstoys novelties booth. Nasstoys is one of the old big-five makers, but I hadn't visited the display, so I paused briefly to see if I had missed anything. I hadn't. Its products looked like all the other mass manufacturers' stuff. (In an incestuous circle, some of the companies make products for the others so the real difference between them is often just packaging.) As I turned to leave, I heard a British accent say, "Can I help you with anything?"

The voice belonged to a woman with startlingly blond hair. Her breasts projected from her chest like huge sea buoys and her tight, white minidress was woefully inadequate to the job of containing them. Her lips were puffy as overstuffed kielbasas. She stood at about my eye level, but then I looked at her feet—it took me a moment to work my way down there—and I saw she was wearing clear, plastic platform shoes of such altitude I guessed her true height to be five feet. Once I recovered from taking all this in, I realized she was wearing heavy makeup. Underneath it, she was about forty.

"I'm Taylor Wane," she said. Taylor Wane is a porn icon, the inspiration for millions of men to take penis in hand. Since 1989, not long after porn first went mainstream with a VCR in every home, she has made over 350 videos. She has her own production company now and a deal with Nasstoys for a signature line. Among other toys, she was at the expo to introduce the Taylor Wane Assturbator Starter Kit (available in lavender or red). "Would you like an autograph?"

"Sure," I said, to be polite. Honest.

Taylor walked around from inside the booth and stood in front of me, making her already imposing persona impossible to ignore. Thinking I was a retailer, she handed a flyer to me. "Nasstoys makes You MONEY with the TOP SELLING TAYLOR WANE COLLECTION," it said. I made some small talk about working in an adult store, and as we chatted, and I looked at the lines around her eyes and the outrageously inflated lips, I felt as if I were encountering an endangered species.

CHAPTER 5

You're a Naughty Daddy

I DISCOVER THAT VIRTUAL SEX ISN'T ALWAYS VIRTUAL

To seduce is to die as reality and reconstitute oneself as
illusion.

—Pierre Baudrillard, 1990

I am stunned by her openness. She lacks any trace of self-consciousness. He, on the other hand, is a little on edge but wants to be brave because she is, and he wants to keep up to please her.

I sit with Susan and Michael in Susan's kitchen, as she talks about her sexual life and her adventures and misadventures with men—and sometimes with women and sometimes with both at the same time. I have come to watch them take some pictures of themselves, possibly having sex. We've left that a little vague. But I want to talk to them first, and the longer I am here and the more we talk, the longer I want to keep on talking. I am in no hurry to go upstairs. We are on the clock because Susan's son will come home at a certain time, so we don't have all day, but I keep stalling.

I sense something going on between Susan and Michael that is not nearly as casual as they have made it out to be.

Before we jump ahead to Susan's bedroom, though, I should explain how I ended up in a Maryland kitchen with the prospect of watching two people have sex.

It started during a conversation with Kim Airs, who has become a helpful Virgil on my tour. I asked her what I have asked others, why there was so much sexual conversation when America was supposed to be a Puritan place rediscovering its religiously restricted carnal outlook.

It's not just the conversation, she said; it's the doing. As my own correspondents indicated, many people were not just watching porn and buying vibrators by the millions. They wanted action.

"One word sums it up," she said. "*Internet.*"

"Yes, yes. I know," I said a little impatiently. Everyone from the folks at Phil Harvey's place to the women in Missouri have said the Internet has replaced school and family and church as sources of information about sex. I rolled my eyes.

I have a prejudice against the Internet. I am sick of hearing how "the Internet has changed everything." I know it's true, but I hate hearing about it from smug know-it-alls in chino pants, the BlackBerrys hanging from their belts turning them into wan gunslingers. I have long thought the rise of the Internet was a self-fulfilling prophecy driven by stock options. To my mind, the Internet as we know it was created by hippies who failed to make utopia in Haight-Ashbury or back-to-the-land communes and thought they could finally carve it out of virtual worlds made possible by digital technology, worlds conveniently free of all the human nature—sex, drugs, self-interest, money, emotions—that mucked up the Haight and the entire hippie-anarchist enterprise. But just as they did before, they turned into prophets for profit, cashing in on promises of a technological nirvana of free information, democracy, and liberty for all.

What nobody seems to be saying out loud is that the Internet has created a new tyranny of technology. What? You don't have a cable router hooked to a 2-gig RAM Vista machine with an Nvidia graphics card and 120-meg hard drive? You read a newspaper? On paper? Oh, man! Refuse to buy an airline ticket online? Pay more. No need to read *Huckleberry Finn.* Kids should learn "computer skills."

Of course it has changed the world, but for every truth that gets out that would not have otherwise been heard, there seems to be a hundred lies. Worse, it has made the world an oyster for Islamic Nazis, hucksters, identity thieves, Lonelygirl 15, and political bloggers who produce nothing original but demand—and receive—obeisance from a political class terrified of what the "blogosphere" might say. The Internet is a black hole into which time is poured.

But I knew Kim was correct. Of course she was correct. The free flow of information on the Internet, not to mention all the porn floating around on it, has probably done more to change sex since the appearance of *Playboy.* Personally I wasn't sure if this was good or bad. Exploding myths was good, I guessed, but I wasn't sure how I felt about the rest. So I asked Kim what she thought.

"Okay, where do I start? The sex act. The sharing of personal information, photos, the anonymity, IMing," by which Kim meant instant messaging. "You can see movies, pictures of naked people, everybody does that now."

By "everybody," Kim meant people who are not pros and not making a living having sex, people who take pictures or videos of themselves and broadcast them to the world. Kim knows because she used to run her own homemade porn film festival to which people from many walks of life submitted videos of themselves in flagrante in a declaration of independence from big-time porn. Nobody got paid, nobody expected a career in the skin trade. It was just the idea that everybody can be a porn star now, she said, thanks to tiny digital video cameras and computers, and the very freedom to do it has led many to take up the challenge.

"The accessibility of sex has changed immensely. I think we are taking action because it is so much easier now. You can go on Craig's List and get laid in half an hour. We are having more sex in all its forms, and that choice is supported a bit more. I mean, go to AdultFriendFinder and you can find anything."

I wasn't sure whether or not to be disturbed or buoyed by the idea that my every sexual desire could be satisfied by going online. On one hand, maybe it could be freeing. On the other, I still worried about the question I asked Candida Royalle and Susan Montani back in North Carolina. "What happens if nothing's taboo?"

So I went to the website of AdultFriendFinder, based in Silicon Valley, the most popular commercial adult dating site (in a realm in which *dating* means "sex") on the Internet. An estimated twenty-four million people from all over the world have registered their profiles with the site and every day tens of thousands join them, sending tiny signal flares into the Web sky. Other members who like what they see can flag the profile, effectively sending their own signal flare in return.

Filling out a profile of myself proved tricky. Since I wanted to attract some responses, I had to make it sound interesting. But I also wanted to be honest and so I could not promise anybody an actual meeting for sex. Besides, I'm more the "meet cute" type. But eventually, I wrote:

> I'm a writer interested in communicating with people who have a variety of sexual interests. Absolutely sincere.

This was completely true, if deliberately vague. In the space for describing who I was seeking, I typed:

> I'm looking for those who wish to share experiences honestly.

Which was also true, though the sharing I had in mind may not have been the sharing a responder might have in mind.

A week later, my first e-mail arrived from AdultFriendFinder, a compilation of all those who had seen my profile and wanted to meet, at least virtually. The first one read: "Young, affectionate couple committed to each other and our relationship. Looking to expand our sexual experiences, fulfill fantasies as well as meet like-minded people and make new friendships." They included a picture of themselves sitting on a couch.

They were pretty tame compared with others that followed. "I have always been that 'good girl next door,'" a woman, who said she was thirty-three, and who sent a picture of her thong underwear–clad butt thrust into the air, wrote. "Now it is time for me to be as bad as I wanna be . . . no more 'good girl.'" In the same batch, another woman, who claimed to be twenty-one, was shown shoving a dildo into her rectum.

Who are these people inhabiting the Web? Who is the woman standing naked in high heels against the kitchen counter, an open box of Wheaties in the background? Who is the man, hands on his hips posing like Superman at the beach, his pale ass gleaming in the sun? Who is the woman sitting spread-eagled in her Barcalounger with the vacuum cleaner plugged into the wall socket, standing ready to clean the living room, which, by the looks of it, could use some work?

In some photos there are needlepoint cushions depicting quaint farmhouses plumped on the couch, and family photos sitting on the piano, or prescription bottles on the bedside table, but the people are always naked or nearly naked and reaching out to the wide Web world.

"I hope you remember me but if you don't, my name is Kitty and I am a 50+ mother of a college student. My first contri [contribution] appeared on April 4th and you all left such wonderful comments. So I decided to submit again. This time I will show you what I like to do right before bedtime." And there is Kitty, reading, or pretending to read, a book, first with a nightie on and then with it off, and then kneeling with her ass to the camera, her breasts dangling.

"Hi Folks . . . ! We are a mature couple living in the Ft. Lauderdale, Florida area. We really hope you guys enjoy our Las Vegas contri. Positive comments are app [appreciated]." And there she is, Mrs. South Florida Sunshine, lying on a hotel room bed, her breasts flopped over her red top, staring out the window over the roof of a Ross discount store, toward the Circus Circus in the background.

They are twenty and sixty and thirty-five. Often they are pregnant. "Preg-O Wife!"

"I had my boyfriend take these pictures," one writes on Voyeur web.com, explaining her series of shots. "I am very shy and can't believe I am actually doing this. Hopefully people will like these."

"This is my hot 26 year old wife," says a newly married man. "She looks hot no matter what she has or doesn't have on, but there is something about a wet t-shirt clinging to her gorgeous breasts. If there is enough positive responses we will post more with the wet clothes all off. Please enjoy, I know I did when I took the pictures and enjoyed even more when I got to put the camera down."

"Hi guys, me again," writes a mature woman with short blond hair posing topless, in panty hose. "You gave me so many hot, flattering comments last time I decided to try again. I thought I was too old for this and had lost my sex appeal when I hit fifty, but here I am eight years later showing my tits for you guys, and hoping you will jack off while you look at me. That is so hot . . . ! I've never been gang-banged but I always wanted to try it. I'm married and have two kids, both of whom are grown up and have kids of their own, so that makes me a granny! Oh my goodness . . . ! Thanks so much."

Like other commercial websites that post amateur submissions, this one has a section that, for a fee, includes X-rated images and videos of some of these same people having sex. Democracy

has come to the Internet, but not in the way its most ardent pro-
moters advertised. Just as happened with the introduction of
Polaroid film, which required no developing from an outside
provider, from the Internet's earliest days, people realized they
could be as raunchy as they ever imagined being without creating
a scandal, because on the Internet, you can be anonymous if you
choose.

Of course, sometimes word gets out, as happened in Snyder,
Oklahoma, when the police chief's wife was discovered posing
nude in front of an American flag on a website. He eventually
quit after citizens demanded a police chief who shared their
moral values. "People in this country do what she does on a daily
basis," he told the Associated Press. He was right about that.

In fact, the commercial websites are just a part of the new
exhibitionism. Influenced by porn, seeking to validate their own
sexual allure, and hungry for experimentation, many thousands
of people have declared themselves freelance erotic icons whose
only payoff is their own sexual satisfaction. They populate photo-
sharing sites like Flickr or private group sites hosted by Yahoo!.
They give themselves names like "Slutmom."

"Very sexy pics, very sexy woman, thanks for sharing. We are an
early 40ish married committed couple. We have also posted our
pics, and we share unblocked pics and vids with other couples?
Interested?"

"Just what we both love! U got us both so hot & horny! Great
tits and with a perfect pussy! We're also in 50s, married, discreet,
looking for good friends. Let's trade pix, talk, then? Love, Sue &
Bob."

The porn world has realized that amateur eroticism, less packaged and seemingly more sincere, holds an appeal that the old-
style skin flicks do not. Your neighbors could be doing it right
now! Sexy Mrs. Dannemeyer down the street might actually be as
hot as you imagined! This is the basis for Girls Gone Wild, those
videos sold on late-night TV and the Internet, the ones featuring

coeds lifting their shirts and dropping their skirts after three Long Island Iced Teas. It has made so much money for the creator, Joe Francis, he is starting a chain of Hooters-like restaurants. A whole new genre of "reality" porn, inspired by the initiative taken by Internet exhibitionists and by TV shows like *American Idol* where Americans routinely subject themselves to what used to be considered shame but now guarantees you a spot on a talk show if you are abused enough, has flooded the adult industry, so much so that sales of traditional, professionally produced porn movies have slumped dramatically, down over 30 percent in 2006.

Bang Bus is the most successful. Dirty Sanchez roams the streets looking for girls and couples willing to fuck in a van for cash (the performers actually apply in advance and sign contracts and releases before being "discovered" on the street). On the Bang Bus website, Dirty Sanchez provides accounts, blog-style, of each encounter.

> German girls are hot. This girls body was smoking. Her ass was sweet and her tits where luscious. From the moment I saw that girl I new she was the one. We picked her up in front of a art museum of all places. I love artsie girls. They give the best head. In my experience they're really wild in the sack too. All this shit was running through my mind as I tried to figure out what to say to this girl . . . She was all up on Blumkin five minutes into it. I started talking to Al-B and I turned around and the two of them were making out. Shout out to Blumkin, that nigga moves fast. Shout out to Hialeah. Shot out to my mom. O.K., enough shot outs. Anyway, Back to the hot German chick . . .

The irregular spelling, capitalization, grammar, and all-around oafishness is deliberate, an attempt to infuse the scene with a gonzo air. Yo! Yo! We're one of you, dudes.

The *Bang Bus* movie and its sequels like *Bang Boat* have been such huge hits that the porn world has been trying to find another series like it. The website Mike's Apartment features download-able movies and photos of girls who show up at Mike's place look-ing to stay a few days for free, but of course, nothing is free anymore. In the movies and website of Shane's World, college frat boys sometimes have sex with female porn stars who show up at their parties.

Companies are harnessing this enthusiasm to package new reality formats.

> *Think You're Good in Bed?* PROVE IT! *The Ultimate Sex Championship Begins* NOW! *Submit Your Amateur Sex Video Today! Hot amateur couples screw for cash! You Could Win $100,000 tomorrow! Cash In On Your Wife's Perfect Tits! Cash In On Your Husband's Giant Cock! Compete Against Other Hot Couples for Mega-Booty! Fuck! Suck! Win $100,000 Bucks!*

Phil Harvey's Adam and Eve staged *The Search for Adam and Eve* à la *American Idol*, except the winner got a porn contract.

My friends from the Las Vegas XBIZ convention, Zach and Anna, had launched their own company, ZAMediaInc.com. They consider themselves entrepreneurs, and Zach especially, who ma-jored in economics, can recite any number of statistics and excerpts from business models to explain why their company is taking off. They are pleasant, good looking, and smart. But as part of their new business, they began producing their own reality porn pro-duction called FuckOrGetFucked.com and advertised it like this:

> *Not just any slut deserves your load, right? That's how we feel here at Fuck Or Get Fucked . . . We make* REAL *bitches compete for the meat and the hardest-fucking slut gets the wad! These are regular girls, totally amateur and eager to please. These chicks either fuck or get fucked; We eliminate the sloppy sluts and give the money shot to the one that's*

worked the cock best. We shoot in Hi-Def and all of our photo sets are Hi-Res, plus we offer multiple video formats for your PC, iPod, PSP & more. Check out some of our latest hoes and then sign up for instant access to see all of the Fuck Or Get Fucked girls in action!

Moffit Timlake has made a small fortune off the desire of everyday folks to show the world they can be erotic players. "These people could literally be your neighbors in the trailer park, and they're hot!" he tells me as we sit in his office. Moffit and his brother, Farrell, run Homegrown Video, the biggest brand name of their company, Xplor Media. Sixty to eighty individuals and couples every month send homemade DVDs of themselves naked and having sex in hopes of making the cut and being included in one of Homegrown's series like Handjobs Across America, Horny over 40, and Housewives Unleashed, available for online viewing or sale in DVD format.

These people aren't your average washouts, with blank eyes and ravaged bodies. Moffit is constantly amazed at how many middle-class, attractive, healthy people want to see themselves in action. As the years go by, the exhibitionists only get better looking, especially the women. Moffit isn't sure exactly why this is, or even why so many couples want the rest of us to see them coupling, but it's a fact and God bless 'em, Moffit tells me, using some of the same language as Kathy Brummitt at the Sinclair Institute, because these folks are showing the rest of us the way toward better sex and communication.

Just as the Sinclair Institute and its competitors try to "give permission," seeing everyday people giving blow jobs, acting out fantasies on the patio, and having sex in public tells the rest of us that all the things we have thought about doing, but never would do, might be doable after all. Some contributors are probably classic exhibitionists, Moffit says, but these days, who is to say who is an exhibitionist? Aren't we all exhibitionists now? Even famous people are naughty, so why shouldn't we have fun, too? "I think it is the whole Pam Anderson tape, the Paris Hilton tape, [former Miss America and onetime nude model] Vanessa Williams, Lindsey, and Britney doing beaver shots," he says of famous paparazzi photos of the pantyless celebrities. Besides, Paris hangs out with Jenna Jameson these days, which goes to show you, he says, that "people just don't care anymore. Porn is not that big a deal and I think that is a good thing."

Moffit thinks many people feel that enshrining their sex into media somehow makes it more real. And if people watch them having sex, all the better, because knowing one's hotness is appreciated helps you stand out in a mass anonymous crowd. "We have a woman—she and her husband have become regular contributors—who goes into their local video store to make sure her video is stocked and announces to people 'Hey, that's my video,'" Moffit says. "She's really proud."

Of all the unlikely routes into the American sex industry I have found, the Timlake brothers' path seems the most unlikely. Both Moffit and Farrell look exactly the way you might imagine they would look if you read their biographies. They both have tousled, dark hair, and a thrown-together preppy style that manages to exude old money without obviously trying. Moffit is an avid golfer, and even in his office he looks as if he just stepped outside a locker room after eighteen holes. Their own names—Moffit? Farrell?— betray their preporn life growing up in a well-to-do family in Connecticut. Both went to boarding school. Farrell, the eldest, attended the Kent School, a redbrick and stone-and-clapboard campus located along the banks of the Housatonic River in northwestern Connecticut. Like Phil Harvey, Moffit studied at Phillips Exeter Academy in New Hampshire. Both moved to California for college, Farrell to Pomona-Pitzer, a small liberal arts school east of Los Angeles, and Moffit to Stanford.

Farrell was always the wild child, so it didn't really surprise his family when he decided to become a Dead Head, following the

Grateful Dead from town to town. He financed his travels partly by selling videotapes of himself and his wife having sex to a small company, Homegrown, that relied mostly on tapes from swingers for its inventory. Farrell didn't plan on making a habit of performing in front of a camera, but it was fun and easy and Farrell had always been sexually precocious, so why not? More tapes followed and by the mid-1990s, Farrell was appearing in mainline L.A. porn productions, billing himself as Tim Lake.

When Homegrown began to crumble, he and Moffit sensed a business opportunity. So they did what generations of WASP entrepreneurs have done. They asked their mother (their father had passed away) for a loan to buy it. She agreed, becoming probably the only backer of a porn production company at her country club. Today their website is one of the most heavily trafficked adult sites in the world, and their DVDs are wildly popular.

Moffit is married, settled, a member of a golf club near San Diego where he tells people he works in "technology." He is a businessman, plain and simple. There is not a single sign of porn in his office, unless you count a golf photo as porn. As far as he is concerned, the product could be socks or bicycle rims or software. In fact, if things keep going the way they have been the past few years, Moffit tells me, he and Farrell might welcome a buyout offer, maybe from one of the porn companies that have already gone public.

Farrell, on the other hand, was divorced a few years ago. His son is being educated in an elite private school where the other parents know he does "something on the Internet," though his son is getting to the age where Farrell and his ex are going to have to figure out a way to tell him Dad is in the porn business.

Farrell also has a new girlfriend, one of Homegrown's more popular contributors. The daughter of a prominent Hawaii businessman, Mahealani was raised Catholic, attended an all-girls Catholic school, did some small-time fashion modeling, and worked as a child psychologist. A couple of years ago, she tells me when we meet, she wound up in a hot-tub orgy and discovered she liked it. It was freeing. She long had a secret desire to make porn, so she decided to make one for Homegrown. "Believe it or not, I told her she is nuts," Farrell writes in his Homegrown blog. "Still, there is no denying that she is a natural hambone in front of the camera and obviously loves the sex. Ultimately, who am I to tell a grown woman with a Master's Degree in psychology what to do? Homegrown video fans went nuts for her in her first video, which she doesn't like that much because it was true amateur porn—full of glorious imperfections. She made another video for one of my amateur porn colleagues, Rodney Moore, and his fans raved about her, too. You just can't keep a sexy mature lady down when her libido is supercharged that way." Like some other Homegrown contributors, she can no longer really be considered "amateur."

Don, on the other hand, is a purist. He has placed a small photo of Johnny Depp as Captain Jack Sparrow on his Yahoo! Messenger screen while we engage in an online chat.

"I will change it to show you what I show women who are looking to cam," he types.

"Okay," I reply.

Whoa! There it is, a man's torso, his hand reaching down, grasping his penis.

"I love the way it feels," Don types.

Uh-huh. Well, Don is waiting for me to type something back, but what does one say to a man holding his own penis? Nice physique? Happy to see me? Don has become so used to showing himself off to other people and to typing graphic dialogue that the words from his side of the conversation flow as easily as a chat about the weather in Russia, where he happens to be at the moment. He is in a hotel room early in the morning, typing back and forth to me before heading out to work as a construction supervisor for an international contractor.

At least that's what he says he does and where he says he is, but you couldn't prove it by me, because on the Internet Don could be an elderly woman in Des Moines or a teenage boy in Hamburg playing God of War II with his other hand. This is precisely the point. Don is not fully knowable or reachable unless he wants to be. So he can display his privates with impunity, without fear of fallout, and have whatever version of digitized sex he wants with whomever wants. Over the past seven years, Don—and I do believe Don is a real forty-nine-year-old man, though I also think Don embellishes for effect (he will tell in one of our chats that he likes to have sex a Herculean three to six times per night)—has had online powwows with about 120 different people. Many of these have become regulars. He estimates that about 40 percent of his sex life takes place over the Web.

At first, Don spent time looking at porn sites, cruising for jerk-off material. Then he discovered a few amateur women using Web cameras. "I searched the chat rooms for more, and found myself sitting in the chair rubbing my cock and wanting more. Eventually, I met a girl from Florida who showed me everything and spread her legs for me and begged me to get a cam. I did, and soon found myself stripping for her, joining in a private digital sex act."

Despite being conservative by nature, a Republican who grew up in the upper Midwest and now has two children and a wife who know nothing about his forays into the sexual nooks and crannies of the World Wide Web, Don has become an enthusiastic performer. When he ends his workday he goes back to his hotel room, switches on his portal into the digital universe, and begins broadcasting himself to anybody interested in watching and joining in, often via Yahoo!'s instant message service, AdultFriendFinder's chat function, or ifriends.net.

"I think of it as pure erotic expression of human desire," he tells me when I ask why. This is better than regular porn, because "we seek escape from our difficulties, from our routine or pres-

sures and this gives it to us. The interaction of two or more sexually motivated people—real people, not actors—is so hot and can
be very satisfying."

Don credits the Internet with being a great equalizer. "Of
course this also allows people—because of weight, or whatever—
to hide what they look like and still have digital sex with hot partners using their desires and minds to weave an erotic digital date
to achieve orgasm and satisfaction."

When I ask Don how he goes about finding virtual partners, he
says it's easy. "If you go into the right room at the right time, all
you need to say is something like, 'Looking to cam with hot lady
that loves cock,' and you will have them begging to watch. Depend-
ing on how turned on I am, I can select one or two of those watching to chat with and see who they are and how sexy or nasty they
really are. So the digital world gives me an avenue of escape [into]
secret desire where I can find fulfillment."

Satisfying. Satisfaction. Fulfillment. People keep telling me
they are finding these online. My anti-Internet prejudice may be
obscuring my judgment, but, really? Satisfaction? Fulfillment?
What bothers me most about the Internet is the way in which it
makes the virtual into reality. I doubt their word because the
Internet offers a mediated, secondhand experience—to my mind,
an impoverished version of fulfillment. Perhaps virtual and real
have so blurred that we can't tell the difference anymore. Perhaps
virtual actually seems hyperreal because all distractions are
stripped away. There are no bills to pay, no nagging partner, no
smells or tastes, or troubles, no risk. The heat of high-speed cable
simmers all that off until we are left with a reduction of intent:
getting off.

Maybe this is all it takes for satisfaction, or maybe this is all the
satisfaction that is available. Maybe it has come to that.

Don does meet real people in this virtual space. To prove it, he
sends screen images of various women, or I should say parts of
various women, mainly breasts and genitals, he has received from

online sex partners. Then he forwards transcripts of his dialogues.
The words were typed with all the ardor he and his partners could
muster, but there are only so many ways to say what amounts to
"Ooh, baby." mmgarcia8: "I want every inch of you . . . balls slap-
pin' off my ass as you ride me." Don's feverish exhortations to
mmgarcia8 and the other women make Prince Charles's infamous
recorded tampon fantasy seem Byronic by comparison, though I
suppose Don might be creatively handicapped by typing with one
hand and masturbating with the other.

All the sessions Don sends end with magnificent eruptions of
bodily fluids jetting across rooms, shattering orgasms, quivering
sighs. "It can be a beautiful experience," he types to me. "Romantic, bubble bath scenes or showers where you mentally wash each
other with lots of soapy water and then go down on each other........
Some like it rough and want to watch you moaning and stroking
your cock...........they long to see you shoot a stream across the
screen to make them lose control themselves.....the best is when
you have cam to cam sex and can see how hot you are making
them.......that really turns me on."

I am a little afraid to ask what the long ellipses signify and to
think of what he is doing while one finger is hitting the period
button over and over.

At forty-nine, Don believes he is much more sexual than he was
at nineteen or twenty-nine. With age comes a dropping of pre-
tense, a greater willingness to experiment. Fantasies and scary
thoughts that went unexpressed rise from the molten center of
the mind to the crust, where in the past they might have stayed.
Now, though, the Internet provides the vent. As a younger man,
for example, Don never realized there were women out there who
"wanted it and were actively seeking raw, hard action." Women
would claim to "be 'shy' or delicate," but thanks to the Internet,
he has discovered that "like me, they had a private, hard core lover
hidden inside an outwardly conservative, intelligent, but obviously sexual being."

Age has had another effect on Don, though, that is not so salubrious. Accumulating experience has taught him that life sucks sometimes. His wife doesn't want sex as much as she used to want sex. She doesn't like to experiment. Life never seems to behave according to your fondest imaginations. Over time you rack up disappointments and then you are forty-nine years old and beginning the downhill slide.

Escaping into his virtual sex world is a way he can live the erotic life he dreams about living, but lately Don has been allowing the virtual to seep into fleshy reality. If he happens to be in a town where one of his viewers or chat partners lives, he might arrange a personal encounter. Don believes in sin and he thinks he is sinning every time he does this, but he has set himself on some sort of sexual journey and can't seem to stop traveling. "Not claiming sainthood, here . . . I am basically a moral person, but flawed major league when it comes to sex."

What does Don want? He can't tell me. Whatever it is, he is unable to type it into words that make any sense. He uses high-flown language about satisfaction and fulfillment and even happiness, but he just keeps describing all the thrilling sex without explaining what he is hoping to obtain from it that justifies his sin. "I love my family, and yet there is this secret side to me that must be satisfied." So he keeps looking.

Recently, he has discovered that he may be a submissive bisexual. He says he found out when he stopped kicking men out of his cam sessions. What the hell? he thought. Let 'em watch. One day he struck up a dialogue with a man and found himself excited. "For a dozen or so sessions I watched him cum as he ordered me into different acts and positions. He asked when I was coming to a town near him, and [I] don't know why, but I told him. The date came and I was on my computer when I saw a message to call him: NOW! he said. I hesitated, but then called and set up a meeting."

Don launches into a vivid description of their sexual encounter, typing so fast I can't slip in a word. "Hey Don! How about . . ." He ignores every attempt. I realize I am just going to have to wait him out, that he is using me as his foil, either trying to get me worked up or that he just needs an audience to get himself worked up, but either way, there is no stopping him now, so I sit back in my chair and watch the words come across the screen and wonder at the power of virtual reality to overcome what we used to think of as real reality. It is a power that Don wonders at, too.

"There I was, on all fours, leaning into it and taking [it] into my mouth . . . sucking his cock and feeling it grow. How did that happen? I thought. How did I end up sucking cock in a Marriott?!"

Susan does not allow her son to have a MySpace page or even to use the Internet unless she is perfectly aware of where he's going inside it. Likewise, Michael will not allow his daughter to have a MySpace page. She did have one for a little while, but then one of her preteen friends was discovered posing in her underwear on MySpace and linking to sexy sites and that pretty much ended computer privileges all around.

This is probably just as well. This way, Susan's son, like the other students in her grad-school classes, the other nurses in the hospital where she works, the members of her mainline church, will never know that she enjoys using her computer to trade digital photos of herself like the one of her sucking a man's penis that she is showing me as we sit in a nearby diner where we have gone for breakfast. In this one, she's bent over a bed, the guy is lying on a floor, his erection in her mouth, though, truth be told, all that can be a little tough to decipher because when you make photographs while having sex in contorted positions, the images come out looking a lot like an ultrasound.

I am having trouble seeing it anyway because glare is flaring off the screen of her laptop, which is sitting on the table between our breakfast dishes. I am also trying to prevent the people in the next booth from hearing our conversation and wondering if ordering the scrapple and eggs—scrapple being parts of a pig you wouldn't eat if scrapple weren't Americana—was a good idea. I hadn't counted on fellatio with my toast. Susan, though, seems oblivious to the neighbors and the food. She's eager to show more, like those she received from one of her male correspondents.

Hello! I won't be finishing the scrapple.

Susan enjoys displaying herself to the digital diaspora because she knows she doesn't fit the usual image of Internet babe. No firm-as-an-unripe-avocado twenty-year-old here. No sir. At forty-seven, Susan is ripe and plump with wild red hair. But her correspondents tell her she is very sexy and that's the point. When you get to be forty-seven, a little positive reinforcement can be a powerful incentive.

"One thing I am *not* interested in losing is my sexuality," she says. "For a woman, that is more of a fight." So she spends a lot of time on her computer, surrounded by her books, inside a charming house built around the time of the Great Depression, on a neat little street in a charming community near Baltimore. She watches other people perform sex acts in front of their Web cameras and sometimes masturbates along with them.

Still, this is no replacement for what Susan calls "skin on skin" with one, or two, or three other people. Men or women. Doesn't really matter as long as they're nice and can give her some direction. Susan, you see, loves "being in service." She enjoys a little light bondage occasionally and being spanked, and the one sure way to find willing partners who can do that is by placing ads on the Internet.

Susan has stopped expecting any connection between love and sex. A divorce, some friction with her family, disappointments from people who do not share her unvarnished honesty, have left her feeling that trust is a rare commodity, perhaps too much to ask. Sex, though, is something you can feel intensely if only for a time, but that's better than not feeling at all.

After her most recent breakup, she took some time to mourn

and then placed profiles on AdultFriendFinder, a Maryland Craig's List, and one or two other websites. Interesting responders from anywhere around the Chesapeake Bay region—a man or a couple—were welcome. If a fellow didn't want a commitment, well, that was okay. Maybe they would have fun. She's not into pressure. Recently, a man, Michael, answered her ad. He's a professional, a tech guy of some sort, who sounded sensitive, caring, intelligent, and best of all, adventurous.

Michael is a tall, thin man with salt-and-pepper hair and glasses, a fit fifty-two. Like Susan, he is divorced.

Looking back, it was the divorce that set him off. Perhaps it would be more accurate to say it was the financial meltdown before the divorce or the increasing sexual frustration he began feeling or any of a number of other things that have melded into a unit of trouble in Michael's mind so that teasing out just what was the precipitating moment is impossible. But Michael clearly remembers a point when his course changed.

Michael was a service brat in a conservative household that, like many service households, led a gypsy life. (I have to be vague about some details of Michael's story—his name isn't Michael—because he has a reputation in certain circles, top-secret clearance through his work for a defense contractor, and children he would rather not inform about this part of his life. He is not ashamed of what I am about to tell you.) Mostly, though, he grew up in this region. He and his dad used to enjoy putting things together, kit television sets, old hot rods, technical stuff, because Michael has always been a technical fellow. In college he started out as a design major in an arty but technical field. This was the mid-1970s, though, when digital electronics were beginning to seep out from labs and into the hands of the rest of us, and Michael was fascinated.

"I got my first calculator and did trig functions on it and it cost me a hundred bucks," he recalls with a laugh when telling me the story. Then he thinks a moment and says "I had a watch *this* big," making a gesture with his fist.

Michael is older than I am, but I remember when my high school took delivery of its first computer, a big typewriter affair that spewed paper tape, like an adding machine. Only the really smart math whizzes were allowed to go near it. One of my best friends was a smart math whiz and so one day he let me watch as he typed in a bunch of numbers and symbols and said, "Watch this!" and then the machine spit tape for a full minute figuring out his equation as we both stood there, dumbfounded and amazed and a little in love with the machine that could think. Like Michael, I remember thinking how good life was going to be.

Michael married his high-school sweetheart. They met when she was sixteen and he was seventeen, then they lived together, and then they got married and had children. He had good jobs because he was a tech guy and everybody who was any good at technical stuff had a good job and Michael was good at technical stuff. This is exactly the way it's supposed to work, isn't it? You get married to the woman you love and work in the field you know and raise strong, healthy children.

In Michael's case, as in the cases of millions of others, the river of life eroded the banks.

"We did not have the opportunity to explore when we were young," he says of his wife. Ostensibly, Michael is talking about sex, but I do not think that's all he is talking about. "When we were young we seemed to agree, but we began to diverge in our sexual outlook. Over time she became much more conservative. You know, hormonal changes go on, she had the kids. Anyway, it caused us to drift apart in that realm."

This is something I have been noticing on my journey, the way people refer to sex as "that realm," a place apart from their regular lives. They make it sound like the old conception of Limbo I picked up in Catholic school, the place where unbaptized babies went, a place I always imagined was located on a Pacific island. There were beach towels. Or, more positively, they make "that realm" sound like a Club Med where you get to behave the way you want to behave but are not allowed to behave when you are home. I wonder if the stories people tell me would be any different if they thought of sex the way they thought of playing golf or a night out eating seared ahi while wearing smart clothes, something fun, but a regular part of life.

Anyway, for Michael sex was an escape. His mind was a logic machine and he lived and worked among others whose minds were logic machines, all highly talented people. Sex allowed him to shut the machine down and think about something else other than calculations and data. By tapping a primal instinct, he could chase away the discipline of logic and lose control. But when sex with his wife became rare and mundane, he had nowhere to go.

The millennial technology financial meltdown took Michael with it. Suddenly it didn't matter how good he was at his job because his job no longer existed. Then his marriage folded. Michael could have absorbed the financial strain, the family frictions, if only the sex was there to provide his escape. "But it wasn't. So there I was, forty-something, which was young to me, feeling virile, and nothing to do. That led to fights. And that led to my ex saying to me one day, 'If you do not like it here, get the fuck out!' 'If you think somebody else is better for you, go!' At that point I said, 'Okay.' I am sitting out on the curb saying to myself, 'What next?' And that is when it began for me, this period of exploration."

Before the Internet, a man going through a midlife crisis had options, but not many and they weren't very practical. There were "swinger parties," and "key parties," those suburban wife-swapping soirees that were supposed to be rampant among the sophisticated and aspiring junior executives of the 1960s and 1970s. But they were far more common in pulp fiction than in real life, and even back then Michael would never have been a suburban, leisure-suited party boy with a too-quick laugh and a martini. He didn't know any swingers anyway, and he is not the kind of guy to walk up to a couple and ask if they would be interested in a three-way. Swinger magazines have been around for a long time, too, but placing an ad, renting a post-office box to receive the responses, was cumbersome and limited and, again, not for Michael.

"Now you can sit down with a computer, and in the anonymous setting of your basement, lie in your bed with your WiFi and with any digital savvy at all, within ten minutes post an ad on something like Craig's List and away you go."

So away he went.

Susan has a bit of New Age about her—she is always entering a "good space" or leaving a "bad space"—and yet she can sound supremely practical. She calls me "hon" without irony nor a hint of flirtatiousness like some crusty diner waitress on a road bypassed by the interstate, a habit she has picked up working as a nurse. When you are sliding a rubber catheter tube up a guy's urethra, it helps if he knows that you know exactly what you are doing, that you won't put up with fussiness, but that you sympathize.

Susan spends a lot of time, or what little free time she has, reading and thinking. So she has thought a great deal about what she would say to a person like me who is sitting back at her kitchen table and asking questions about her life. She has a strong impulse to make me understand that her life is not so very different from anybody else's; she just happens to crave experience. Sometimes the experiences are good ones, sometimes they are bad ones, but harboring regret is a waste of time. There have been reasons to regret, for sure. Romances have gone sour. Some were just strange, like the guy she lived with for eighteen months who turned out to be a cross-dresser but never told Susan he was a cross-dresser, and if there is one woman on the planet a man could tell about his cross-dressing, Susan is that woman because she would say, "Well, that makes you special; how can we have fun with this?" but he didn't tell her and she was hurt by his lack of trust. Plus, he complained about her job. All those penises she looked at every day played on his mind and made him jealous. She still laughs out loud when she tells the story, because if you have seen one shriveled little penis you have seen them all. In the context of nursing work, penises aren't sexy.

When she tells stories of hurt, she never frames the plot to focus on pain. Instead, they serve as little illustrations of the ways in which everybody gets hurt if they step outside themselves and what fun would it be if you just kept yourself locked in all safe and sound? All in all, her wounds have not been any more deadly than most other people's. Her siblings are the safe-and-sound types. They haven't experienced half of what she has, and haven't been hurt half as much, but she suspects they aren't as happy as she is either.

Susan has had to make a peace with her family. They have not always approved of the way she has lived her life and have not hesitated to criticize. So she is skeptical of professions of love. She is skeptical of media, too. And the medical profession she is part of, and business, and religion, and especially politicians of all stripes. Our society no longer breeds trust, she tells me.

And yet she insists she is happy.

Life is too short not to be happy. You can wait all your life for the good stuff to start, or you can do something to make it happen and Susan is the kind to make it happen. Like now, for instance. She was in that last relationship until a few months ago, was crazy about the guy, but it didn't work out. So she took a breath, saddled up, and went online.

Men outnumber women online by a wide margin, but Susan is picky. A lot of them snap a digital image of their penises, and Susan isn't exactly impressed by penises. Many say something crude in their ads, thinking a blatant come-on will attract, but she skips right past those. She liked Michael's response because he sounded intelligent and straightforward and never mentioned sex, at least not outright. He said he was a middle-aged man, professional, educated, and was looking for somebody who thought like he did. He said he wanted to spend time together.

She answered. "I told him he was intriguing, and he said, 'You don't know me well enough to say I am intriguing.'"

"Hard to get, huh?" I say to Michael, who is standing nearby. "Were you giving her sass?"

He laughs. "Like, 'You can't have that.'" He glances over his spectacles. "I got that bad boy thing goin' on!"

Susan and Michael exchanged a series of e-mails, each slowly courting the other with banter and the slow dance of revelation. They made it clear to each other that sex was the point and if something developed besides sex, that was all to the good, but sex, the kind of sex that has a few twists and turns, was the agenda.

In the days before online chatting, digital ads, and the ability to send photos of yourself performing sex acts screaming around the world, Michael and Susan would never have met. And if they had, they would have talked on the phone and likely never broached the subject of kinky sex. That is the wonder of the digital revolution, Michael says, why it has become a vital tool enabling sexual experimentation. When Michael talks about the Internet, he uses words that remind me of Don, words like *convenience* and *freedom* and *self-expression*, but he sounds less giddy than Don.

"It is a double-edged sword sometimes. It puts it right in your face."

What's "it"? Sex? Loneliness? The fact that you are a middle-aged man alone on your bed scanning a computer screen for "intimate connections"? "You do search in solitude. It's not like in the days when you were part of somebody or part of your social group when you went to church, or had people you went to school with. I think as you get older, you lose those kinds of friends. As those things change in your life, you realize there is this portal into a parallel universe."

In the parallel universe, the intimacy that used to grow over a lifetime snaps to life in a flash. You say what you want to say and tell other people exactly what you want because there is no chance she is going to throw a glass of cabernet in your face or spread the word among your mutual friends that you are a weaselly pervert. There is very little time wasted. The long discussions over pasta dinners on first dates are replaced by keystrokes sent into cyber-space. You don't even have to dress up. You can sip a cold beer and pitch woo in your boxer shorts.

If Susan detects too much drama in a guy online, she moves along to the next one. If Michael senses a woman won't be up for his brand of sexual shenanigans, he won't bother to send another e-mail. In chat rooms, they say, you can always tell who is for real and who is posing and get a pretty good idea of their education and their openness to whatever it is that they want somebody to be open to.

"I work with hospice nurses, and you do not talk about sexuality in these terms and you cannot talk about who you are," Susan says. "It does not work that way, at church or school or wherever your community is. You cannot be real open and talk about your sexual-ity, but you sure can online and you can find somebody who is interested in the same things you are without exposing yourself. For me, online, the freedom I get is that I can talk about all the intimate deep, dark secrets. If I meet a guy at church, I cannot be sitting there in church going, 'You know, sex is so important to me!' That is probably just not gonna fly. They are not going to expect it. I do not know if I would feel comfortable doing that. Now, there could be individuals like me at church, but I am not gonna sit there and talk about my sexuality in a public setting. Online it is a public setting, but the anonymity is there and I can be 100 percent who I am."

Because of all the online spadework and revelation, when they finally did meet in person for lunch, they spent three hours talk-ing and never mentioned sex.

"We talked about who we were in the world," Susan says.

"I was looking for a new friend," Michael tells me. "A new friend who had some of the same thoughts in her mind as I did. You have to have other interests after you climb out of bed."

"Or you don't," Susan interjects, "but then it's not as good."

"Friendship is important and intimacy is important," Michael says. "But if you meet someone and you have nothing else in common, but the sex is great, well, is that so bad?"

"Exactly," Susan says. "You know what it is, and it is never gonna be anything more than that, but that's not a bad thing."

For Michael, the Internet is a reflection of the human mind, and so, to anybody who would condemn his own behavior, he would say, "Take a look inside your own mind if you think we are the freaks." The Web, he argues, gives him "the freedom to be free to think things you want to think and not only think them, but go and act upon them. It's self-actualization."

"Wow, I had never thought of it that way," Susan says, "self-actualization as being part of this, but yeah."

"I mean, how cool is it that you can dream the dream, then go make it real?" Michael asks.

"You can find somebody to make it real with," Susan enthuses.

At the moment, Michael is hoping to self-actualize with another woman named Christine and Christine's boyfriend. Last night, he arranged a meeting with Christine after she answered an ad Michael and Susan placed on Craig's List looking for a couple. Susan was upset that he went to the bar without her, though she does not use the word *upset*. Disturbed, maybe. Chagrined.

Michael scrambles to explain himself. "Look, the female half of the other couple called me and we talked on the phone and she said—Susan was working, by the way—and she said, 'Why not come and meet me at a bar? My boyfriend can't come because he works a night shift.' So I went and met her at this bar last night."

Susan smiles. When Michael told her he had met Christine, she asked for a conversation with him. "That only took three hours to work through. I brought baggage. He brought baggage. We got back to some good space."

Not perfect space. Not enough space. Susan has paused for the first time in an hour.

"So tell me about her. Come on," she says to Michael.

Michael is on the spot.

"She was interesting. She was cute. She has a health-care background." Michael looks at Susan with hope in his eyes. "She's not an EMT now, but she spent time with EMTs." Michael tries a segue. "I tend to find there is a little correlation between edgy kinds of sexual behavior and the jobs some of these people do. You see trauma nurses, EMTs, police officers, firemen. My gut tells me there is some correlation there between that adrenaline-pumping kind of job and other areas of their lives."

Susan refuses to take the bait to change subjects.

"We are going out, maybe tomorrow night, all four us *together,*" she says, "to see if we like each other. We don't know yet. We have not made formal plans. Maybe we'll get drinks and snack and meet her boyfriend."

"Christine is a bit younger, about forty," Michael says. "She is interested in bisexual experiences, in trying it. Susan has some experience with that."

Susan does have experience with that and she has experience with swinging, so that's not what bugged her. It was the fact that Michael met with Christine alone. Now she doesn't sound keen on the setup at all.

"What about that other girl?" she asks, referring to another responder to their ad. Michael and Susan sent a few photos to her and she was supposed to have answered. They have been waiting for her e-mail. "What did she say?"

Michael makes a few clicks on Susan's laptop computer. There is an e-mail waiting.

"I was wondering if I am the only dirty, kinky little girl who finds that sick sort of role play oh so hot," the e-mail reads. "How big is your dick daddy? And I am glad I can make mommy watch as I fuck my daddy. I am a redhead, too. How fun is that? And I have red pussy hair to prove it."

"Well, that's pretty explicit," Susan says, frowning.

"So do you like that or not?" I ask.

"It can work both ways." Susan thinks. "To me, that is a big, drama-filled response."

Earlier I had asked how these two would define their relationship. "What are you? Lovers?"

"*Lovers* is a good word," Michael replied. "I prefer the phrase *intimate friendship.*"

"Which is different than friends with benefits," Susan interjected. "It is intimacy on several different levels."

Susan seemed a little nervous about words like *love.* She told me several times before I even arrived in Maryland that she is not "in love." They have never talked about love. Usually, when Susan finds great sex, and comfort with a man, she falls in love rather hard and rather fast, and the interesting thing is, she is not doing that with Michael. No, she is not in love. What a relief. "We are not future-oriented people," she said.

They seemed to work hard at not being in love, and now there is this hint of jealousy or mistrust the way somebody in love might feel vulnerable. Personally, I think they are in love, and fresh with the memories of how thin the ice under love can be. They are skating as fast as they can to avoid falling in.

That's why I have been stalling about going upstairs, I guess. Susan has been sincere since I first made contact and I have grown to like her. Now that I have met Michael, I like him, too. I came all the way to Maryland to see how they took photos of their sexual escapades to share with others, and how they navigated their own sexual terrain through the Internet and then made it come to life. Both of them, especially Susan, who is a gleeful exhibitionist, have welcomed me to watch, but now it feels wrong. This isn't porn. I think I could intrude on sex, but I have no desire to intrude on love.

Susan is palpably straining to go upstairs and get going, though. I follow them up, and after some initial awkwardness, they kiss passionately, knocking Michael's glasses askew. I see some things and I hear some things and a few photos are snapped, but I am not going to tell you much about any of this. Instead, I am going to point out that I am kneeling outside Susan's open bedroom door trying to make myself unobtrusive and I am not really looking at them. I am scanning the books in a bookcase. Robert Heinlein's *Time Enough for Love* is there, which I know well. Susan told me earlier today that it was a big influence on her thinking. In it, Heinlein's hero, an especially randy immortal, rejects all sexual taboos, even managing to have sex with his own mother thanks to time travel.

A book on Anselm of Canterbury, the father of Scholasticism, is there, too.

I am telling you about these books because I am comfortable around books. I am not comfortable watching two people I have come to know have sex. This surprises me perhaps as much as it is surprising you. Still, I am supposed to be reporting, and so I see enough to get the gist of their style and to notice when Michael pulls out one of those wooden sticks used to stir paint, but before Michael has taken off his trousers, I close the bedroom door softly and walk out of Susan's house.

The next morning I pick Susan up and we go to the diner. "Are you sure you aren't in love?" I ask. She admits that she would like to be in love with Michael. And to make a solid go of it, whatever that means. Not marriage, probably. But what? Getting this right is important to Susan because she knows I will be explaining it to you and she thinks there ought to be far more understanding about people who don't conform to a traditional conception of sex and love. But we have to leave the thought hanging in the air because there isn't really a good box into which such a relationship should be placed. In any case, Michael is not ready. She doesn't want to force him to prematurely confront the idea of love. Right now, he is full of wanderlust and has picked Internet World as his terra incognita.

The next day, I receive a phone call from Susan. They have met Christine and Christine's boyfriend.

Susan and Michael arrived at the bar where they arranged the meeting only to find Christine plowed and maudlin. It was ten thirty. There was no sign of the boyfriend.

A few minutes later, he arrived. He is a county cop and there was a delay back at the station, so he wasn't able to leave on time. He is older than Christine, about Michael's age, which complicates matters with Christine because she is more than a decade younger. The fact the cop is married and has a family and that his wife has no idea he is screwing Christine, not to mention cruising for group sex, doesn't help either.

Michael suggested they all go to a different bar; maybe a change of scenery would lighten Christine's mood, though more booze didn't sound like a good idea. So they drove in separate cars to the other bar, and when Michael excused himself to go to the bathroom Christine announced that Susan and her boyfriend should kiss. She pushed their heads together. Michael saw the kiss but didn't mind, of course, because kissing other people is the point of the exercise.

Outside, there were roadblocks all over the place. The local police were trying to nab drunk drivers. So they all elected the county cop to be their free pass through the roadblocks and Susan got in the cop's truck, while Christine poured herself in Michael's car and they caravanned in tight formation. Just a few minutes into the drive, however, Christine began sobbing.

When they arrived at Michael's house, Christine sat on his

couch and cried. Susan told Michael to go hang with the cop while she had a woman-to-woman chat with Christine.

"Look, hon," she said in that way she has. "There is no pressure here. It's no big deal. Just relax, nothing has to happen." Susan got up, retrieved some tissues, and handed them to Christine.

"Take off your underwear," Christine barked.

Susan took off some of her clothes. Christine grabbed Susan's hand and said, "Where's the bedroom?"

Susan heard the men searching for the women but couldn't say much because Christine was mauling her. After Michael and the cop found them, all four spent the next five hours in every conceivable combination. Man–man, woman–woman, man–woman, man–man–woman, man–woman–woman. Vin Scully couldn't keep track of this game.

"It was awesome!" Susan tells me later. "Everybody had a really great time."

But Christine called Michael the next day, upset again, arguing that she did not receive enough attention. "Too much drama," Susan says. "We want it to be easy and we think it can be easy."

They have not seen the couple since. On the other hand, Michael did pull out a bunch of sage, burned it, and then smudged himself and Susan and the room to "re-create the sacred space between us." Susan took that as a very good sign.

There have been other fun nights since then, like the time Michael and Susan went to a sex club in Washington, D.C., and Michael stuck his penis out of his fly and Susan held on to it like a raver's glow stick and danced and danced.

"We are in love. Absolutely. Oh, absolutely we are in love," she tells me months later. "We were probably in love when you were here, but I just did not use the *L* word or the *C* [commitment] word.

"We are brother, sister, lover, friends, confidant. We both do not like the words *soul mate*, but we are pair bonded and really solid together. He can talk to me about anything. Everything about this relationship is fulfilling."

Michael changed jobs again and makes a little more money now, and he works closer to Susan's house. He comes over for lunch sometimes and all they do is eat and talk. Michael gets lonely going to his own empty house. There have been hints about moving in together.

"Michael and I have a tremendous amount of trust, and there are few walls there. Most of the people I know in relationships have very, very little trust, or respect for that matter, for each other. That is hard to get anywhere. Very few people have that level of trust with me. If he asked me to marry him tomorrow, I would say yes."

Wait a minute. Susan has contradicted herself. She claims to value trust above all, and yet she has sex with a man, and that man's mistress, when the man's wife remains clueless at home with kids.

"The primary relationship must be one of trust," she explains. So as long as she and Michael trust each other, they don't worry about lies a playmate might be telling to somebody else. She realizes this is flimsy. "To be honest, that level of drama with mixed people or couples has proven a hindrance to having a good relationship with another couple. We have decided that only unencumbered people should be considered or their partners informed or involved."

That may not be much of an issue in the future, because "We have a girlfriend," she tells me, someone they found online. "She is wonderful so far, and actually, she is my girlfriend, and I share her with Michael. We are all clear on our individual roles and responsibilities. She is subordinate to me so the dynamic is great for Michael who directs traffic."

"You know," she says, "I think this is as good as it gets and it is pretty damn good."

CHAPTER 6

Beat Me, Shock Me, Call Me Artist

I WATCH PORN ARTISTES TRY TO MAKE SEX AVANT-GARDE

Tits, cock, pussy, whatever. That's old.
> —Johnny V., Internet porn consultant, 2006

Joe Obenberger plays it to the rafters. "I never feel as charged and proud as when I stand in front of this audience that shapes the sexual fantasies of the world!" he tells the online pornography producers. "You are the cutting edge of liberty!"

His voice, made imposing by a pronounced Wisconsin accent, and amplified by a frame bulked with decades of bratwurst and beer, fills the room at the XBIZ convention inside the Hard Rock Hotel in Las Vegas. "Heroic!" Like the minutemen at "Lexington and Concord!" You are not just fighting for American liberty, he shouts, you are advancing human enlightenment! Like "Prometheus! You developed the technology that will keep kids in classrooms! I think you are patriots!"

Greek mythological figures and doughty Revolutionary War

fighters are not the usual metaphors used to describe pornographers and so most of them smile and nod, bathing in the warm
affirmation of their importance to the world. The huzzahs Obenberger sprinkles like holy water on the heads of the faithful are
not so much an acknowledgment of their role in keeping humanity supplied with naked eighteen-year-old hotties from Ukraine
and middle-aged MILFs (mothers I'd like to fuck) as for the way
these entrepreneurs have shaped the Internet and defied government oppression. Obenberger is stroking their self-image. Shop
online? Well, that's because porn sites figured out how to collect
charges, see? Got high-speed service to your house? Well, porn
drove that. All those pictures and videos take up a lot of band-
width. Porn defeated Betamax! For a long time, the princes of
online porn have been the dirty street urchins of the digital age,
and by God, they think it's time to join Bill Gates and the Google
guys in the gilded halls of business.

Obenberger may be their most vociferous legal champion. He
was a star prosecutor in the U.S. Army's Judge Advocate General
(JAG) Corps, held small-time elected office for a while, but now
has laid his body down in the path of the moralists and the Republicans who have declared war on naked people having sex online.
He defends obscenity cases partly because he believes "fucking
and the Trinity are the two most interesting things to talk about"
and partly because he is a civil libertarian, a free-speech absolutist,
who believes porn is the thin wedge being driven between our
liberties and the censor's red pen.

He overplays his role, but rhetorical flourishes are necessary
sometimes. Like right now, see? He is sighing heavily. Perspiration
breaks out on his brow. His neck strains against his shirt collar and
tie. This is the transition moment, act 2 of what amounts to a
parental speech. A second ago he wanted his audience to know
how proud he was of them so when he makes this sad face, they
know he only scolds them because he loves them.

In a much quieter voice, he says, "Some of you are delusional."

You're sending spam to computer users that "has a woman's face looking like a glazed ham!" You're putting porn in front of people who haven't asked for porn because "you want to become the next twenty-seven-year-old millionaire!" Why antagonize people? Why ask for trouble? The government is gunning for you because porn is a red-meat issue for the Republicans and the Christians, so "if you have incestuous bukkake scat midget tossing, you will be prosecuted."

Most of the people who should be hearing this bravura performance aren't. This being Las Vegas, not to mention the middle of summer when the temperature outside is 111 degrees, most of those who might actually be creating incestuous bukkake scat midget tossing are already out by the pool ordering up margaritas and beers. Most XBIZ attendees are not, apparently, worried about jail.

In the porn Stone Age, producers and consumers used to pretend that sexy photos were about sophistication and sipping good scotch while sitting through a Coltrane set with the gorgeous "girl next door." That was the *Playboy* ethic, sex as part of a cultivated life. These days, nobody pretends porn is about anything other than getting off and exploring the next coolest, most radical thing.

Outside, the pool cabanas are occupied by "content" companies, which produce images and videos, and billing companies, which collect user fees. These big fish in the cabanas are trying to attract minnows, the Web masters (a grandiose name for a guy who runs a website) who offer short doses of free porn but include links to the big sites where, for a fee, a surfer can see hard-core action. Every time a surfer "clicks through," the big site pays baksheesh to the little guy.

This system creates a problem. There are now so many free porn sites, nobody has to pay for it. The one way to be sure you get customers, and customers who stay, is to offer something unique, like incestuous bukkake scat midget tossing. This is another reason why, as Kim Airs told me, "the Internet has done a lot of normalizing."

* * *

"Oooh . . . what do I like?" Madison Young pretends to think, milking the slightly wicked grin on her face, though she already knows the answer to Princess Donna's question. "Rope would be number one on my list. I like rope and I like pussy. I like rope and pussy and pain. Single tail [whips]. One of my favorites is hands. I like hands around my throat, hands around my mouth, hands smacking my ass, smacking my breasts. Grabbing the hair. All the things you can do with hands."

"Yes," Donna replies. "I am a big fan of hands also; they are great." Donna pauses, working up another question.

"How old are you?"

"I'm twenty-six."

"How long have you been doing porn?"

"Mmm . . . I've been doing BDSM porn for the past four years. BDSM is pretty much where my heart is."

"Are you nervous at all?"

"Holt!" Chuck, the cameraman, says, meaning "halt" or "stop" or "cut." Something like that. He says this every time he needs to change his position for another angle, which is quite often. "Say it again from 'Are you nervous . . .'"

"Are you nervous about anything? About me and the electricity?"

"I am a little nervous about the electricity," Madison replies.

A little, yes, but not too much. Madison is an artist. Actually, Tina Butcher is the artist, although it is possible, I suppose, that Madison, as Tina's alter ego, is an artist, too. So she is willing to make sacrifices. Last night Madison and I walked from her apartment in San Francisco's Castro District to Café Flore, one of those oh-so-precious little places dotting the city. I was hoping for a steak, maybe, or a plate of pasta because I was starving, but Tina wasn't feeling quite as chipper as she might. Her TMJ was bothering her, for one thing, and when your temporomandibular joint is sore, aching, really, as Madison's is pretty much all the time lately, you don't have a big appetite. Madison did see a dentist for it and he explained that all she had to do was use a smaller-diameter ball gag. TMJ is a common occupational hazard of being a queer bondage model, he said.

Madison was cramping a little, too. She had an IUD placed in her uterus a few hours before we met, and as her gynecologist said would happen, she was feeling achy in her abdomen. So just some chai latte, please? she asked when we ordered. We sat down outside and she wrapped her cardigan tighter around her petite body and curled into a catlike lump on her seat. She sipped from her chai latte and explained that the good news from the gynecologist was that being suspended naked upside down by her ankles, having an electrified dildo inserted into her vagina, being shocked by a cattle prod, ought to be okay because the IUD won't conduct electricity and fry her insides. Another doctor told her that the irregular heartbeat she has had since she was a kid shouldn't be affected by the amount of electric current running through her body either. She's probably not going to have a heart attack or anything. See, the great advantage of San Francisco, Madison told me, is having such knowledgeable health-care providers. "It's one of the beautiful things about living here."

The IUD represents something of a moment for Madison. She has started sleeping with men, or rather one man, James, her new boyfriend, her first male lover. This created some confusion, both for Madison and for the label-rich San Francisco lesbian/queer/ transgendered/transsexual/gay/bisexual/bicurious community of which she considers herself an important part.

When Tina Butcher opened an art gallery in San Francisco she called it Femina Potens (Latin for girl power, or powerful woman). She has a talent for naming her own art, too, like a 2005 work called *Big Hard Meat—Why I Became a Vegetarian Dyke*, which is, according to Tina, a "Web intervention piece exploring the boundaries of art vs. porn. In this piece I sexualize the destruction and capturing of a phallocentric piece of meat. Meat in this said piece signifies a greater power construct and destruction of that meat signifying the destruction of that same power construct. Madison Young uses sexual signifiers to capture the viewer's attention and 'meat.' This capturing of one's 'meat' leaves the viewer in an unsettled and uncomfortable weakened state. While the subject, who is often viewed as 'a piece of meat' and objectified for the enjoyment of others, turns the table, objectifying the viewer and the power and privilege of the viewer for her own enjoyment."

So you can see why the people who know Tina Butcher, to say nothing of Tina Butcher herself, might be troubled by a phallus-equipped boyfriend. She is still a vegetarian, but she can't really call herself a dyke anymore. At one time she tried the descriptor "pansexual," but now she prefers "queer," which leaves a lot of wiggle room. And you can see, too, why Madison and Tina can be easily confused because Tina Butcher's art is all about switching roles. Madison is Tina's alter ego, and when you see Madison performing it might be just Tina making art and turning you into the subject of the art. Or maybe not. Tina doesn't seem entirely clear on this point either.

At the moment, Madison is wearing a conservative, print dress not unlike one I would picture her wearing back in our mutual home state. This fits with Madison Young's identity as the cute, tiny, farm-bred girl with the red hair (she has let her hair grow out to play down the dyke image and play up the midwestern girl-next-door image) who finds herself in all kinds of distressing situations.

Currently she is handcuffed to an overhanging pipe in a basement room of a big building in the Mission District catercorner and across the street from the *San Francisco Chronicle* building and a block away from the James R. Browning federal courthouse. It's known by the people who work in it as the Porn Palace, the home of Kink.com, one of the most successful and popular porn sites on the Internet. The room has big sewer conduits hanging from the ceiling, an electrical junction box, a bank of electric meters on another wall. The walls themselves have been painted to appear as the dark and forbidding bowels of an abandoned industrial building, a place where a girl could wander in and fall into the hands of an evil sadist like Princess Donna, a recent graduate of New York University who studied photography and human sexuality, and who has just grabbed Madison by her hair, released her from the pipe, and forced her to kneel on the floor.

"You want me right where I am?" Madison asks.

"Action!"

Donna, who is wearing nothing but a minidress that looks like it was made from a black volleyball net and patent leather platform boots that make her about six feet tall, and who has a heart tattooed on her left upper arm—not a cute Valentine's heart but a heart out of a *Gray's Anatomy* illustration—says yes, then pulls up Madison's dress so Madison is mooning the ceiling.

Smack!

Madison groans.

Smack. Smack!

"Oohoh oh ah ha."

"Holt!"

Chuck and still photographer Lisa Mackie scramble to get a tight shot of Madison's butt, which is already pinking nicely.

"She can scoot over for you, too?" Donna asks Lisa. "Is that okay here?"

"Action," Chuck says in almost a whisper.

Smack!

Donna leans over and spits into the cleft between Madison's cheeks.

"Um um oh ahh."

Smack! Smack! Smack! Donna is slapping Madison's labia.

"Holt!"

Chuck, dressed in a mechanic's coverall for some reason, is already working up a sweat as he scrambles for a shot directly over

Madison's ass. Lisa is kneeling on the floor, her lens about a foot from the silver ring piercing Madison's labia.

"Action!"

Smacksmacksmacksmacksmacksmacksmacksmacksmacksmack.

"Oh ah ah ah oh oh oh . . ."

"Holt! Action."

Smacksmacksmacksmacksmacksmacksmacksmacksmacksmack.

"Ha ha ha ha ha ummm. Ooohhhhhhh OH! OH!"

"Stand up," Chuck instructs. "Holt!"

Standing up proves awkward for Madison, whose wrists are still handcuffed. Donna releases them.

"Action."

Donna slaps Madison's face. "Come on! Take your dress off, and go get me the Hitachi."

"Holt!"

Tina Butcher loves rope. She sleeps with a coil of rope next to her pillow so it is the last thing she smells at night and the first thing she sniffs in the morning. She masturbates with rope. "Just the smell of rope makes me wet," she says. She has always liked rope, sure, but this thing of using it as a sex toy is only a few years old.

Tina Butcher grew up in the small neighboring towns of Goshen and Loveland just north of Cincinnati, Ohio. Her dad had a tree service there, and so Tina was always around rope. Tree guys use it to haul down big branches, sling over limbs, hoist themselves and their chain saws into the air. "Rope smells like home. It smells like autumn leaves and trees and sex."

Tina was a good girl, an extraordinarily good girl. She earned straight A's all through grade school and even in her performing-arts high school. She almost never dated, though she certainly had some opportunities, being a smart, cute redhead who can, when she wants, strike a very sexy pose. But Tina wasn't much interested in striking sexy poses. Her first kiss did not come until after her eighteenth birthday. As a matter of fact, she had a reputation for being an untouchable girl, a little fragile even. Other kids protected her. "I was always known as the virginal one," she recalls. This was just fine with Tina's mom. After the divorce from Tina's father, her mother didn't like the idea of boys anyway.

"If any guys come near the house, I am going to get the shotgun!"

Tina's mother would come to regret this no-boys policy when she discovered one of Tina's journals. It was a compilation of Tina's dreams, and wow, did Tina have some dreams. There was the one about being forced to have sex, the one about being kidnapped and blindfolded and raped. Tina would wake up wet between her legs after those dreams. "I had no idea what to make of it, why I was having this funny feeling. I was kind of afraid of my body." She was also a little afraid of the fact that her dreams were populated by women. Tina was especially obsessed by Catwoman, not Michelle Pfeiffer or Julie Newmar or any of the women who have played Catwoman on film—all of whom inspired deep, abiding crushes in me—but the comics iteration. She masturbated to the pen-and-ink drawings of Catwoman.

One day after Tina had left for college, her mother found the dream journal. "She read them! When she found out, she was like, 'Oh shit, I never should have told you men were so evil!' I got in trouble for my dreams! I was so pissed off, I mean I am not even getting to do this, I am just dreaming about it."

In fact, by then she was just beginning to get to do it. Tina chose to attend college just up the road a ways, at Antioch in Yellow Springs, Ohio, about sixty miles from where I grew up. I used to run cross-country meets there.

Antioch is one of a handful of small liberal arts colleges in Ohio, some of them so-called Midwest Ivys, like Oberlin, Dennison, Kenyon. Antioch was founded by a local Christian church group before the Civil War, but the church dissolved its association with the school after it hired abolitionist, educator, and former congressman Horace Mann to be the first president and found him to be far too liberal. Mann is considered the school's spiritual founding father, and his motto, "Be ashamed to die before you have won some victory for humanity," served as the school's guiding creed.

Antioch became known as a tiny laboratory of political correctness. This meant that if you were a white, middle-class, straight male kid and you couldn't at least pretend to be interested in Emma Goldman and anarchist theory, you might have been happier at the nearby University of Dayton. (In fact, so many students *were* happier at other schools that enrollment collapsed and Antioch College announced in 2007 it would shut down in July of 2008.) Antioch's most famous adventure in the politics of sex came in the early 1990s when it developed the nation's most comprehensive "dating code" after being pressured by a group called Womyn of Antioch.

The code, formally called the Antioch College Sexual Offense Prevention Policy, is, says the preface, "about empowerment, changing our rape culture, and healing." There are a lot of steps you have to follow to escape our rape culture, like asking for explicit verbal permission at each phase of a sexual encounter. Moaning and pointing to your genitals don't count. Unspoken Cary Grant–Deborah Kerr kisses and the pounding hearts of *An Affair to Remember* are also out. On the other hand, the code does state that it will not "restrict with whom the sexual activity may occur, the type of sexual activity that occurs, the props/toys/tools that are used, the number of persons involved, the gender(s) or gender expressions of persons involved."

Antioch was an ideal place for a girl like Madison who had dreams of sex with girls. She majored in theater and women's studies and had her first real sexual experience there, with a woman. She also used handcuffs once, but really, she knew very little about BDSM until she moved to San Francisco with hopes of making her way on stage.

Not long after arriving, she met British expatriate Peter Acworth, who asked her to "do a suspension," to be tied up in an elaborate web of knots and suspended off the floor, a technique known by its Japanese name, shibari, for a website Acworth had started called Hogtied.com, the first of the family of Kink.com porn sites. Tina made a good shibari model because she was tiny and easy to wrangle, plus she had that midwestern girl innocence going for her, but most of all, after leaving home, she had decided to be the kind of girl who was willing to try anything once and being tied up naked certainly fell under the rubric of "anything."

"Peter Acworth tied me up and tortured me well and I discovered that indeed I was flexible and indeed I did love pain," she tells her fans on her own website. "I connected with the rope. It became part of me and the pain became a beautiful electric current that tickled as it ran into and out of my body. I found immense pleasure in the freedom of bondage, the spaces that it allowed me to explore outside of my body. It was a spiritual and challenging experiment in which I was able to document and get paid for."

She continued to model, and the proceeds allowed her to partially fund the opening of Femina Potens in a small garage. Over the next several years, Tina became acquainted with, and inspired by, an earlier generation of art-porn fixtures like Annie Sprinkle, famous for her one-woman show involving chocolate sauce, a speculum, and audience participation, and writer and performance artist Carol Queen. Both were among the first group of female performers who argued that it was possible to be both a feminist and a porn star. They insisted that pornography could be empowering to women, could allow women to control their own sexuality and to depict it as powerful and natural, not something to be repressed. They became popular speakers on college campuses in the late 1980s and early 1990s. Sprinkle gained fame as the focus of a political backlash by conservatives who decried the grant of National Endowment for the Arts stipends to theaters where she performed. The backlash, of course, turned Sprinkle, a minor underground celebrity, into a world-famous influential authority on sexual and artistic rights.

Today, Femina Potens, run by volunteers, is located in a tiny space tucked down the side of a larger building in the Mission District. I visited it before heading up to the Castro to meet Tina at her apartment. A continuous loop of a video, *Drawing Complaint: Memoirs of Bjork-Geisha*, was running. A flyer informed me that I was witnessing a meta-art moment, a "guerilla performance" by two women protesting a San Francisco Museum of Art exhibit related to another work of art, Matthew Barney's film, *Drawing Restraint 9*.

As if this were not confusing enough, in the film, Barney, known best for his multipart Cremaster series, and Barney's girlfriend, the Icelandic composer-singer Björk, visit a Japanese whaler, undergo a Shinto wedding ceremony (sort of), and wind up cutting each other's legs off with flaying knives. Whale tails grow out of the stumps. Meanwhile, a giant blob of petroleum jelly slides around the deck of the ship. The film lasts two and a half hours. Apparently, the artists in *Drawing Complaint* did not approve of Barney's film, so they dressed up as a geisha (the Björk character) and a fur-covered whaler (Barney's character) and conducted "unsolicited performances of fan dancing, lip synching, samurai whaling, and chopstick hara-kiri amidst crowds of confused viewers and gallery guards."

Over by the desk, manned by a young woman who had just moved to San Francisco from Salt Lake City, a small magazine rack offered flyers, notices, cards, pamphlets, and zines covering the gamut of lesbian and queer protest and social events. A column in a zine moaned about the commercialization of pornography, citing a website called Suicide Girls, which was supposed to be a revolutionary free-form porn collective of tattooed, gothy, powerful women but which turned out to be run by a man for money. Or maybe not. The details were controversial and hotly debated by online bloggers, but the writer of the column seemed pretty sure porn idealism had been sold for cash.

"From 'Go get me the Hitachi' . . . and . . . action!"

"Go get me the Hitachi!"

"Yes, ma'am."

"What's my name? Ma'am? Is my name ma'am?"

"Yes, Princess Donna."

"Holt!"

"Can you put her over here?" Lisa asks, trying to get a better angle on a still photo.

"Action."

Donna forces Madison to the floor and puts a knee in her back. Madison's rear end is high in the air. Donna spits on her labia and pushes the large Hitachi vibrator up against Madison's clitoris. Then Donna shoves most of her hand into Madison's vagina.

"Ha oh oh uhh uhhhh uuuuhhh ha ha ho ho mmm mm hmm hhmm hhmm ha hmmm ham mmm hammmm oh oh oh ho ho ho ho . . ."

"You know what you do when you wanna come here, right?"

"Oh! Oh oh oh . . . I . . . oh . . . oh . . . ask your permission?"

"Right."

Buzz, buzz, buzz, buzzzzzzzzzzzzzzzzz. "Fuck oh fuck ohmmm oh oh ha ha ha ha oh oh ho ho ho uh uh uh hu huh phhh oh can I please come . . . may I come?"

"That's not the whole sentence!"

"Please miiisss aha ha ha tress Dahhh nahhh caaaan I coooom-mme?"

"You can come."

"Oh oh ha uh uh haha uh uha ho ho ho haha ha ha ha ha ha ha ha ha ah oh hmh hm hah ah ah a ha hi hi eh he he he eh ehe ehehe HEEEE! ho ho ho ho oh oh oh oh oh oh oh OH OH OH OH ha oh oh oh oh my god oohhhhh oohhhhhhhhh oohhhhh oohhhhh fuck

hah ahahahhhhhoooooohhhhhhhhooooooooggod yes yes god yess
oh oh thhhaaaannnnkkkk you hhahahh hhhahaahahahahaha-
haaahhhhhaahhhhhhahhhhhhhhoh OH! OH! OH! OH! OH! OH! OH!
OH! OH! OH! ahah ah hhh aaaaaaaaaahhhhhhhhhhhh."

"Did you come, slut?"

"Oh yeah. Mmmmmmmmmmmmmmmm . . ."

Smack!

"At its core, the undergraduate Program encourages students to
question the meanings of 'male' and 'female,' as well as of sexual
norms, in both Western and non-Western societies," reads the
description of New York University's Program in Gender and Sexuality Studies. "Courses seek to unravel the ways in which ideas
about gender and sexuality shape social roles and identities, in
addition to the ways in which race, class, and ethnicity function in
the experience of gender and sexuality within a culture. Gender
and Sexuality Studies challenges the privileging of some categories (i.e., male or heterosexual) over others, along with the
social and political implications of such hierarchies. Our curricu-
lum makes gender and sexuality central rather than peripheral
terms of analysis and seeks to complicate what is often presented
as 'natural' or 'normal' in traditional academic curricula."

Donna, a stage name, is twenty-four, still fresh out of NYU,
where she was an enthusiastic student who absorbed the theories
and now believes that sexuality is "socially constructed." "I really
don't think I was born with my sexuality," she tells me when the
taping breaks for a change in setup. "I think that I have never
liked anything that was normal. I always hated things that were
expected of me or expected of women."

So she went into porn. Her career began as a "sub," a model
who undergoes what Madison is undergoing now. She was popular
because she was tall and pretty with a curvy body and wild, jet
black hair. First she worked at a website in New York called

Insex.com and liked it there, she says. At Insex, you could actually mark people with bruises and cuts, make them cry, use real blood and real syringes in "needle play." At Insex, she could shove meat hooks up a girl's nostrils and practically lift her off the floor. Insex was just the place for a girl who likes to write poetry like this from Donna's MySpace page:

How to get Gay Married

Step 1:
Gather all the kitchen knives together
Sit across from one another at the kitchen table
Cut the top of each others hands
Keep cutting in the same spot over and over until you have used
*   each knife*
Step 2:
Smoke cigarettes together
Rub the cigarette ashes into your open wounds
Giggle . . .

But a few months ago, Insex was bought out by a Dutch company and Donna moved west to run Kink.com's Wired Pussy site as the reigning queen of electro-torture sex. She finds Kink.com a bit limiting, though, a little too soft. Acworth doesn't permit crying or drawing blood, or needles.

"I was hypersexed as a child," she tells me as she begins prepping Madison for the next scene. While growing up in Sacramento, "I used to get in trouble for my slumber parties. I used to like to do strip shows for, like, the boys in the neighborhood. I use to like to play games, like, you pretend to be sleeping, I get to do whatever I want to you, and if you wake up you lose. And I never woke up."

When she saw her dad's porn stash "I thought that was, like, disgusting. I would think, 'This is horrible!' So I would, like, steal it from him and look through all the pages and be, like, 'Ugh! I will steal this for him so he does not have to look through this any more because this is disgusting,' but it would totally turn me on at the same time."

Her parents were "naked all the time," she says with a note of approval, and "not, like, super uptight or religious. They were open-minded. One time I asked my mom what oral sex was because I had heard it in a movie, and she said, 'It is when, like, you kiss someone all over their body' so this is what I thought oral sex was for a long time." Donna demonstrates by kissing her arms and hands.

"She really said that?" Lisa interrupts with a note of indignation. "I feel that's really deceptive."

This isn't the effect Donna was hoping for. "No, but it *is* when you kiss someone all over their body! I thought it was really sweet."

Like Tina Butcher, Donna identifies herself as queer. I am still a little confused about what, exactly, queer means.

"What does that mean?" Donna repeats, looking at me the way Anna Wintour might stare down a rube at a Paris fashion show who asked what the hell "rouching" is. "It means I do not generally date biological males. I date people who think of themselves as queer. It is more of a political and cultural stamp than purely what kind of sex I have. No matter who I am having sex with, it'll be queer."

"Uh-huh," I say. Donna senses my uncertainty.

"It'll never be straight."

This doesn't help. If I like to have sex with my wife when she's wearing, say, one of my white dress shirts and a tie, does that make me queer? What if I think it'd be fun to have sex on a tree stump in the Gallatin National Forest? How about a guy who dates only women but likes bondage? Is he queer? Or straight? Or a woman like Susan who prefers men, says she's straight, but will include women, sometimes, and likes being spanked? What about my new friend in Missouri who's a Baptist, has tried threesomes and foursomes and anal and likes to have a good time, but is married and happy being married, and says she's straight?

"Well, what does straight mean?"

"Vanilla. Normal," Madison says.

"Yeah," Donna agrees. "Vanilla." And then, recalling her NYU training, she adds, "Normative." She strains to clarify. "I think straight is, like, an unmarked category. Straight is people who do not really think about their sexuality," she says, looking at me and my wedding ring, "people who think their sexuality is naturally occurring and not a social construct. That would be straight to me."

"Oh, I see," I say, though what I see isn't exactly what Donna wants me to see. What I see is that I have met a lot of people who think deeply about their sexuality; the Christian Joe Beam does, and thinks about everybody else's, too, and the pornographer Phil Harvey does, and so does Kathy Brummitt and most of the other people I have met, and as far as I know none of them are queer. I'm not queer. Or am I? No, what I see is that Donna needs to be special and to be seen as being special by being outrageous. I have no idea what normal means when it comes to sex. I am coming to the conclusion that nobody in America does anymore, and if everybody is not "normal," then we are all queer, or none of us are, but either way, Donna isn't so special.

"But if you want the nuts and bolts of who I have sex with, that would generally be women and trans men."

"Uh, men to women?"

"Women trans to men." But she says this with too much definitiveness and backtracks. "Or, men trans to women, although most people who are trans men really want to be thought of as men."

Madison isn't so sure. They huddle. "Not all of them," Madison says. "I think trans men identify as trans generally."

"But that is not to say I don't do it with a boy here and there," Donna adds. "Queer is a little bit more all-encompassing, because otherwise it is pretty limiting. I mean, like, saying I am a lesbian?" She rolls her eyes in that "soo last century" way.

"Well," I suggest, because I am completely lost in Donna's gender shell game, and because I don't really care all that much and am sorry I brought it up, "how about pansexual? Would that be accurate?"

Donna is losing patience.

"No. Queer is the only way to describe my sexuality. You always have to ask whoever you are talking about," she instructs. "Pansexual is not how I define myself, but somebody else might. Not many people in the queer community do," she says with pedagogical authority. "Not any that I know."

Lisa says she's queer, too. "We have a lot of queers in the office."

"Queer is a political statement more than a biology issue," Donna insists again. "But Chuck is straight," she says, as if trying to find me a bro. "Or vanilla. Heterosexual. Married."

"Vanilla!" Donna and Lisa say, kidding Chuck.

"No, I got kink!" Chuck whines defensively.

"You're married, you're married!"

Chuck is married, and happy to be married and have a job making decent money. He used to work in public access cable, and then for the state of California, but this pays better, it's local, and he gets home every night to his wife. She doesn't mind the nature of his work; she just doesn't want to hear about it.

Donna's parents don't mind either. She told them recently, over Thanksgiving dinner, exactly how she earns her living. They knew she worked at a porn studio but had not known she was on camera. "My dad said, and I quote: 'That's okay, I don't have any problems with sex work.'" Lisa is impressed. "I know," Donna says. "I was, like, 'Wow, Dad. Cool.' And my mom just had a bunch of questions, um, about, like, tying people up. And she was, like, 'Why does it matter to you?' And she was, like, 'Anybody can tie people up.' And I was, like, 'No, Mom. This is different.'"

Donna does have other ambitions. She is planning to create an instructional video on yoga for bondage models.

Tina Butcher's family still doesn't really know what it is Madison

Young does. An uncle back in Ohio did find a few online images of Tina from an art performance piece and was shocked to find her naked. That prompted a call from her father, to whom Tina explained that she was sometimes nude for her art. That wasn't a lie, exactly.

Chuck volunteers that his parents have no idea where he works and what he does, so could I please change his name? But he likes working at Kink. "This is as close to family as I have come in any work establishment," he says as Donna finishes roping Madison's naked body into a web of knots called a torso tie. She is also trying to affix tubular glass suction devices over Madison's nipples, but this is proving challenging because Madison has pierced nipples. Then, like some mad dentist with a grudge, she buckles a steel mouth expander around Madison's head. This forces Madison's jaw wide open. She cranks a winch labeled "Not for Movement of Humans," to lower a steel ring from the ceiling, hooks Madison into it, and then cranks Madison off the floor while Chuck continues his thought.

"This is a very family atmosphere."

Donna grabs Madison's labia and swings her back and forth.

"Action."

"Ahh ahha oh . . ."

Donna cranks Madison higher. Clackclackclackclack . . .

"Ooh oh oh hah ophah oh no."

"Moaning? Are you moaning?" Donna asks.

"Oh! OH OH!"

"You know what, Madison, let's put this in there . . ."

Lisa's camera clicks rapidly. Clickclickclick.

"And get that little pussy stretched out. Spread your legs! Mmmmm."

Donna rubs lubricant on a large dildo and slides it into Madison's vagina. A red wire leads from the base of the dildo to an electric box on the floor. There are dials and a digital readout on the box. Next, Donna clamps heavy chains onto Madison's labia and hooks four old, rusty padlocks through some of the links. Madison is hanging vertically now, her ankles tied together, her arms tied behind her back, a rope harness wrapped tightly around her chest so her breasts are squeezed out between the rope coils, the glass tubes dangling off them. The chains and locks pulling her labia rattle along the floor like a pornographic Jacob Marley's.

"See those numbers? See it?"

"Holt! 'See those numbers.' Action."

"See those numbers? What number is that?"

"Hiii." Madison can't pronounce *nine* because the steel expander is keeping her mouth wide open. Drool runs down her chin.

"Nine?"

"AHH! . . . Heehee-ix!"

"Fifty-six?"

"Hurhy-hree . . . Hay-heen . . ."

Donna hits Madison with a black leather flogger.

"OH! OH! OWWW! OH Gah . . . Hurhy . . . oh oh."

"Holt! Do another reading of those levels. Action."

"Horhy-hore . . . Hihhy . . . Hurhy-hoo . . . Huhee-ree . . . Huhee-hor . . . Oh OH! Gah oh gah huhee-hive!" Current jolts Madison's body, making it jerk upward.

Now Donna is using a pneumatic pump to create intense suction on Madison's nipples, sucking them far into the glass tubes.

Chuck is really sweating now, shouldering his camera and jumping all over the set to get the right shots.

"Action!"

"Have you learned? Think you have learned your lesson?"

"Hesh! Hesh! Hesh! Ohhh oh oh . . ."

"Say nice things about me when you are hanging up there."

"Eah. Eah. Eeoo r hah. Eeoo ha hate hans. Eeoo eel reahhy ood. Eeo uck ee o ice."

"I am not thoroughly entertained yet. Keep going . . . I am still turning it up until you think of something better to say."

"Oh eah. Eeoo r ucking hah. Eeoo r o ucking hah." Long rivulets of drool hang from Madison's chin.

"I think you can be a little more enthusiastic! I have a setting at ninety-nine! That could make you much more enthusiastic when it is up to ninety-nine!"

"Argh argh eeoo so hah eeoo so argh hah! oh oh ah ow ow ow ow."

"Holt!"

Click, click, click. Clack clack clack. Donna winches Madison higher.

"You all right?"

"Uh-huh."

"I am going to turn it up. Just say 'Unh-hunh' whenever it's too high. They are going to think it is going up to ninety-nine, which is, like, hot wires."

"Hey, I believed you," Lisa says.

"Well, I will if she doesn't say 'unh-hunh' before then."

"Action."

"You wanna please me?"

"Uh-huh."

"What would please me is if we turn this all the way up. I am going to turn this all the way up. Then we are going to count to one hundred. There it is at ninety-nine."

"Holt! Repeat there it is at ninety-nine. Action."

"EEEOOOOOHHHH!" Madison squirms as if trying to climb out of the ropes. "OH! HE! EH! EH! EHE! EHE! EHE! EHE!"

"There it is at ninety-nine."

Smack! Donna hits Madison with the flogger. Smack!

"Count!"

"Unh, oo, ree, or, hie . . ." Madison is on the verge of tears.

Smack. Smack.

"OH! Huahhuha . . . huhee-oo, huhee-ree . . ."

"Holt! Twenty-six. Go."

"Huhee-ix . . . Hurhee-ix . . . Horhee . . ."

"Keep counting," Donna instructs. "I will come back when you are done."

Madison counts between sighs and cries and yelps. "Hayhe hor, hayhe hive . . ."

Click. Click.

> Pornography is defined as the graphic, sexually explicit subor-
> dination of women in pictures and/or words that also includes
> women presented dehumanized as sexual objects who enjoy
> pain or humiliation; or women presented as sexual objects
> who experience sexual pleasure in being raped; or women pre-
> sented as sexual objects tied up or cut up or mutilated or
> bruised or physically hurt; or women presented as whores by
> nature; or women presented being penetrated by objects or
> animals; or women presented in scenarios of degradation,
> injury, torture, shown as filthy or inferior, bleeding, bruised,
> or hurt in a context that makes these conditions sexual.

Andrea Dworkin wrote this for a 1989 preface to her 1981 book *Pornography: Men Possessing Women.* It parallels the text of an antiporn law she and lawyer Catharine MacKinnon were campaigning for in cities around the country.

Dworkin, a radical antiporn feminist, was not subtle in her writings. "In contemporary American pornography, of course, the Jews do it to themselves—they, usually female, seek out the Nazis, go voluntarily to concentration camps, beg a domineering Nazi to hurt them, cut them, burn them—and they do climax, stupendously, to both sadism and death."

Madison Young was a newborn when Dworkin first published her screed on porn. It was an ideal time to mount an antiporn offensive because Ronald Reagan had just been elected with help from a new Christian conservative movement. He appointed Edwin Meese his attorney general. In what was one of America's most unusual political alliances, Dworkin, MacKinnon, and other antiporn feminists found themselves working with Meese and fundamentalist Christians to advance the law in one battleground city after another, making porn a national issue. Meese formed a special commission to investigate it and began putting the weight of the U.S. Justice Department behind prosecuting it (until suffering defeats like the one administered by Phil Harvey). Dworkin was happy. "This law and the political vision and experience that inform it are not going to go away," she boasted in 1989. "We are going to stop the pornographers."

"Who is Andrea Dworkin?" Lisa asks when I wonder out loud what Dworkin and MacKinnon would say if they were here.

"They did those antipornography sex ordinances, that whole confusion that being antiporn, antisex work was feminist; it was antiwoman, actually," Donna interjects as if Dworkin, or the very idea of such a thing as an antiporn feminist were phlogiston, a quaint, wrongheaded notion from the history she learned at NYU. "It is so funny. That was the one time that feminism became completely confused with right-wing politics. Like the church and the right wing? And feminists making laws that were supposed to support women . . .

"I just laugh about it when people ask me how I can make porn and consider myself a feminist. I make porn *because* I am a feminist."

Donna turns to Lisa and asks, "Is my hair okay?"

"Action!"

"OH OH mmmm oh gah, oooh oh gah oh oh ooohh uhh ooo hmmm ah oh hmmm . . ."

Donna has hung Madison upside down by one ankle. She bends Madison's free leg back with rope, wraps the rope around her ankle, and threads it through Madison's mouth so Madison looks like a masochistic ballet dancer in inverted airborne attitude. She turns Madison's labia into a Baskin-Robbins French vanilla cone by spitting on them and then licking with gusto. Chuck and Lisa surge forward for tongue-on-vulva close-ups, the money shots.

Clickclickclickclickclick.

"Ah ah ah ooo ah ooooo mmm m m ohh ahh."

"Holt!"

Donna retrieves clothespins attached to electrical wires and attaches one to each of Madison's labia. Next comes a glass dildo wired for electricity. She slides this into Madison's vagina, then crouches down onto her hands and knees so her ass is in front of Madison's inverted face.

"Action!"

"Oh OH HA HA oh oh oh oh ah ha ha uuuuuhhhhhh."

"I am not asking for you to do it!"

Madison somehow manages to slip her tongue from behind the rope in her mouth to lick Donna while Donna masturbates.

"I want to make sure you are really turned on before I fuck you."

"Holt!"

There's a mad scramble to get the girl-on-girl oral shots. Lisa splays on the floor; Chuck leans over, dripping sweat off his nose. They are inches away from Donna's organs of reproduction, a phrase that occurs to me because they remind me of medical interns at their first gynecological exam.

"Action."

Donna is a screamer.

"Oh OH HAMM HAMMM oh oh oh oh ah ha ha oh ahh ooh ahhh hahh oh mmmm mmm hmm hmmmm oh oh hmmmm oh oh ha ha ha ha hooooooo oh ha ha ooh oh OH OOIHA OHA SMMMMMM OH OH OH OH OH OH OH OH OH OH OH . . ."

Things are moving quickly now and it's tough for me to keep up. Wait! There's Donna with a cattle prod. Zzzzut! Zzzzut! Zzzzut! Miniature static lightning bolts race across the gap between the two copper nodes at the end, and for the first time Madison's expression betrays some genuine fear.

"AYEAH! YAEAH! OW! OW! OW! OW! YWEAH!" Is she being shocked by the prod? The thing in her vagina?

Clack clack clack clack clack. Donna and Lisa rush to winch Madison to the floor. Madison can take a lot of pain; she thinks being a redhead gives her more pain tolerance. But even Madison has limits to how long she can dangle upside down, contorted, with her breasts sucked into glass tubes, electricity shooting through her body.

Madison is standing now, awkwardly because she's got her hands tied behind her back with rope. Donna has it looped over . . . what? The ring in the winch? A pulley? And she's brought it down to tie it into a big knot of Madison's hair. Oh, I get it. Every time Madison lowers her bound hands, she'll pull her hair.

Diabolical.

But there's more. A lot more. The finale is coming soon, I gather, because there is some serious gearing up. A candle is lit. Objects are brought in from the storage room next door. In all the fussing, however, somebody has forgotten to remove the dildo from Madison's vagina. Finally, Lisa notices it's still in there and she and Donna laugh. "I always forget those things," Donna says.

Peter Acworth is thirty-six years old and favors the slightly stodgy fashions of a clubby banker working in the city of London. His shirts are usually buttoned down, his brown hair neatly trimmed, his soft face closely shaved. He can often be found standing with his arms folded across his chest on the periphery of a clutch of people, smiling congenially. He is, in fact, a congenial fellow. If it hadn't been for the Internet, Acworth would have been one of those unassuming chums Britain seems to grow as regularly as the barley harvest, a well-to-do, educated banker with a small country house, an appropriate wife, a loyal dog, and a kink for bondage and domination.

In 1997 he was living in New York earning a graduate degree in business at Columbia. He had already graduated from Cambridge where he studied mathematics, and he had worked at the staid British investment bank Barings, so his future seemed set: maybe a stint in New York after Columbia, some time in Singapore to learn the Asian markets, then back to London and the pinstripes. But then he latched on to the idea of throwing a few bondage photos he had purchased onto a website he created, Hogtied.com, figuring to make a little extra money. The hit counters on his Web page started moving the first day. The money followed. America, it turned out, contained many people like Acworth who appreciated the sight of people being tied up for sex.

Soon thereafter, Acworth became a full-time pornographer. He moved to San Francisco and happily rode the boom—bust—boom cycles of the Bay Area's wired economy, virtually immune from the panics that decimated other dotcom businesses. In what amounts to a small-time re-creation of the old Hollywood studio system, with Acworth as Louis B. Mayer, Acworth built his own studio, hired the talent, and exhibited on his own websites. Now, his fifty or so employees churn out up to four or five new productions per day for the Kink family of sites. There is Wired Pussy, of course, and the original Hogtied, but also Whipped Ass, Fucking Machines (in which women, typically, ride mechanical devices equipped with dildos, something like the bucking mechanical bull from *Urban Cowboy*), Men in Pain, Water Bondage, Sex and Submission, and Ultimate Surrender, a female wrestling site. More are planned. Madison's boyfriend, James Mogul, is producing one called The Training of O.

The popular sites gross about $300,000 per month. If you're a good site producer, you could make up to $150,000 per year. That sort of money attracts people like Reena Patel, vice president for marketing. She joined the company four months ago after working in the Bay Area's pharmaceutical industry. In fact, about half the employees are women.

When I arrived at the Porn Palace this morning, there was no evidence of this success. I wasn't even sure I was standing outside the right building. It was completely anonymous without signage of any kind, on a run-down block. But inside, success was obvious. On the top floor, offices lined one wall and in the open floor spaces, where another company might have stuffed cubicles, about ten video editors sat in the dark in front of banks of large flat computer screens. Each wore headphones. The soft tapping of computer keys and mouse clicks provided the only accompaniment to a mosaic of body parts floating unconnected in digital space-time.

When Madison arrived, we walked down a flight of stairs and into a realistic-looking castle set Acworth obtained from the Walt Disney company. This level also contained a jail set, a barn, a functional bar, an operating room—a backlot crammed inside a building in the middle of San Francisco.

In the basement several heavily tattooed guys pounded on wood and steel, backed by a heavy-metal sound track. They were building new set pieces and creating new fucking machines or servicing old ones. The other half of the basement contained a storage room for supplies and equipment, some technical, like cameras and lights, and some props and safety devices like surgical gloves, lube, dozens of ball gags, dildos, chains, handcuffs, leather straps, whips, and electrical devices whose functions I could only imagine. Madison is shooting in an attached dead-end corner room.

But even as I am watching Madison and Donna work, Acworth is negotiating for much larger space. He is arranging to buy the landmark San Francisco Armory building for $14.5 million so he can turn the former home of the California National Guard into the new Porn Palace.

After our walk-through, Madison and I went to the "green room." Literally. It was painted green. She sat down for makeup and costuming, not that there was much makeup to apply or any-thing elaborate to fit. While the makeup artist, a woman with green hair and spiderwebs tattooed behind both knees, worked on Madison, I couldn't help noticing a stack of empty enema bottles, a one-gallon pump jug of Platinum Premium lubricant, and a supply of Ocean Spray cranberry juice.

The customer and set designer, who works for San Francisco's American Conservatory Theater when she's not working in porn, picked out Madison's dress, and Madison swallowed an ibuprofen; her IUD cramping was better but hadn't disappeared. Not that she'd notice in a few minutes anyway.

Donna hobbles Madison by affixing a wooden dowel between Madison's ankles. She sticks weighted clamps to her nipples, turn-ing Madison's breasts into a parody of an ancient Bantu matri-arch's. Then Lisa and Donna apply little round patches like those used for medical monitoring onto Madison's butt, her labia, her inner thighs. Wires lead from the patches to the electrical generator.

After some discussion about ball-gag diameters, Lisa picks out a smaller one than Madison used to prefer in deference to her TMJ. Donna straps it around Madison's head. Then Donna straps a giant black silicone dildo around her own waist. As she walks, it flops up and down, back and forth as if it is trying to escape the steel ring holding it into the harness.

"Action!"

A black leather flogger flies back and forth through the hot, still air, the strips beating against Madison's already crimson bottom. With every stroke, the strap-on waggles, Madison moans and yelps, the electricity hums and buzzes.

"Oh oh hmm hmmmm oh oh oh mmmmmm . . ."

"That's making your pussy wet, isn't it?"

"Uh-huh . . ."

"Holt! Repeat that . . . 'is making your pussy wet.'"

"Can I get a pussy shot here?" Lisa asks.

"Action!"

"Oh ahh ooh ahhh hahh oh mmmm mmm hmm hmmmm oh oh hmmmm oh oh ha ha ha ha hoooooooo OW! oh ha ha ooh oh OW! OH OOIHA OHA Shhthththt OW! OH OH OH OH OH OH OH OH OH OH OH . . ."

Donna turns on the juice. "Is the fuck doll dancing for me? I can see it shaking your ass."

"Oh ahh ooh ahhh hahh oh mmmm mmm hmm hmmmm oh oh hmmmm oh oh ha ha ha ha hoooooooo oh ha ha ooh oh OH OOIHA OHA Suuuuuhhhh OH OH OH OH OH OH OH OH OH OH OH . . ."

Donna then picks up the lit candle and pours hot wax from it onto Madison.

"OW! OW!"

Sure as the sun sets, Donna points the floppy dildo strapped around her waist at the target of Madison's vagina.

"OH HAM HAM OH OH OH . . ."

"Holt! That was good," Chuck says, apologizing for stopping the action. "I just thought I was going to trip."

No wonder. The floor has become a puddle of spit and lubrication. Chuck has to skate across the surface while shouldering his video camera.

"Can I just get the insertion shot?" Lisa requests. Donna obliges, backing up and then pushing forward again.

"Can you, uh, maybe if you go back and forth a little bit?"

"Action!"

Donna drives the strap-on in and out of Madison.

"OPHS OHS HA AH AHA HA HA AH OH OH OH OH MAH AHA HA HA AHA HA AH AHA HO OH OH OH OHA HA OH OH OH AHAH AHA AHA OHO OH OH OH A A A A A A A A AH AHA AH AAHAAHA A . . ."

"Holt!"

"Need something?" Lisa asks.

"I got some lube on my lens," Chuck says. Now I know why Chuck is wearing coveralls.

"Okay," Chuck says after wiping his lens. "And . . . thrusting action!"

"Hmmmmm HMMMM OH AHA AH AHA HOOO HO HO OH OH AW AH OO! OO! OO! OO! OH OH OH OH yeah mmmm OHO H ah ah ah aah ah ha OOO! EE EE EE EE!"

"Can you come one more time for me?"

"Oh ah wawa um. I wawa um. I wawa um, Mishresh Hanhah!"

"Okay, so you do some work. Come on! Come on! Do more of the work."

Madison is trying to move her hips back and forth, but she has nowhere to go, being roped to the ceiling and all. Still, she makes a brave effort.

"OOOHHH OH OHOHHHHH OH OH HA AH AOHA HA AH EEEEEE AH AHAH A HEEE HA AHA AHA HJAEER HO HO HO HO HO HOH OH OH HJAEER EAH UCK EAH UCK OPH OH OH OH OHOH OHA HHHAH AHA HA OHA AHA HA AHA HMMMMMMMM HM MMM HMMM MM haha aha HAMMMMMMMMM OH OH OH OH OH OH OH AAA AAA AA AAA AAA AAA OH OH HO HO HO HO MMMMMMMOHHH HA AHA HA AHA AH AHA AHA HA AHA AHA AHA AHA AHA AHA AH AHA HA HOH OH OH MMMMMMMMMMMMMMMMMM HMMMMMMMMM OHHA OOHAA eeeaah-hhh eeeaahhh oh uck eah oh eah oh eah oh eah eah eah eah aye AYEAH YAEAH OW OW OW OW EAH . . ."

"You gonna come? Hmmm?"

"Esh, Mishrish Haa uhh."

Thunklurp thunklurp thunklurp thunklurp thunk . . .

"You wanna come for me? You wanna have an orgasm for me?"

"Esh, reeze."

Thunklurp thunklurp thunklurp thunk . . .

"Tell me how fuckin' horny you are!"

"Ah mm uck ee horhee."

"Keep saying that until you are done!"

"Ah mm uck ee horhee. Ah mm uck ee . . ."

Thunklurp thunklurp thunklurp thunklurp thunklurp thun-klurp thunk . . .

"Horheeahmmuckehhorheeahmmmuckehhorhee aooh hah aha-haha aha ooh oho ohohoh oh ahahah mmm ahahha aha ha uckeh horheeuckeh horheeuckehhorhee AH AH AH AH AH AH AH AH AH AH ahhhhhhh!"

Midori is the undisputed queen of American BDSM models. A graduate of the University of California at Berkeley, Midori was born in Japan and speaks fluent Japanese, which gives her enormous credibility, to say nothing of popularity, among a generation of Americans fascinated with Japanese pop culture and kinkiness. But Midori rarely models anymore, choosing instead to travel the country—sometimes the world—giving shibari seminars and BDSM lectures to neophytes who want to turn manga comics into real-life scenarios.

Today there might be a dozen or so well-known extreme BDSM models like Madison in the U.S., almost all of them under thirty. But the power of the Internet has hugely magnified their influence on the pop culture mainstream and they, and the fetishes they depict, have now become sought after among people who regard irony as king and modern hipsterism as religion.

In 2006 the *San Francisco Chronicle,* a Hearst newspaper, desperate to appeal to a younger, hipper generation than the typical readers of its "dead-tree" product, hired a woman named Violet Blue to be a sex columnist. Blue, a porn blogger for a website called Fleshbot (a division of the snarky mainstream Gawker site) and a sometime performer, is one of Madison's acquaintances and a friend of Acworth's.

"As a sex writer and online sex personality, I'm not any kind of 'safe' pastiche you see in mainstream media," she wrote on her blog, trumpeting her hiring. "I have chipped black nail polish, work on lethal robots for fun, have tattoos, am a fetish model, am a pro-porn pundit, a tech fetishist, and make no apologies about sex. I'm constantly in some kind of online controversy," all of which makes her very, very badass and very, very cool. "And now I write a column for the Chronicle."

Later, in a very cool column for the paper's website, she interviewed Eon McKai, wonder boy of the so-called alt-porn phenomenon, whose first big success was a DVD called *Art School Sluts*.

"Down the street, we found comfort in an empty, unhip café with broken, squeaky overstuffed chairs and a server who rolled her eyes at us no matter what we ordered. I'd met McKai a couple years ago in Las Vegas during the Adult Video News porn convention, amid the circus of porn stereotypes, when a small group of us younger, paler, decidedly less straight porn intellectuals, directors, performers and bloggers found each other and clustered at crappy hotel bars and in dank casino hotel rooms, marveling at being outsiders within what we realized was a corporate porn bubble."

Efforts to evoke scenes like Paris in the twenties—Man Ray and Hemingway and Fitzgerald and Dos Passos and Josephine Baker and Marcel Duchamp and Kiki of Montparnasse—are common with alt-porn habitués eager to paint a rebel artist sheen onto skinny, tattooed people fucking each other.

Anyway, McKai explained alt porn this way: "Altporn comes from the Web: sites like fatalbeauty.com, profanepirate.com, Suicide Girls, raver porn and on and on. To break it down more, let's just say that altporn features performers that are a part of a subculture or a 'scene.' As a part of that, they dress a certain way. It's Goth, punk, emo, raver, shoegazer—and so its permutations are endless. Throw in some bitter hipsters, heat that up until you get some Internet drama . . . and you have altporn."

Cool.

The built-in flaw, of course, is that cool expires when enough people sign on and what is underground nudges its way to the surface. Whereas the once very cool Johnny Rotten is supposed to have said, "Sex? Aah fucking hippie crap!" thirty years ago, now sex is ironic and indie and alt. Another young woman named Joanna Angel, "writer, journalist, producer, director, model, and an AVN award winning adult film star," as she describes herself, created an Internet site called BurningAngel, "an independent site that celebrates the intersection of sex and rock 'n' roll with erotic photos and hardcore XXX movies alongside her interviews with punk and indie bands including Marilyn Manson, My Chemical Romance, the Bouncing Souls, and Bad Religion, among many others."

As with Violet Blue, self-congratulation on media saturation is very cool, too. "Referred to as the 'queen of altporn,' Joanna has been featured on Playboy TV's 'Sexcetera,' Fuse TV, KSEX Radio, and in numerous editorials, including the The New York Times, The Village Voice, Time Out New York, The New York Press, Esquire UK, Penthouse, SCREW, XBIZ, Fleshbot, AVN, and Heeb, which featured her on their cover and named her an 'up and coming Jew.' Joanna holds a B.A. in English from Rutgers University—among her numerous professional and provocative roles, she considers herself a writer above all and documents all her life's experiences in her BurningAngel blog, which is revered by intellectuals, hipsters and rock n' rollers across the globe."

Sid Vicious was dead before Joanna Angel was born.

Candida Royalle's first porn movie was released four years before that. She was an art student, like Eon McKai, and chuckles at the revolutionary rhetoric of the kids. Her generation of porn pioneers and their older free-love siblings "lifted the lid" of Pandora's box, she told me "and now it has come flooding out."

Kiki de Montparnasse died in 1953. Her name is now on a chichi sex toy store in New York City selling overpriced silk bondage ropes, riding crops, and titanium vibrators.

In fact, there are other signs that this scene has already gone kitsch besides upscale sex stores and the hiring of Violet Blue by the *Chronicle*, that it has been kitsch for a long time. Madison, for example, has a friend who lives in Los Angeles named Claire Adams. Claire describes herself this way on her MySpace page:

Just a young innocent thing born far away from where I ended up physically but not mentally! I have been a pervert for as long as I could remember, relishing and celebrating the processes of unconditional love, sadism, and bondage:)

I enjoy meditation, yoga, nature and hiking. Watching movies in good company, sharing life with my partner, meeting people from all walks of life make this all worth doing and takes up most of my free time. I think a lot: consciously, deliberately, in depth thinking. Something I cannot avoid. It has rewards and also fulfills some sort of masochism I've yet to find a definition for.

My passions lie with psychological innuendos. I like the attempt of understanding the boundaries of my intellectual, emotional, and physiological, and erotic existence. I love bondage and sm and the challenges and wonderful experiences represented in those categories. It is a mainstay in life for me.

Claire is well known in BDSM both as a model/actress and for doing her own rigging on other people. She worked with Insex, appears with Madison on Madison's website, and she works with Kink's websites. She also travels and lectures at fetish gatherings. But Claire's most recent big moment came in 2006 when she worked with fashion designer Tom Ford and photographer Art Streiber to suspend actor Peter Sarsgaard for the March issue of *Vogue* magazine. For Tina Butcher, this was proof that what she does in the guise of Madison Young is important. Finally, shibari, bondage, S&M, "sex positive" culture in general are receiving the artistic recognition they so deserve. They may not be mainstream yet, in that boring Ohio-ness mainstream sense of the word, but they are becoming mainstream among the really cool people who count, like Tom Ford.

But twenty-five years ago, designer Thierry Mugler created dominatrix looks for haute couture, and twenty years ago, Gianni Versace evoked bondage. Today couture routinely takes its easiest inspirations from BDSM porn. Mugler designed an overt domina-trix look for that most obvious of bourgeois Americana, the Las Vegas extravaganza, Cirque du Soleil's *Zumanity*. The Gucci "plat-form runway sandal" ($850) and the silver-spike-studded Dolce and Gabbana spike heel ($560) can be found in the *New York Times*. Goth-metal icon Marilyn Manson shot a fashion spread for "Vogue Rocks," a special edition of *Vogue*, wearing spiked boots and capes and his trademark makeup.

"Another day, another homage to Mad Max and the Thunder-dome," fashion writer Cathy Horyn wrote in a 2007 review of a Milan show. "That was the scene at Dsquared, where the design-ers Dean and Dan Caten ran riot with sexy black leather, rough-looking fur and chain ornament. It was all fun and perfectly banal."

"Awesome!" Donna says. "This is your first time on Wired Pussy. How was it?"

This is the postgame interview, a standard feature of videos shot by Kink, meant to convey the idea that the model was willing and enjoyed the whole the thing, so no harm, no foul, see? We were just playing around.

"It was great!" Madison answers. "It went by way too fast."

"You'll get to do it some more. What was your favorite part?"

"Oh, gosh. Well, I really love suspension and I really enjoyed the ankle suspension."

"That *was* cool."

"I also really enjoyed the cattle prod actually, and it was pretty fuckin' hot being suspended and having your pussy pushed into my face. I think I could deal with that happening many many times."

"oooh, so could I!"

"That was pretty hot. I also really loved the beginning scene we did, having your hands on me. I liked just being tossed around and having that sort of energy, so that was pretty cool."

After she has dressed and we are walking around the building, searching for our way back to the offices upstairs, Madison tells me, "Nothing we did today was that intense. It's like a dance. There is an art to it. You can have a beautiful experience." When she works with other people, Donna or anybody else in her career as a bondage model, whether it's in London or Los Angeles or here, "it's important that intimacy is being shared" because that intimacy comes across on camera. Having an orgasm can't be faked and still look real, so you have to let go.

The drawback, of course, is that Tina Butcher has become hard to please. "Sometimes I do think I am a bossy bottom," she jokes. She has requirements. Rope, hitting, slapping, spanking. All done just right and at the right time. She doesn't always need them to achieve orgasm, which she regards as the goal of sex, but she has been disappointed whenever she has dated anybody outside "the industry" and so now she only dates people who can give her what she wants, like James.

When we find the offices, we sit with the talent coordinator, who asks, "Was this vaj rate or anal?"

Madison and I try to remember if there was, in fact, anything anal and I am amazed to draw a blank. The only part of her body that was not penetrated, shocked, slapped, or flogged, I guess, was her anus. Madison seems surprised, too. Huh. How about that. The coordinator hands Madison a check for $700; it would have been $800 for anal.

Madison and I are supposed to return to Kink tonight for the company holiday party, but we've been here since ten o'clock, it's now five, and neither of us has eaten. So I invite her for an early dinner. She suggests a Thai place a couple of blocks away.

Rain is starting to come down as we leave Kink. A storm is blowing into San Francisco, one of those windy, wet, cold storms.

We walk with our heads down and Tina talks about writing a book—memoir of a bondage model—and her artwork and her bondage website where members can sign up for regular subscriptions just like Kink. She would like to travel less, control her own destiny more. After all, there are only so many variations on a theme and after Madison Young has been seen in thousands of photographs and hours of video being bound and punished in dozens of different ways, what's left? Branching out and becoming your own boss like Midori is the only way to make it in this business, though art is really what she would like to do. The problem is that Tina Butcher has become inextricably bound to Madison Young.

"Sometimes I'm not sure where Tina ends and Madison begins," she says. "I forget which one I am." She is finding the task of running two personalities, two identities, to be more complicated than she had first thought. Who is the subject of the art now? Is she the viewer or the viewed? Is the art porn, or the porn art, or neither?

Tina the vegan orders noodles and vegetables. She pulls out her cell phone and calls James, who is recovering from a bad cold, and coos into phone, "Hi, baby. How are you feeling, huh?"

Later I walk back to Kink for the party, which is already going strong by the time I arrive. The caterer is setting out turkey and mashed potatoes and gravy, and broccoli, a very traditional holiday meal. There are mini pecan pies.

A few people are kitted out in fetish attire, some are wearing jeans, some fancy party clothes. Acworth is wearing a striped buttoned-down shirt and jeans. He spends a lot of time standing by the kitchen door, smiling at his employees having a good time.

Somebody announces a puppet show is beginning in the barn set, and I imagine PVC-clad puppets with Mohawks and codpieces, but in fact it is a standard *Punch and Judy*–style show playing for an audience of ten small children and one smart-ass ten-year-old who keeps saying, "Yeah, sure." They are employees' kids, mainly.

Back in the bar I meet a fellow named Bruce, who happens to be from Ohio, also not far from where I grew up, and so we laugh about all the Buckeyes in the Porn Palace. Bruce was "in computers," which is what computer guys say when they instinctively know you are incapable of understanding what it is they really do. I ask him what, exactly, he does, and he explains it, but of course I am incapable of understanding anything. This is partly because the computer terms are so much gibberish to me and partly because Bruce appears to have swallowed a dozen Ritalin. His eyes are bugging. The mass of brown curly hair on his head has turned into nervous little springs mounted on his skull and he speaks without punctuation. But I gather that when Bruce was in college back in Ohio he invented some sort of computer program, and then ended up working at Apple and making fistfuls of money when twenty-year-olds could still show up in Silicon Valley and make fistfuls of money, but blew it all on good drugs and hookers and professional dominatrices in Europe and Asia, but it was worth it, man, you know? Because you got to live, man, and you don't want to wait to do that stuff until you're old, and now he works here at Kink and really likes it because there is so much state-of-the-art gear and he can't seem to stop talking like this and staring wide-eyed and unblinking and grinning at me as he describes his debauched years that I've stopped understanding anything he's saying, except that BDSM is like a higher existence, you know? Practically spiritual, but it runs up your credit card debt and you gotta pay that off so you need to get a job.

I managed to offend some of the queer employees earlier in the day when I suggested that labels on sex seemed a little old-fashioned, that I didn't care if somebody was queer or gay, or bi, or straight, and that as I traveled around the country I didn't find many people who cared much either. I said something like, Gee, seems to me you sort of put yourself in a ghetto by waving the queer flag and not just living your life however you want to live it. This was taken as a signal to lecture me on the oppression they were suffering right now—not thirty years ago, or twenty years ago, or ten, but right now. In San Francisco? I said. Are you kidding me? How oppressed can a queer in San Francisco be? But I had underestimated how important it is to be oppressed, and questioned their right to feel oppressed, and they got mad at me.

Now a few of them are eyeing me from the bar, so I move to a big red couch and sit down, trying to disappear. A pretty woman with coal black hair, about thirty, wearing a red corset and diaphanous white blouse and black pants, sits next to me. Does she work here? No. Her name is Domina Selina Raven. She wants to know who I am, why I'm here.

"I'm hanging out with Madison Young for a couple of days."

"Oh, Madison. She's one of the smart ones. She has a good head on her shoulders about this business."

Selina's a good judge. She's a professional dominatrix who has taken over a dungeon formerly run by an older pro-dom who is semiretired—seen people come and go, you might say.

I ask how one becomes a pro-dom, how one goes about becoming semiretired. Is there a 401(k)? And just how does one find oneself on such a career path? She laughs and says, "I went to Catholic school," as if that explains it all in a simple declarative sentence.

In fact, she graduated from the same Catholic high school in California where I once briefly taught remedial English, the same Catholic high school golfer Phil Mickelson and screenwriter and director Cameron Crowe attended, though I suspect the school doesn't brag much about Domina Selina Raven. "My Catholic upbringing instilled the following concepts in my mind: pain is educational, the end result of pain and suffering is redemption, and it is possible to achieve a state of spiritual enlightenment through mortification of the flesh."

After high school, she attended Mills College, the highly regarded women's liberal arts school near Oakland. She's been going through a rough time lately, partly because she recently broke up with a woman after having been with her for a year. "But then I realized I just really like dick."

"There seems to be a lot of that going around," I say.

Selina asks if I have been to the roof yet; there's another bar up there and a hot tub. I haven't, so we climb the stairs and, yes, there is another bar on the roof and a hot tub steaming, and white fluffy towels at the ready, but nobody is using the towels or the tub because of the wind and rain. Donna is sitting at the bar, necking with a stocky young woman—or transfolk—dressed in a suit and a fedora that make her look like a Sam Spade impersonator. She has created sideburns by arranging strands of her hair and pasting them to her temples.

Two guys spark off some dope and use a Coke can as a pipe.

"How did you like your visit here?" Raven asks.

Others have asked me this same question all day. I'm not sure what they were expecting, but I sensed disappointment when I used words like *fascinating* or *interesting*, noncommittal words meant to get me out of the conversation. I think they want to hear that I was appalled, shocked, horrified, outraged, turned on.

But I wasn't. I was bored. I sat behind the bright lights, stayed out of Chuck's way, and was bored, bored, bored. I was surprised at being bored, because you wouldn't think a guy would be bored watching a cute girl get tied up by another cute girl and then be hit with a cattle prod and fucked by a giant dildo, and spit on and licked and electrocuted, would you? I mean, something in that mix ought to have stimulated some reaction in me, no? But I got nothing. My sensitivities were not shattered, my libido was not plucked, my moral indignation remained happily asleep.

I was bored the way I am bored by monster truck rallies, big wave tow-in surfing, Wal-Mart, glazed Krispy Kremes with added sugar, the giant animated robot warriors and fireworks and blasting music of the overture to *Monday Night Football*, car chases on the news, Internet bloggers, violence, Hillary Clinton and Britney Spears and Paris Hilton and Dick Cheney and 50 Cent, bling and

cribs, the Ford Expedition, extreme soft drinks, liberal piety, conservative insanity, and twenty-eight-ounce sirloins at an all-you-
can-eat buffet.

But the people at Kink are genuinely nice. I like them, even the
queers. I mean, though I unintentionally offended them, they
didn't throw me to the ground and kick me with Doc Martens or
anything. And everyone did try so hard at shock I did not have the
heart to deflate them.

Now, though, standing on the roof talking with a weary-
sounding Selina Raven, I say, "Sometimes I think we're all just
incredibly bored."

"Yes," she says with a rueful smile. "Hell yes, we're bored."

As I walk out the door, I see Chuck and I grab his hand and
thank him for letting me sit in.

"Hope I wasn't in the way."

"No, man, it was fine." He smiles the way the only kink-free
straight man in the room could smile, and says, "Some crazy shit
around here, huh?"

"Yep. Pretty crazy."

The next morning I take the BART train over to Oakland to
watch James and Madison create some content for her website.
When I arrive at James's virtually empty loft atop a commercial
building near the *Oakland Tribune,* he is prepping his cameras.
Tina has not yet become Madison.

James used to run his own website, Nawshibari.com, but he
gets health insurance and something close to $100,000 working
for Kink. He's forty-one years old now, and health insurance and
six figures mean a lot more than they did when he was knocking
around as a carpenter back east or up in Washington State experi-
menting with fetish photography and learning shibari rigging.

Since his cameras are all digital he can shoot as many images as
he wants and toss out most of them without sacrificing any dough.
So he and Madison improvise. She only needs a few good shots for

a decent website update to keep the paying customers happy for another week.

Compared with yesterday, these are glamour photos. She wears makeup and lip gloss and high heels. She takes her panties off and poses in a pink satin camisole with her hands against a wall, sometimes taking suggestions from James but more often directing him.

James pauses to put some music on a CD player. There are no chairs, so Madison, waiting, crouches down on her heels, her elbows on her knees, to think. She is wearing her camisole and her high heels, and the silver ring in her labia dangles a few inches above the floor. I suspect, for just a moment, this is a pose for my benefit because to me this is sexier than anything I saw yesterday. Then I tell myself, No, Madison Young is just used to being naked in front of people, so stop being so vanilla. But James keeps calling her Tina, and then catching himself and saying Madison, as if I'm not supposed to know Tina Butcher, and so I wonder if I am an art project, if Tina Butcher is using Madison Young to reinforce and then destroy my socially constructed view of women and sex. Either way, thinking about it has made it pretty unsexy.

She and James decide they need a video clip for her site and it ought to be a suspension. Since Madison is a little sore from yesterday, nothing too fancy. James ties her up and suspends her from the hooks in his ceiling and pulls her off the ground and takes the video of her squirming and moaning. The CD playing in the background is from a trip-hop band, Portishead. The girl singer whispers, "Nobody loves me it's true . . . Not like you do."

CHAPTER 7

Apple Pie Days, Latex Nights

I Learn the Ropes at a Fetish Convention

> If he doesn't return to consciousness within five minutes or so, call 911.
>
> —*The Seductive Art of Japanese Rope Bondage,*
> by Mistress Midori, 2002

I have been here for exactly ten minutes and already a woman I do not know has grabbed my crotch and licked my ear; another woman in a 1940s-style pinup dress—all polka dots and bosoms—has pressed her chest against my arm and demanded I buy her a glass of wine; an elderly woman wearing an evening gown, pumps, panty hose, heavy pancake makeup, rouge, and an ankle bracelet casts flirty glances at me and I'm pretty sure she is a man; and right now there is a guy wearing a rubber hood over his head, crawling on all fours licking the black steel-toed boots of a woman in a mesh dress who is leading him around by a chain attached to a collar around his neck.

And this is just the meet-and-greet.

Seriously, my balls hurt. All I did was ask a question. A woman was handing out the paper title sheet for a DVD. She gave one to me. It said, "Cock and Ball Torture." A how-to, I gathered. I got the gist; the words *cock-and-ball torture* are self-explanatory. But never having had my cock or my balls tortured (unless you count riding a Sting-Ray bike with a banana seat), I did not know how one went about it, so I said, "What does cock-and-ball torture mean?" admittedly an imprecise question, which apparently constituted an invitation to grab my treasures and squeeze with the force of an angry NFL lineman. While I was gasping for air, she leaned into me and licked my ear.

I staggered to the bar so I could lean against it and buy a drink to numb the ache. A forty-three-year-old redhead in a polka-dot dress named Rachel Steele sidled up to me and introduced herself as a MILF. She wasn't always a professional online MILF; she used to work for Wal-Mart. But posing for naked pictures for her own site, or doing bondage and fetish work for others, beats standing around on your feet all day, and if I was a gentleman we would not have talked this long already without my offering to buy her a plastic cup of wine. Judging from her red-stained teeth and the way she seemed to struggle to focus her eyes, she didn't need another cup of wine. Then she shoved her boobs into my shoulder and said I was handsome.

"Oh, come on!" I said. "If you really want me to buy you a wine, okay, but don't bullshit me."

She laughed and winked, and when the bartender handed her a new plastic cup full of red wine, she almost put it down my shirt. "Thanks," she said, before slipping me her business card and hobbling away.

So now here I am, still clinging to the bar, my balls throbbing, watching women in rubber dresses and men in capes and the guy on all fours crawling back and forth. My first fetish convention is off to an interesting start.

I have come to Fetish Con in Tampa, Florida, an event that attracts hundreds of attendees and scores of exhibitors of fetish-related products to the downtown Hyatt, because some readers have written things like this, from a fellow in Chicago: "I have an odd fetish, and want to know if it's something to be concerned about. As an adult I like wearing diapers and babyish things. I guess I would consider myself more of an Adult Baby. Is this or any fetish dangerous to have? Thanks."

Exactly what fetish is gets very complicated. Psychiatrists, and especially Freudian psychoanalysts, use it to indicate a paraphilia. (If you can masturbate only with a woman's shoe, you've got a paraphilia.) But these days fetish is an umbrella that includes BDSM and pretty much anything else kinky.

I think fetish has become part of our conversation thanks to the work and passions of people like Madison and the folks at Kink.com and other Internet porn sites. They push the edges further away and the void between the edge and the middle fills with the constant churn of pop culture, bringing shibari to *Vogue* and fetish to TV. My adult baby wrote to me after *CSI*, then the most popular show on network television, ran an episode about a murdered tycoon who was also an adult baby fetishist. So I have come to Tampa to see if all this "content" isn't pushing mainstream sex beyond toys and porn and AdultFriendFinder hookups, if mainstream America is wrapping its arms around fetish in real life.

So far so good.

Once I've caught my breath, I roam around the meet-and-greet to meet and greet, being careful to say nothing that could endanger my genitals. Eventually I find Vesta, one of the event's organizers. She is dressed in purple tights with a face mask and a cape, a short, pudgy, blond superhero. When she is not a superhero, she works as a nurse with a military affiliation and lives with her husband, a retired military man. When I introduce myself, she hugs me warmly but I cringe—a little posttraumatic stress—until I'm sure she's just being friendly.

Vesta and her friend Genesis Lynn have been running Fetish Con since 2001, making it part of a circuit of similar events with names like Thunder in the Mountains (in Denver) and Beat Me in St. Louis that have arisen as bondage, fetish, and S&M have grown in popularity. Fetish balls (think Cinderella in rubber) have been popular for some time, especially in Europe, but they are typically one-night party events. Fetish Con and its brethren offer educational seminars, parties, fashion shows, shopping, and networking. (I am hoping that tomorrow I will learn about "mouth stuffing" with Bond Dave, a master scarf bondage expert.)

The meet-and-greet is going on in space that has been cordoned off from the rest of the hotel, but some of the fetish convention-eers have gone down to the lobby bar and are mingling with guys in jackets and women in slacks, some of whom are attending a legal conference. The lawyers are casting sidelong glances at the tight corsets and Morticia Addams dresses of the fetish women, but I can't tell if the looks show fear, humor, disgust, or admiring curiosity. All the above, I think.

I order a beer, and a woman wearing shorts and a T-shirt makes way for me at the bar. I ask her what she thinks of these fetish people. But she is part of the fetish group. Her name is Sheridan Nicoll, she says, and then quickly adds that this is the name she uses for modeling purposes. Her boyfriend, the marine who just left for Iraq, knows her by another name.

Sheridan has moved to Tampa recently from Cleveland. I have met many Buckeyes on this journey, and I have been astounded by the number of Catholics I have encountered, so I take a wild swing at the ball and say, "I grew up in Ohio. You aren't Catholic by any chance?"

"My family is *very* Catholic. I went to Catholic school."

Sheridan introduces me to another woman, also dressed in a plain vanilla wrapper, who identifies herself as Paige Turner. (Cute noms de fetish are common, I learn.) Paige, forty-six, is something of a mother hen to local fetish models, and when I explain what I'm doing at Fetish Con, Paige enthusiastically welcomes me to the fold and promises to provide whatever guidance I might need. She led a vanilla life herself for a long time, she says, but while working in a boat factory in Connecticut, she turned kinky.

Unlike Sheridan, who isn't really a fetishist but is happy to play one for money while she studies criminal justice, Paige would do it for free. Not unlike Susan back in Maryland, Paige loves the idea of being forty-six and having men get erections at the sight of her pictures. Most often she does straight bondage, getting tied up in cute costumes, for example, but she has also made a specialty of "forced orgasm," a bondage practice in which a woman has a powerful vibrator like the Hitachi applied to her clitoris, as Donna did to Madison. The difference, however, is that the "top," the person in control, doesn't release the vibrator after the "bottom" has an orgasm. The machine just keeps buzzing away and the bottom comes again and again in a mixture of agony and ecstasy.

"I should be doing a forced orgasm while you're here," Paige tells me. "Come and watch." Then she introduces me to her husband, Jerry, known in local fetish circles as "the Bad Man." Jerry won't be the one to give her a forced orgasm; that would be another guy. Paige's son is here, too, with his girlfriend. Fetish is a family affair.

Other than possibly losing my ability to have children, the night has gone well, I think. I had been concerned that I was so vanilla, I might be an unwelcome presence. Instead, people seem eager to help and to explain. I hear over and over again how much misunderstanding exists about fetish and about BDSM. Most attendees think it is long past time to shed the scary, freaky image those of us outside the fetish world have of those inside it. When Paige talks about it, she can sound like a woman talking up a small-town bowling league, just a bunch of people with a common interest getting together for good clean fun, a little knot-tying, and some dress-up.

* * *

T he six-foot pink bunny refuses to speak because rabbits don't talk. But I persist with yes/no questions until he cocks his big bunny head to one side and heaves an exaggerated sigh and uses pantomime to tell me that he works as a bartender, lives in Talla-hassee, bought his bunny suit on eBay, has a girlfriend, and is a male somewhere between the ages of thirty and fifty. Oh, and being a furry is his first real fetish. He has dabbled in fetish—he made a "so-so" gesture with his paw—but being a furry is his first immersion. I won't swear to any of this because I am not fluent in rabbit sign language, but I think I'm close.

As far as I can tell, he is the only furry here. Exactly what a furry is gets very complicated, and furries themselves don't seem to agree. In fact, there has been a furry rift. After popular media (*CSI* did another episode featuring furries and they've been pro-filed in magazines) got hold of furries and emphasized the erotic side, some in furry-dom insisted they want little or nothing to do with sex; they just like to make pictures of anthropomorphized animals. But others do dress up in furry costumes and gather in a furry group and "yiff," or have some form of sexual encounter. Sex could mean humping on each other in a group scrum until furry orgasm, which makes a mess inside the furry suits, or it could mean slipping the human genitals outside the costume and yiffing with somebody you know only as the gray grizzly bear. Furry sex can be awkward, as you might imagine, which is why the website Second Life, a virtual reality world, has a large and growing furry community where she-foxes and he-bears can yiff any way they want with realistic-looking animal parts.

I don't know what the big rabbit does for sex and I'm not about find out, because it was tough enough getting him to pantomime making a martini.

In the land of this convention, the rabbit falls somewhere near the middle of the fetish devotion scale. On the far end, there is a blue-collar factory worker from Louisville, Kentucky, who is being pushed around in a wheelchair, because having been mummified in black electrical tape, he can't walk. His dominatrix, Miss Mia Voraz, is keeping him supplied with liquids by holding the straw of a juice box through a tiny slit in the tape and into his mouth. Miss Mia, a young former art student, is heavily tattooed. She wears a corset that has squashed her breasts almost to her chin. She is very serious about being a dominatrix, which is a good thing for the guy in the wheelchair because he could die of suffocation if she's not careful.

In snippets over the next two days I will learn that he has had a tape fetish since he was nine years old and that he feels truly secure and safe only when he is encased in it. The mummification takes over half an hour for Mia to accomplish, starting with a layer of plastic wrap and then the tape. He can last about four hours in his cocoon. Mia, who clearly operates as a surrogate psy-chotherapist, tells me that "he has made a lot of progress" over the past few months and has recently begun opening up to his family, coming out of his shell, so to speak.

Goddess Heather straddles both vanilla and fetish worlds. Christine Auer grew up deaf, the daughter of an aerospace engi-neer who always told her she could accomplish anything in life. She discovered athletics, but after high school she began gaining weight. Joining a gym helped, and, inspired by the bodybuilders she met there, she lifted heavy weights and eventually began taking steroids. She bulked up to enormous dimensions. When she discovered some men like being dominated by Amazonian women, she birthed Goddess Heather and entered the fetish world. She shows some of her photographs to me and they are what I expect, lots of mean grimaces and riding crops, huge breast implants, a buzzed flattop haircut, and bulging muscles. Then I turn a page and go breathless with surprise.

"I have the most unusual vagina on the planet!" she announces.

The woman has a junkyard hanging from her cooter. Every one

of her fifteen labia piercings holds a chain that reaches the floor, or an old, heavy lock. She is stretched like a Mursi woman's lower lip.

Yet Heather isn't scary. She ought to be, but even in the pictures, she can't quite make me believe in her viciousness. In person, she is earnest, sweet, and thoughtful. We talk for half an hour about her life, about how devastated she was when her first husband died, and how at forty-six she believes she can be a unique advocate for health and fitness among older women, presumably through some means other than genital weight lifting. She has set up a mainstream fitness business to try.

Many attendees show no outward kinkiness at all. I meet a man in his fifties ("Call me Sir Arthur") dressed in casual slacks and shirt with thick glasses with a trim graying beard, in Bond Dave's Scarf and Sari Bondage seminar. At first he chases me away but then apologizes for his abruptness and explains that he and his wife are "very private people when we come to these things." I tell him that's fine, I wasn't offended at all, and begin to walk away, but he grabs me and keeps explaining himself further and further until I conclude that for some reason it is important to him that I understand. For the next thirty minutes he swings wildly back and forth, talking first about how conservative he is ("I watch Bill O'Reilly all the time") and so is his small town, and then about BDSM. At one point his wife incongruously interjects that her son is an honors student. Unlike most people I meet here, he seems tormented. "I really hate it when all the gays are out marching," Sir Arthur says at one point, but then he backtracks immediately to say that he understands the concept of glass houses and stones and that "a lot of my friends would probably call me weird" for being here.

Foxy, on the other hand, "don't give a shit what anybody thinks." He's happy in his big cowboy hat and showy gray handlebar mustache, driving a couple of sturdy mares, his wife and a neighbor. They have tassels on their heads, hooves on their hands, blinders on their faces, bits in their mouths, and leather thong "saddles" around their middles. Foxy lives in rural central Florida. He's the kind of guy who votes a "straight NRA ticket" because "it just ain't a good day unless you snuffed the life outta somethin'." Snuffin' the life outta stuff keeps Foxy working. He's a taxidermist.

Foxy and his team would seemingly have nothing in common with Chloe, a male university biology professor with an interest in Buddhism, whose long, luxurious tail keeps getting in his way. But they are all part of the same pony play group.

For Chloe there is no sexual gratification from dressing up in nearly $1,000 worth of tack and showing it off or being trained by his girlfriend, his "handler." Chloe just likes the escape he feels when she puts him through his paces, when the only thing on his mind is being a horse.

"So we'll do lunge line circles where she'll check my step, make sure it's all right. I do show work, so she will go through all the behaviors I would do in a show."

"Like dressage?"

"Yeah. Full dressage. The whole bit."

Chloe, being highly bred, can be temperamental. "If I have a day where I don't want to prance around and listen to what she is saying, I will be unruly." Some ponies do have sex. For example, a pony might become angry at his or her trainer and attack and "have their way with them," Chloe says.

His girlfriend had no idea he was into pony play or even what pony play was until they had dated for some time. "It has been very cool, another way we can really be close to each other. It helps with trust and it has to be intimate, because you are really putting yourself in someone else's hands."

Superhero fetish is a subgenre specialty, one Vesta has explored for years. She now runs an ongoing series on her own pay website called League of Amazing Women. She hires a photographer who uses a simple point-and-shoot digital camera to create an episode in comic serial form. The whole production takes about an hour.

The league operates in Tiedsville (Get it? Somebody always winds up bound and often topless) and features a revolving cast of super-powered women and female villains. The League of Amazing Women is deliberately silly and there isn't even an attempt at creating a set. Vesta will shoot an update just about anywhere she happens to be; I watch one being made in an empty conference room at the Hyatt. But Vesta still makes a profit from people who join her site.

Superbecca is even more low-budget. Rebecca Edwards, a fifty-year-old North Carolina housewife, loved reading comic books as a child. With support from her husband, she started her own website featuring herself, a quasi-superwoman, battling evil in the woods behind her house. Becca gets chloroformed, tied to trees, or captured and bound by rope and held hostage on her living-room couch. Superbecca requires an arduous suspension of disbelief and she is never nude, but fans are devoted. Frank, a twenty-eight-year-old artist in the video game industry, joined her site because Becca is "sincere." It's gratifying for "a guy to feel he is in control, especially of a superwoman," he says. "That's part of the fantasy."

Dave Gibson, forty-five, is a short, slight man just beginning to nurture a middle-aged paunch. He wears his dark brown hair in a tight trim. His clothes are neat and basic, his glasses squared with metal frames. Dave lives alone in a house in Pennsylvania, in a town of just over five thousand people, a pretty place of red brick and trees that turn gold in the fall. His sister lives nearby.

Dave is an electrician for a railroad, the one that used to be the Pennsylvania Railroad. The old PRR is long gone. Today it exists only on Monopoly boards. The locomotives are a lot different than they used to be, too, much more sophisticated with circuit boards and high-tech electronics. Dave received his first electronics training in the military. He spent eleven years in the service. For more than two of those years, he lived on a satellite-tracking station, over one hundred miles from the nearest town. Yet despite his years of experience in the military and with the railroad, the electronics on the locomotives are changing again, becoming even more computerized and finicky, so Dave is having to be retrained.

As Dave explains this to me, he excuses himself for a moment. "Have to wet my whistle," he says, one of many anachronistic phrases he prefers.

He's an old-fashioned guy, Dave is. He carries no debt except for his mortgage. He calls women "ladies," as in "when a lady is wearing heels." He is diligently polite. Politically, Dave leans far right. He's an enthusiastic supporter of Pennsylvania senator Rick Santorum, who has made the restoration of America's moral values a personal crusade. (A few months from now, Santorum will be defeated for reelection, gravely disappointing Dave.) He also reads the conservative writers, especially Ann Coulter. He's a big fan.

"I am very, very Republican," he says. "I vote what is best for the country."

Every guy needs a hobby. Dave enjoys photography. He reads the how-to magazines and has invested quite a lot of money into new digital cameras and props like ropes, ball gags, handcuffs, leather restraints, blindfolds, chains, and duct tape.

Dave likes to take photos of pretty girls tied up, gagged, and helpless.

"I'm a pervert!" Dave exclaims. This makes Sheridan laugh, even though her arms are bound tightly behind her back, her ankles roped together. I am in Dave's hotel room with Dave and Sheridan. I feel as if there is another guest in Dave's room, too. There is a copy of Ann Coulter's *How to Talk to a Liberal (if You Must)* sitting on Dave's bedside table. Ann is looking up at us. She is wearing a purplish leather top that would fit right in here at Fetish Con. Dave is wearing shorts and a T-shirt. Sheridan, lying on Dave's bed, is too, but her shorts are significantly shorter than Dave's.

Dave's T-shirt is black. It is one of his favorites, with a cartoon drawing of a sexy dominatrix schoolteacher named Miss Behaving standing in front of a chalkboard and holding what looks like a paddle. "Miss Behaving's Driving School," it reads. "You've been a very, very dangerous driver." Ann is standing in front of a chalkboard, too. It's pretty crowded in this room.

There is a trunk by his bed. It and one of the drawers in the room are as meticulously packed as an obsessive fly fisherman's tackle box, containing ropes in various colors and dimensions, safety scissors in case of a bondage emergency, ball gags in different colors and sizes, duct tape, white cloth gags he has ripped into precise lengths, chains, vet wrap (a form of restricting bandage used by veterinarians as on the legs of horses), and more. Dave keeps an eye out on Internet sales to get the best bargains.

Having managed to get Sheridan's elbows to touch behind her back, Dave is pleased. "Not everybody can get their elbows together like that," he says admiringly.

"I roll on my shoulders to keep them flexible," Sheridan says.

Knot tying is a vital part of Dave's hobby. He's spent several years working to create better knots, and now, as he leans over Sheridan, he pauses, making sure the knots are big enough and symmetrically aligned. The work is consuming, or at least Dave's focus is consuming; he doesn't notice that he is already perspiring and we're only about fifteen minutes into his two hours of time.

Sheridan has done this enough to know what Dave is looking for, so she turns her head to look over her shoulder with a mixture of seduction and fear. Dave's Sony Cyber-shot starts whirring.

When he was a little boy, Dave used to sit, rapt, in front of the TV during *Batman* and old westerns because women were often tied up, left squirming and in peril. There was something exciting about the idea that he could rescue a damsel in distress. On the other hand, there was also something exciting about imagining himself the villain who put her there in the first place.

Growing up in a small town, there was very little chance of Dave's seeing much bondage porn and there was no Internet. It wasn't until he joined the military that his interest truly flowered. Working in that tracking station wasn't much fun. You practiced for Soviet missiles, you kept an eye on NASA missions, all very important, but being over a hundred miles from anywhere in a military installation gets boring and lonely. So when he had the chance, Dave made the trip into the town and purchased his first bondage magazines. They were very expensive because they were imported from America, but Dave, who is no spendthrift, bought them anyway.

Bondage imagery featuring women in underwear, bound in ropes, had something of a heyday in the 1950s, most famously through the work of Irving Klaw, the man who made Bettie Page an icon. The business shriveled in the wake of government investigations into juvenile delinquency and the availability of fully nude women in the new men's magazines like *Playboy*. It survived mainly on the covers of lurid detective pulps that depicted women tied up, supposedly by crooks and maniacs. A California outfit named Harmony Concepts helped revive the genre in the 1980s. Rather than forcible bondage like that depicted in the pulps, Harmony advocated consent as part of the "Harmony Philosophy":

> What is most discouraging about this business are the prevailing social misconceptions concerning bondage, at least the benevolent, romantic type of bondage that we produce. For the unenlightened, what we represent and advocate really needs to be clarified. In that spirit, the following general explanation is at least a start.
>
> It has never been nor will it ever be our purpose to depict women as mere subordinates to men. These pictures and articles are not about that. The materials we produce are carefully and, we think, obviously designed for men and women to whom bondage is an important mutual diversion, a

recreational and benevolent experience, a fantasy with a happy ending, a good-natured game in which everybody wins.

For Dave, the sexual attraction isn't so much nudity as it is seeing a woman in jeopardy. He gets sexual gratification from looking at his pictures and imagining his "damsel in distress." "A fantasy aspect to all this is being the hero and rescuing the damsel, and sometimes I like to do that. But I also like being the villain, the guy who gets to do this."

Yesterday he shot with Tomiko, a former third-grade and kindergarten teacher who now does non-nude bondage modeling and is known for playing the businesswoman-in-glasses. Dave especially likes that look. "You could call that a fetish, like the girls on the Weather Channel. They look nice and neat and look so attractive."

I steal a glance over at Ann in her long blond hair and leather.

Dave will spend about $2,000 on models during the three days he is in Tampa. He began arranging appointments months ago by putting up a profile on the Model Mayhem website. Paige did him a big favor by giving him a shout-out.

"05/25/06 7:00pm Hey Dave! Glad to see you here! The Badman and I are looking forward to seeing you at Fetishcon again this year... great pics on the profile...none of me tho...:(JK.....I believe you'll do well.....girls......if you want to shoot with a really great guy Dave is your man! He's lot's of fun and really sweet! Hugs and kisses,

Paige.

The trip to Fetish Con has become an annual pilgrimage for Dave, his big vacation of the year. He comes down to the lobby bar, and he'll visit the show floor of the convention to check out new fetish equipment displayed by manufacturers and to see the professional fetish and bondage models who are here promoting their DVDs and websites, but mainly he will watch his pennies and stay in his room shooting every day, adding to the thousands of images he has already accumulated.

Sheridan, hog-tied now, lies down on her belly and Dave snaps away. She looks back at him and compliments his knots.

"That's really pretty what you've done there."

Dave beams. "I have only one thing on my mind."

We all laugh, except Ann.

Dave has never done nude photography. "I am still relatively new. I am feeling my way along, what I am comfortable doing. I have done topless, but that is about the limit to what I feel I am ready to do so far. As I do more, maybe I will. It's like, 'What's the rush? Why be in a hurry?'"

His sister is the only person outside the fetish community who knows of his preoccupation. Ideally, Dave would find a girlfriend who shared his interest, but if she did not, "I would have to carefully gauge her feelings. If she objected, it would end the relationship." He could never be public about his fetish, he says. He could never assert his right to take pictures of pretty girls tied up in rope just to gratify his own masturbatory fantasies.

As Dave shoots, and ties new knots, and shoots again, and poses Sheridan in new ways, he becomes increasingly eager and even more solicitous of her. "Everything okay?" "Does that hurt?" "How are you?" Models are understandably cautious about going to an amateur photographer's hotel room or home. They rely mainly on word of mouth from other girls, and the mere rumor that a photographer has acted inappropriately will get him black-balled. Dave would behave like a gentleman anyway, but he makes a show of it because it doesn't hurt to be thought of as sweet and unthreatening.

"Are you warm?"

"I'm hot, actually," she says, and I'm grateful to her because I'm sweating and all I'm doing is sitting in a chair and talking. But Dave hasn't noticed at all.

He turns up the air-conditioning and says, "What do you say to a topless shoot? Is that all right?"

"If Brian's all right with it, I'm all right with it," she answers. Me? Why do I count? This is the first time in my life a woman has asked if I would mind if she took off her top.

"Do you expect me to be offended?" I ask, laughing, which makes Sheridan laugh, and Dave takes the opportunity to snap off a half-dozen photos. He likes happy faces on tied-up women.

"I was being polite. I don't want to take my top off in front of anybody who is going to be offended." I assure Sheridan that I can take it.

Dave is unprepared for the quick assent. "I guess I better figure out what I am going to do." Dave is getting a little overeager, rushed, jittery.

But Sheridan is helpfully making suggestions. "How about taping my ankles? You can use the chair here. You can tie my arms to the chair and feet together," she says, demonstrating. She puts her hands on the bottom of her T-shirt and starts removing it.

"Do you want me to turn my back?" Dave asks, carrying his punctiliousness too far even for Sheridan.

She sighs. "Oh, come on." Sheridan pulls off her shirt.

Dave almost stops trying to direct her. He snaps away as if at any moment Sheridan will evaporate. He begins sweating again, leaping to stand on the bed one moment, straddling the space between a chair and the room's desk the next. Sheridan runs on automatic, mostly, delivering smoldering looks, smiling, laughing, pretending to strain against the ropes.

Dave takes a few shots of her butt. Her shorts have gone wedgie and Dave zeros in to capture the rope, her cheeks, a hint of labia.

In her book, Ann says, "It's hard enough to resist temptation without feeling like you are the only person on earth being asked to engage in the Herculean task of not committing a mortal sin." Dave does not think this is a sin, though, or if he does, the sin only makes it more fun. He may love Ann Coulter, but when it comes to sex he doesn't obey her any more than the Southern Baptists back in Missouri were cowed by the diktats of preachers.

When it's all over, Dave releases Sheridan from the final tie, and while she changes clothes in his bathroom, he cleans up the used ball gag, the ropes, the cloth strip he used on her mouth. Sheridan returns. Dave thanks her profusely and hands her a hundred dollars in cash. He'll probably send her some of the images, too, so she can forward them on to the boys in Iraq. She has developed a fan following among the guys in her boyfriend's outfit.

Dave tries to say good-bye by giving Sheridan a hug, but he makes such an uncertain, tentative move, she is not sure what he's doing and so she reaches out her hand to shake his, which he assumes means no hug for him, and it all winds up being a little awkward.

Dave Gibson has been naughty. Tonight, in Ann's book, he'll read, "Character is developed out of a lifetime of choices. Almost every decision you make, however small, will be a step closer to God or a step closer to the devil." But though his mind might belong to Ann Coulter, his heart belongs to Miss Behaving.

I am sitting in the back of a shuttle bus as it drives through Tampa on its way to nearby Ybor City and a nightclub called the Castle. Carl, a lawyer for a social services agency in a Florida county, and his new girlfriend, a young nurse (maybe Michael was right—I seem to be meeting a lot of nurses), are sandwiched next to me. Paige Turner assured me that I would pass if I wore black to the Vamps and Vixens Ball, so I'm wearing black jeans and a black T-shirt, not very fetishy, but I've got Carl beat. He looks . . . actually, he looks like a lawyer, a preppy lawyer. His girlfriend is wearing a black flared, pleated dress made out of PVC cut low across her chest and heavy black eyeliner and black boots. Everyone else on this fetish troop carrier is geared up in some version of PVC and leather and rubber. We are all packed so tightly that when somebody rubs against another passenger, you can hear the PVC squeak.

We ride for a few minutes in silence—Carl and the nurse and me. Finally, I say to Carl, "You don't look like you belong."

He grins. Tension ebbs from his face. "This is my first fetish event. This is my girlfriend," he says, introducing us, "and we haven't been dating very long. She wanted me to see what it's like."

"And?"

"It's interesting."

Carl's girlfriend seems a little disappointed by the word. She brought him to Tampa so he could understand something that has become part of her life in hopes of a conversion. Carl doesn't oppose anything he has seen so far; he kind of admires the fetishists' freedom to go a little nuts, but he makes it clear that for him to embrace his inner fetishist will require a profound mental adjustment.

When the bus pulls up to the Castle, there is a line around the block waiting to get in the front door. Most everybody seems to be under thirty and they are decked out in gothy, fetishy costumes, scores of them, a tribe standing there with varying levels of patience.

As Fetish Con attendees, we have been granted special access to the Castle, so we climb a set of wooden stairs and enter through a back door. Industrial metal music blasts over a sound system. Trent Reznor screams, "I wanna fuck you like an animal!" Colored spotlights bounce around the cavernous dance floor, which is so jammed with people dancing isn't even possible. Giant flat TV screens above the bar are playing scenes of old black-and-white movies by Irving Klaw. Bettie Page is up there in her underwear. Over in a corner a body painter named Pashur has set up a mini-studio and is quickly painting topless girls and their faces. One girl, her torso elaborately painted by Pashur, is dancing on a platform behind him, doing a trancelike sway. A man sits beneath her, his hands cuffed behind his back, a collar and leash around his neck, an American flag captioned "9/11 Let's Roll" tattooed on his shoulder.

"There is a bumper crop of creative newcomers," the party's promoter, Jsin, had told me earlier. "The younger kids, the next generation, are open people. They take all this for granted. It is nothing for them to walk around in bondage harnesses." Here was Jsin's proof, a hundred or so kids—mainly kids—ready to party.

Marilyn Manson marries (and subsequently divorces) Dita von Teese, a fetish superstar as Jenna Jameson was a porn star who, like Jameson, went mainstream and is now considered a chic symbol of the new popularity of fetish. She has been on the covers of the *New York Times* style magazine and *Paper*. She has been nominated by the readers of *Elle* as a "style icon."

The Matrix movie series was a fetish-style apotheosis. Everything was fetishized: the violence, the technology, the hardware, but especially the fashions. The imagery is everywhere now, marketed like Red Bull and hip-hop and cell phones.

In the old days, like ten years ago, a kid wanting to find a fetish party had to get to a record store that carried flyers about underground events. "Now there are party images on MySpace," Jsin said, and announcements of future happenings all over the Internet. (Even the Internet itself has become an object of fetish. Cyber-fetish attempts to transform you into a living digital avatar with accessories like neon-colored wig attachments resembling dreadlocks, and shiny metallic PVC and latex.)

I have been told over and over how the Internet has unleashed fetish, providing a place where enthusiasts can find each other. Barb, a sixty-two-year-old woman from Shreveport, Louisiana, explained that as a child, she used to enjoy spankings. If she couldn't sleep at night, "I'd think about spanking. That would give me a warm feeling and I'd go off to sleep." She was married for thirty-one years, but "I couldn't get my husband to hit me for anything." There had long been spanking fetish magazines, but she never saw them. Then she finally got a computer and hooked it to the Internet. She typed "spanking" into a search engine. "I knew then I was not the only one." She left her husband and became "romantically involved" with "Master Mac," who owns the Kink Shop in Shreveport. A Southern Baptist, she justified her fetish to me by saying, "I do think this is biblical. The man is the head of the household, right? Well, this is just taking it a step further."

Joy Berger, a self-described "little Jewish grandmother," couldn't be happier about the fetish boom. She owns Le Chateau Exotique, a fetish-wear store in New Hope, Pennsylvania, one of the largest in the country. Fifteen years ago she stopped teaching high-school biology and started selling fetish fashions and equipment. Business has never been better. She wouldn't say just how much she sells every year, but she did say that she never imagined fetish would become so mainstream. "I now sit at the mayor's table," she told me, referring to chamber of commerce meetings.

But pop culture appropriation of fetish, its omnipresence on the Web, and the resulting trendiness have generated some grumbling in the fetish world about arrivistes who just like to play dress-up. "Oh yes," a professional BDSM porn star named Anastasia Pierce told me, "they're being rebels! They will sit around and smoke clove cigarettes." These people miss the point of fetish, argues Mia Voraz, and Voraz's mentor, a longtime fetish expert named Sir David Bane. The latex, metal, and leather clothing, the encasing rubber suits, may be sexy, but they are also supposed to be transcending.

"It is a transformative experience," a professional fetish model named Kumi Monster told me. Kumi, who has thousands of dollars' worth of latex dresses, takes on a new persona when she wears them. "It's different than putting on a suit and tie. Your attitude changes, your posture changes, whether or not you have heels on, for example. Heavy corsets force you upright. You are not slouching." When she is wearing her fetish clothes, she said, "I feel in power wherever I go."

While fetish is all about sexuality, often it is not about sex. Instead, fetish makes sexuality a theatrical experience in which the entertainment payload is dropped before the denouement. Orgasm may be necessary, and momentarily pleasing, but it is also a defeat, even a death, because it brings you out of the fetish moment and back into the ordinary.

BDSM is often more mental than physical. Voraz, for example, won't have sex with her duct-taped client; instead, she'll play with his big head. The idea is to give power up to the dominant, or top. Submissives, or bottoms, often talk about "entering sub space," a kind of endorphin-fueled mental flight free of any worries or cares because they have yielded all responsibility to the dom. This is why, in a very real sense, the sub is often the one in charge. They are being serviced by the dom.

Some people object to the conflation of fetish and BDSM, but popularity has made "fetish" an increasingly meaningless word. This helps explain why nobody really knows how many fetishists there are in the United States. If you use the looser definition, it could be about two hundred million, or just about every adult. For obvious reasons, I have always had a little thing for Catholic schoolgirl uniforms, which is painfully hackneyed in the age of shibari, I know, but there you go. Is that a fetish or just a quirk? Do women who dig men in tool belts or cop uniforms have a fetish, or just an interest in tough guys? Understand that fetish also comes in degrees, from full time to only on your husband's birthday, and you can see the problem.

Using a much stricter definition, given to me by the principal partner of Diversicor Media Group, publisher of fetish magazines like *Skin Two, Bootlovers,* and *Domination Directory International,* about 7 percent of Americans are hard-core fetishists. He is extrapolating from his circulation, but that would be about fourteen million adults. I have no idea if his number is an accurate reflection or not—there has never been a reliable survey. I've seen estimates that say 15 percent of Americans have a foot fetish, but I don't know if that's accurate either, and I'm not sure it matters. I think it is enough to say that many people, far more than most of us recognize, are at least a little kinky and the numbers are growing.

Many of the Fetish Con attendees tell me they weren't always able to express themselves this way. Just as Madison dreamed of Catwoman as a girl, they saw a superhero or a fantasy character like Conan the Barbarian in a comic book, or they watched a movie where somebody was spanked or slapped and then kissed passionately. A half-dozen tell me that, like Dave, they loved old westerns on TV, especially the parts where somebody got tied up. Chloe said that as a boy, he would watch a cowboy on a horse and wish he were the horse.

A man named Bob tells me that when he watched cowboy-and-Indian movies, he wanted to be the Indians. At the moment he is wearing a black leather hood over his head, a collar around his neck, and he is being led with a leash, by his wife, Melissa, who looks like a plump Robin the Boy Wonder thanks to the black mask on her face. Like Bob, she also points to an early interest in BDSM. She was eight when she watched a movie on HBO and saw a clothed man spank a partially naked woman in a hallway. "It spoke to me," she says.

I am tempted to tell you a lot more about their childhoods and to say that Melissa drags Bob around by a leash because both of them lived through baroque family melodramas. There were sledgehammers through car windshields, and drug addiction and alcoholism and a kidnapping by Mafia-connected goombahs in New York, and life in a trailer in a redneck town in central Florida, and some sexual abuse from a relative, and a private eye beating up a dad, and something about a chain saw. But the fact is, Bob and

Melissa aren't sure what, if anything, the childhood traumas have to do with leather and leashes.

Secret yearnings are the most powerful of all. You nurture them unshared with anyone else and in the closed hothouse atmosphere they grow until you can't suppress them anymore. Both Bob and Melissa went on with life despite their childhoods and their inner passions. When Melissa could no longer suppress her yearning for BDSM, she initiated an apprenticeship under a bondage master so she could properly learn the system for using rope. During a brief first marriage, she dominated her husband, and other people—mainly other women, but sometimes men— but he never seemed to understand that when she said she wanted a submissive man, she did not mean she wanted a doormat. A subtle point, perhaps, but vital. Bob had much less experience when he placed a profile on Bondage.com, part of the Adult-FriendFinder network where Melissa found him.

"On our first date we went to a restaurant, then drove to a lake," Bob recalls. "It was soon after July fourth and there were kids there shooting off bottle rockets, so forever after I have been able to say that fireworks went off on our first date." They kissed on that date. Melissa squeezed his nipples a little.

They go on telling me the story of their courtship and I keep waiting for the bacchanalia of kink. Instead I hear about their second date and how Melissa screwed up her courage to ask Bob to spend the night at the town house she shared with her sister because she already knew she was nuts for him—"Hey, I'm a stud!" Bob says, laughing, at this point—and when she did, she announced her fear by saying, "I am trying to work up the courage to ask you to stay the night but nothing will happen and we will not do anything and I would like you to stay with me" all in one breath.

"Does your sister wear contacts?" he asked.

"Excuse me?" she replied.

"I cannot wear my contacts all night long," he explained. He was hoping there was contact lens fluid in the house. There wasn't, so they drove to Wal-Mart. Bob bought a NASCAR toothbrush, too.

"Then we watched *Finding Nemo,* my favorite movie, and the next morning he left." To Bob and Melissa their story sounds romantic and epic the way yours probably does to you, but as far as everybody else is concerned, you sorta have to be there, you know? So I'll skip the rest of the courtship and fast-forward.

They dated, they were engaged, they got married. Now Bob and Melissa are in their midthirties. Melissa works in a technical capacity for a military contractor and was a regional campaign volunteer for George W. Bush. Bob, funny enough, is a corporate controller. Bob drives an SUV. They bought a house they can't really afford, but they love it and work constantly to pay the mortgage. One recent Christmas, Melissa bought Bob a new Wii video game machine. Bob bought Melissa a Prince Albert.

Ahh, now we get to the kink.

Bob's Prince Albert is a piercing in the head of his penis that will attach to a chain Melissa can use to lead him. The Prince Albert was a big deal, because Bob is not into pain. Even scarier for Bob, they ran into the guy who was about to do the piercing, at Kmart.

"We went to buy some Lysol," Bob recalls, "and we saw him and he said, 'Hey! How you doin'?' and Brian, I am not kidding you, the guy had facial tics! Like Tourette's or something. He kept popping his neck, doing these half turns, and circles with his neck! It was a surreal moment." Bob went through with the piercing anyway, a testament to love.

They've also done a little home improvement to their new place. They have added a bondage table, and a custom-made hoist for rope suspensions, and, in an extravagance they feel guilty about because it's so financially irresponsible, they bought a custom wood and steel cage. Bob spent Christmas night curled up in it. They are redoing the garage and will incorporate the cage and the hoist "so they are plausibly deniable" as handyman equipment.

Melissa uses all this on Bob, but not all the time. They have regular old vanilla sex, too. But if Bob acts especially cocky, she'll "verbally degrade him. I spit on him, urinate on him, absolutely anything I can think of to take that smug little look off his face."

Bob and Melissa lead monogamous lives together, but have a different definition of monogamy than many people might. They will do BDSM with another couple, but there will be no intercourse or sexual touching. Group play happens rarely, though, because they look for fellow BDSM couples the way you might look for compatible golf partners—you want a couple you get along with off the course. Melissa, being bisexual, sometimes likes having a woman join them for sex, which Bob doesn't seem to mind, and which doesn't count as not being monogamous either.

Most of Melissa's friends know about her sexual life. When she worked for a previous defense contractor, she had security clearance in a government facility. "All had to be on the up-and-up, so I came out at work. Everyone wanted to be my friend and find out about it. A lot of people said, 'I am so jealous of you. I wish I could do anything I wanted and not be afraid.' Out of about sixty people, ten said that to me."

Bob has been much more circumspect. Fetish Con is his first real outing in public and he feels "like a scared kid in a candy shop. It's like such a big part of my life that has never been talked about, it's been considered taboo."

When I contact Melissa and Bob some months after the convention, they will sound even happier. "Really, we are so happy it's ridiculous. It is quite disgusting." Just one problem, though. Since they both work full time, they will look for a maid, but with the debt burden they already carry, they can't pay cash. Instead, Melissa will interview men who want to clean house in return for being dominated. "I'll have fun pointing out all his mistakes with the paddle!" Melissa will say. And Bob will approve because look, man, he wants a clean house and "if Melissa has to beat him, that's okay."

* * *

"Ladies, we are being far too nice to our men," Chanta Rose scolds. Her accent, Australian by way of England, makes her sound appropriately authoritative in that British public-school way, and her modest floral-print dress, the way she has fixed her blond hair in a bun, reminds me of the teacher of the Junior League dance lessons my mother made me attend at the Knights of Columbus hall. The memory makes me shiver. I had a tough time in dance lessons. Being twelve, dressing up in my orange sport coat and a clip-on tie, and bowing at the waist with my left hand over my belly button to ask a twelve-year-old girl for a dance struck me as absurdly unnatural, like mixing peas with Hershey's chocolate sauce. It just wasn't done. I hoped this was not going to be mandatory in order to get girls.

I suspect some of the men in the meeting room of the Hyatt, where Chanta, who happens to be a friend of Madison Young's, is teaching Bondage for the Male Submissive, can relate to the feeling. Their arms are being tied behind their heads by women using hemp rope and a very elaborate technique demonstrated on a male volunteer by Chanta from atop a wooden platform set up in the middle of the room. Most guys are laced up in an array of complicated knots, their elbows now pointing toward the ceiling, their wrists crossed, their palms somewhere near their scapulas.

Doubtful looks shoot up at Chanta as she exhorts the women, especially when she tells them this would be a great bondage position to start the day.

"Yeah," one guy interrupts, "but I'll be late for work!"

"Being late for work because you are tied up and being sucked off is not a bad thing," Chanta barks impatiently.

Yes, well, there is that. He gives a little nod and tries to shrug his immobilized shoulders.

Others need no cheerleading. A man about forty is being tied up by a woman who has to be at least sixty. She is dressed in a one-shoulder black Lycra top and tight, stretchy pants. He seems eager. An elderly couple, each about seventy, he with a long white ponytail, she with giant hoop earrings and a beehive hairdo, are being downright studious. The other twenty or so couples are a mixed bag of ages and experience. Some are novices.

None of them, though, are meeting Chanta's demanding standards. So she explains again why it is important to get it right. "You know when a guy is eating your pussy?" she begins, suddenly sounding not at all like my dancing-class teacher. "Well, his head can't quite get the right angle." The men and women splayed around the room nod in recognition of the problem. Yes, we see. Yes. "This is that clit-in-his-face position."

The goal, she explains, is to create a weblike contraption of rope and forearm behind the head, forcing it up into the desired attitude. Some of the women adjust their ropes, mainly trying to make the bonds tighter, but Chanta is still dissatisfied. The women are not following directions with enough gusto. The fact that the men are not adolescent Romanian gymnasts may have something to do with the current troubles, but Chanta will brook no excuses.

She grabs her model and spins him around, pulling on an elbow. "Do you see? He can't wiggle." Sure enough, the elbow barely moves. On the other hand, the skin on his arms is beginning to plump like water balloons between the bands of rope. The women in the room, seeing this, are unable to call upon their inner hostage taker.

Chanta scans their faces, gives a subtle cluck, and steps off her stage. She roams from couple to couple. "He could get right out of this!" "No, no, no." "Oh, dear. He's not a baby, love. He's a big boy. He can take it." The women nod, like Boy Scouts learning the bowline who finally see the bunny's route. A few release their knots, tug harder on the ropes, and retie, some achieving impressive results.

Chanta returns to her perch, spins her model around again, then crouches behind him. She begins reaching up under the inseam of his shorts. "Now," she continues, "you can incorporate cock-and-ball torture into this." (Hey! Maybe I'll finally learn cock-and-ball torture!) Chanta stands up quickly, interrupting herself. "Oh, and that reminds me. If you"—she indicates the men—"are someone's demonstration bitch, and you have a drippy cock, for God's sake wipe it off. Especially if you've just come from the bathroom, wipe it!" This man isn't naked as her eager volunteer models often are, this being the Hyatt and certain regulations against naked public cock-and-ball torture being in effect, but I gather this is something of a professional hazard for bondage instructors, something like dance teachers who remind twelve-year-old boys to dab their sweaty palms. A few of the guys laugh, but I am grateful for the tip, reckoning it just the sort of social wisdom like "Never walk in the line of another's putt" or "Shirt cuffs should show half an inch" that might come in handy someday.

"Okay, so I am all for tying down the balls . . ."

This is not a class to teach you how to handcuff a lover or use old neckties to tie their ankles to the four-poster, or even Bond Dave's scarf-tying seminar. A few of these guys are on the verge of a dislocation. Yet nobody is decked out in their fetish wear. Nobody looks like a lost cast member from *Texas Chainsaw Massacre*. I haven't seen many of these couples around the convention. Most of them look like they read the Sunday paper events listings to each other over coffee this morning and figured this Bondage for the Male Submissive workshop sounded more fun than a flower show or a contract bridge lesson.

A young couple near me at the back of the room is being especially serious. She is petite and pretty in a tube-top dress of black-and-white paisley, and flip-flops that show off a new French-style pedicure. He is tall and handsome, dressed in jeans and a T-shirt that says "Professional Gaming League." His hair is cut short, like the young professional I imagine he is. They wear wedding rings. I picture them driving a Volvo station wagon.

She is a good student, studying every knot, every twist and bend Chanta Rose demonstrates, and then duplicating them almost exactly on her husband. Such precision is her nature, she says.

Linda is twenty-seven and works as an investment banker for a big-name financial institution. Like her husband, Chris, who is thirty-one, she studied finance in college back in Tennessee where they both grew up. They have come to Chanta's seminar after seeing a BDSM and fetish show at a nightclub. One of the models asked Linda if she would be a model for an upcoming event, something Linda did not pursue, but the show and the invitation made them curious about Fetish Con. Bondage for the Male Submissive just happened to be on offer when they arrived. It's the first time Chris has been tied up.

Neither of them dreamed about being tied as youngsters or considered any alternate meanings to old westerns. As far as they know, they have not harbored latent fetish drives. Nor have they ever attended a fetish convention. Coming to one wouldn't surprise any of their friends, though. "Homosexuality, bisexuality, transsexuality—it's all accepted and welcome," Chris says. They do have friends they won't tell about being here, the ones who lean fundamentalist, but not because they feel ashamed. They don't want to make anybody uncomfortable.

Both were raised in churchgoing families. "I was a Bible beater," Chris recalls, from Joe Beam's old denomination. "Church of Christ. No music, no dancing, my Christian high school did not have a prom." There was no sex education in his school or from his family except "fire and brimstone" about the evils of premarital sex. "I knew early on I did not identify with that personally. As time has gone on, you find a middle ground, what's okay with you, with your relationship with God, and you incorporate that into your personal life. I think I have a personal relationship with God that is part of my life structure, but it would be non-denominational. I would go to any church to get a chance to worship the Lord."

Religion and sex are not connected in Chris's mind. But he does believe that "when we are intimate together, that is the highest celebration of my love and his word. If I did it with a rope tied around her wrist or a clutching embrace, what does it matter?" He and Linda, who happily had premarital sex, also use porn sometimes, of many different genres. It's just another instrument, like rope.

Both say they are liberals who happened to vote Republican in 2004. They often feel torn between their liberal social leanings and conservative economic philosophy and wish they didn't have to choose. Someday, they won't, they believe, because they find people their age just aren't concerned about the way other people have sex. They cite reasons I have heard before, like digital media and an omnipresent sexuality that serves up every possible variation. To be sure, they do have concerns about the sexual climate in the country, mainly the sexualization of children, especially young girls. "I hate seeing a third-grader looking like a twenty-five-year-old out at a club," Linda says. But the sexual terrain they are navigating as newlyweds is vastly different from any generation that has come before, even the vaunted "free-love" generation.

"People our age and younger are not scared to explore many different parts of their sexuality," Linda explains. "Being bisexual or homosexual is just much more widely accepted than even five years ago."

Nothing is off-limits for them. "Everything is open for discussion," he insists. "If there was just something she absolutely desired, I would probably try to overcome whatever personal issues I had to get there because it would be important that she feel fulfilled, and I think vice versa."

The party on the final night of Fetish Con, Guilty Pleasures, is more manageable than the chaos at the Castle. The sound track is the same—fetish seems to have an official list of industrial and goth music—but Club Chambers is less nightclub and more "play space" as designed by Hieronymus Bosch. The entire second floor is given over to instruments of torture, and many people from the convention are using them.

When I arrive, Mia Voraz has her submissive, duct-tape man, strapped to a big steel X-shaped structure in the middle of the room. He's out of his tape and stripped to a black jockstrap and black socks, a steel collar held fast with a padlock around his neck. Mia is hitting him with a hairbrush.

Wait. Now she is caning him like a sadistic schoolmaster, creating a cross-hatching of diagonal red stripes on his butt, his legs, his back. She works on him for about fifteen minutes, then releases him and orders him to pick up his pants and shoes and get dressed. He follows her dutifully as she walks away.

In one corner, an elderly man lies curved over an incline, his ass shining up through leather chaps. His wife, kitted out like a dominatrix French maid, her reading glasses perched at the end of her nose, is using a kitchen whisk to transmit electricity from a violet wand to his back, butt, and legs. Blue sparks fly out of the whisk as she rolls it over his body and he jerks up and down. Then she shocks the bald spot on the back of his head with the attentiveness of a grandmother knitting.

A woman lies tied up in a coffin on a small stage. A man, about six foot five, with a chiseled body is prancing around in his socks and a tiny white G-string, chatting up women, which seems to be working pretty well for him.

A professional flogger—there is such a thing—a thin man, with long black hair, his naked torso gleaming with sweat, his black eyeliner beginning to run, is making a show of twirling two cat-o'-nine-tails across the backs of young women who take turns in his iron cross. This is a show, really. It is performance and an audience is appreciated, because, like the theater, the object of fetish is to create a new world to escape into, a place better than reality.

But there is a determined self-consciousness about it all that feels forced. For three days I have been noticing a young woman, tall and thin with extraordinarily black hair, walking around the lobby bar of the Hyatt and at these parties. I have been noticing not because she is beautiful, but because she always has a dress or a top that reveals a big tattoo on the small of her back: "God Forgive Me," in gothic print. Like the name of the party promoter, Jsin, it seems too precious. I spoke to the sales manager of the Hyatt yesterday and he said he liked having the fetish people there because they bought rooms in August in Tampa and they policed themselves and were better behaved than a lot of other so-called mainstream business organizations he has hosted. The Hyatt doesn't care if she is into fetish. So she appeals to God.

Tonight, while we were waiting for the shuttle bus to take us here, about twenty of us had gathered outside the lobby door of the hotel facing the street. It was hot out and PVC doesn't exactly breathe. So people sat wilting on a flower bed, griping about when the bus was coming or chatting desultorily in small groups. A carful of local young men drove by slowly, the occupants staring at us and then shouting, "Freaks! What a bunch of fuckin' freaks!" To which everyone stood and whooped and hollered and shouted, "Yeah! We're freaks! Betchur ass!" and they remained enlivened, standing outside the Hyatt hotel in downtown Tampa, their sin reaffirmed, until the bus arrived.

CHAPTER 8

Playing with Fire

I DRESS UP, BUT AT A SEX CLUB,
CLOTHES DO NOT MAKE THE MAN

It is very important that I feel in control.

—Paradox, 2007

I want to beat the asinine grin off his face. He is lying there in her arms curled like an infant against a mother's breast and all I can think of is wanting to slap him so goddamn hard he'll know what real pain is. Get up! Stand up, you pathetic noodle! You giggling little schoolgirl. You mewling, murmuring, disgusting kitten.

I feel such an overwhelming contempt I am alarmed. This man has done nothing to me. I don't even know him. He is in computers—that's all I have been told. Maybe he's the nicest guy in the world, but he is really pissing me off.

This is it? This is the end of my journey and I get this guy, a white-haired, bearded, sixty-something "computer guy" nuzzling into her lap as if he's trying to return to the womb? This is what we've all been looking for? Mommy? Come on, you sonofabitch, tell me it's more than that! Tell me we're looking for heaven or hell or enlightenment or something to replace flat-screen TVs and McMansions. Tell me this huge burst of sex we're living through is about something more than wanting to chuck it all for milk and cookies and a pat on the head.

Maybe it's just my pants. They are punishingly tight. My testicles are aching yet again, screaming at me because they have been turned into a meatball panini by the PVC inseam. When I take these fucking pants off, I expect my boys to have become two-dimensional. I am also sucking in my gut because I am wearing a clinging muscle T-shirt with a skull on the front and I am too vain to show my body fat. Goddess Heather explained how to produce washboard abs, but I have not had a chance to implement her program. I'll get right on that.

Not that anybody would notice or care. Nobody else here seems at all concerned about their own bodies. Over on the dance floor, a topless woman, about thirty-five, wearing a short, flippy pleated skirt, is swaying hypnotically to the music. Metal again. Several feet in front of me, three obese people, two men and a woman, are taking turns lying on a mattress as one partner or another works their nude bodies over with a violet wand. Two feet behind me, a mostly naked woman is lying across the lap of another woman who has made a fist of her right hand and is shoving it in and out of the naked woman's vagina as if churning butter. Meanwhile, a tall, bald man in his fifties, wearing a sleeveless reptile-skin shirt and leather pants, is throwing jabs at the back of the mostly naked woman's thighs—jab jab jab, Joe Frasier working the heavy bag—as the fist churns in and out.

Jab jab jab. In, out, in, out.

I arrived in Seattle several days ago to put myself in the hands of Allena Gabosch. I had asked Allena, the director of an organization called the Center for Sex Positive Culture, popularly known as the Wet Spot, to mentor me. I wanted to know what it felt like to be a member of a sex club where BDSM, fetish, swinging, pretty much the entire gamut of America's sexual menu, played out. I thought becoming one with my inner perv, overcoming my intransigent vanilla persona, would allow me to reach a new depth of understanding.

Allena was a good choice. She is hopelessly funny and has a sense of humor about the scene and the people in it. Yet she is also a big, dominating, tattooed, tender, earth mother, with long, dark, stringy hair and a gapped-toothed smile and a lot of pounds she would like to shed because she thinks skydiving ought to be her next adventure. Finally, Allena has the advantage of having been around awhile. She has seen how much sex, and our attitudes about sex, have changed over the past decade. Mostly, she is encouraged, but she is no blind cheerleader.

Before I arrived, we talked about my travels so far and how sex had become such a cultural focus. I told her about the mail I received and she wasn't surprised. A new era of sexual experimentation had clearly taken hold, she said, and not just by the usual suspects of free-love hippies and dissolute hipsters with too much money, but everybody from all walks of life were starting to show up at the Wet Spot seeking information about sex that heretofore had been considered edgy and rare. She wasn't sure exactly why this was happening now—we talked about the Internet and pop culture, but these didn't seem completely satisfying—just that over the past five years or so, her clientele had boomed. The Wet Spot now had eight thousand members in the Seattle area, the eldest eighty-one years old. All of them had redefined "normal" for themselves. Allena was most excited by the center's new status as a 501(c)(3) charitable organization. Many companies in the area have programs that match employee contributions to 501(c)(3) charities, and Allena was joyful from knowing that companies like Microsoft and Boeing, both of whom have employees who are Wet Spot members, could help subsidize the organization's operations.

"Bill Gates is going to be supporting Sex Positive!" she said several times. This was a sign to her that sex-positive culture, a vague term that implies a celebratory attitude about all kinds of sexual variation among adults, had arrived and was now an ineluctable part of mainstream life in America.

On the afternoon of my arrival in the city, I drive over to the Wet Spot. It is situated not far from downtown Seattle almost under a bridge overpass. From the outside, it's not much, just a white concrete-block building with a rutted, mainly dirt, parking lot and a small sign by the steel front door saying SPCC. Not just anybody can walk in. A small reception desk inside the front door is always manned and there is paperwork to fill out and identification to provide and releases to sign stating you know what you are in for.

People are also asked to provide a name to be used by the organization in case they prefer their real names never to be spoken. There are a few prominent citizens who belong despite the risk that some unscrupulous fellow member might contact an employer, say, and out a member. The fake name option is a layer, albeit thin, of protection. I fill out my paperwork and show my identification. I promise to abide by strict confidentiality rules.

Despite never having seen Allena in person, I recognize her right away. Though a half-dozen or so other people are here, late in the afternoon, nobody else could possibly be her. She runs up to me and gives me a hug as if we have known each other for years.

Allena shows me around with all the pride of a woman who has built something from virtually nothing. She and her volunteer staff overcame the obvious social and political barriers, and constant financial troubles, to create a place Allena feels is safe and welcoming to everyone. The club resembles spaces I have been in before, places where under-the-radar rock bands play for one hundred cognoscenti. I saw Liz Phair a long time ago in a place almost exactly like this. A small snack bar with soft drinks and bottled water and juices is built into the wall closest to the front of the building. Facing inward, three rooms line the right-hand side: Allena's office, a small library offering reading materials on sex, and an operating room with medical equipment.

The operating room isn't just for show. When I ask about it I am told that they "don't actually remove any organs or anything" but small bits of tissue might be taken or incisions made. (If you want some serious operations, you'll probably have to go to Mexico. They do amputations down there. A few years ago, a guy with an amputation fetish died in a San Diego motel room after his leg was cut off in a Mexican clinic. You could say he had a paraphilia.)

The far left side of the building has a small shower and locker room, an after-care room with a futonlike bed where subs recovering from a sub-space trip can be comforted, and a play space with BDSM gear. A custom-made steel and wooden bondage bed, more gear, and a cubicle with a regular bed where people can have sex await in a back room.

I have come this evening specifically for the Fire Play seminar. I'm not sure what fire play is, and having learned my lesson after the cock-and-ball torture incident, I have not asked for details. But Allena tells me I'll love it because it is one of the edgier modes of BDSM action. I will learn from a man named Paradox. I find some of these BDSM names a little annoying, like Dungeons and Dragons identities, but Paradox has a good reason for adopting his BDSM handle. He is the forty-five-year-old dean of libraries at a major state university where the administration has no idea their dean is well known in BDSM circles for lighting naked women on fire. Paradox thinks this news might cause consternation because at his previous university, a large midwestern institution, somebody outed him to higher-ups. That partially explains why he moved jobs.

As people begin arriving for the seminar, I think I notice a type.

A short, muscular, bald man in a canvas kilt and Doc Martens
stands off to one side. He introduces himself to me as Fandar.
Another man, tall and bald (the same guy I will see later punching
the woman's thighs), arrives wearing a black leather tricorn hat,
a silky black poofy pirate shirt, leather pants with a codpiece
attached, and leather boots that extend over his knees. The T-shirt
on a large woman reads: "I let my mind wander and it never came
back."

"These are Renaissance fair people," I say to Allena.

"Oh yeah, and sci-fi geeks. Totally. I know I was. It's all about
fantasy."

We all settle down into folding chairs in the middle of the Wet
Spot. Paradox begins. "Fire touches our inner core, our animalistic
side, our fear. But it also touches our intellectual core . . ."

I spent a half hour talking with Paradox while he set up and he
seems like a fine person. Everyone here seems nice. Once again, I
am amazed at their openness. They know I am not one of them,
necessarily, and yet here are people who no doubt have reason to
fear condemnation, who fully realize their sexual tastes are different from those publicly expressed (though perhaps not privately
indulged in) by most people, and yet they will answer any question, tolerate any intrusion. Still, I'm bristling.

At first Paradox was afraid to play with fire. But nine years ago,
a dom in Nebraska (a dom in Nebraska? I'm not sure I ever
expected to hear that exact pairing of words) taught him how to
do it safely, and ever since he has considered it "one of the more
fun aspects of BDSM play. This is very much edge play," he says
ominously. "It is very easy to screw something up badly. With this
stuff, safety protocols are all important . . . Play with fire long
enough, you will get burned."

Fire and nudity are two things I would have thought are best
avoided in combination, but Paradox keeps emphasizing the fun.
He starts with a list of safety precautions, explains the importance
of using 70 percent isopropyl alcohol as our fuel source (30 percent

of it is water that acts as a barrier between the alcohol and the skin), and explains why the head of the submissive should be covered: burning hair puts a damper on the mood.

Still, "a male submissive I knew in Kansas, a big bear of a guy with a hairy back, loved to get torched across his back because for the next two or three weeks, he felt it as it grew back, and it itched like all get out. That was a turn-on for him."

Paradox is a handy fellow. He makes much of his own equipment, mainly from stuff he finds at Home Depot. Bob, of Bob and Melissa, told me he calls the store "Dom Depot." Paradox says he walks down the aisles looking for "pervertibles," hardware ostensibly for one use that, with a little imagination, can take on entirely different uses. For example, a few wooden dowels, some cotton batting, and string can be used to create "fire wands," small torches. Paradox has a half-dozen of them arrayed on a stand next to a table where his demonstration model, Jenny, is lying topless, a long skirt still tied around her waist. Each one of these constructions must have taken Paradox fifteen minutes to create, and that was after the trip to Home Depot. Yet the flames will last seconds. BDSM is a lot of work, which may be one reason why I've never taken to it. I'm more the "feed me grapes and bring me wine" sort of hedonist.

First, Paradox applies flaming Q-tips to Jenny's naked back. This is the "warm-up period." He rubs them up and down her spine until the flame dies, then repeats with another, a series of blue and yellow dancing fairies tripping up and down her body.

Next he lights his fire wands and gently beats Jenny. The flame wooshes through the air, the wand hits Jenny with a thud, and the wand goes out, usually after one or two hits. Jenny stands up. She's a short, fleshy young woman with a number of healing bruises. Paradox whaps her, not very hard, with the fire wands, and I look around to watch the dozen or so people observing Jenny being hit by the wands and the flames. They like what they see, but I sense no erotic charge at all.

Fire wands are just the beginning, the easy intro. Over the next half hour, Paradox uses canes, exploding flash cotton of the type used by magicians, and then twin floggers made of Kevlar that he soaks in alcohol, lights, and uses to flog a naked Jenny as she stands up against a big wooden X. Allena dims the lights so we can appreciate the full effect of the whirling, flaming floggers.

"Whoa!"

"The sound is just so great."

"Cool!"

"That is awesome!"

Woosh, woosh, woosh, the floggers fly in big blazing circles, hitting Jenny and then wheeling back in an arc of fire.

For his pièce de résistance, Paradox lays Jenny back down on the table and forms trails of alcohol in patterns across her back, butt, and legs. He orders the lights dimmed. Then he fires up a violet wand and lets the blue and yellow sparks zzit zzit through the air. The glass tube at the end of the wand glows purple. Holding it just above her back, he activates it again and a spark flies from the glass tip onto Jenny's back, igniting the trails of alcohol.

"Aww! Brilliant!"

But he's not done. While she is still lying down, Paradox uses soft wax to form a bowl on the small of her back. He pours in some alcohol and lights it. Jenny has become, one audience member says approvingly, "a human candelabra!"

"That is so sexy . . ."

As a brief encore, Paradox gives everyone a quick lesson on fire cupping, the practice of using Chinese glass cups to create a warm suction on the skin. He places a cup where he wants it on Jenny's back, lights a match, lifts the cup slightly off her back, holds the flame under it, removes the flame, and then tips the cup back fully onto her skin. As the air inside the cup cools, it sucks the skin up into the resulting vacuum.

"Gwyneth Paltrow does this," Paradox informs us. The effect is like giving somebody an enormous hickey. "You will get a very nice bruise there."

"The smaller cups are great on nipples," Paradox says. "This is a very fun thing to do, especially if you have somebody who is lactating."

"You are a very sadistic daddy," Jenny says, smiling. Paradox glows at the compliment.

"Aren't you worried about the bruising?" I ask Jenny.

"Oh no," she says. "I like to be marked."

After the seminar has concluded, Allena introduces me to Debra and Craig, a middle-aged couple who don't resemble the others in the room. I don't see them attending any Renaissance fairs. Debra is petite, thin, elegant looking. Her nails are perfectly manicured, her lips glossy. She is wearing a glittery camisole top and black pants. Craig is tall, thin, blond, handsome, and well dressed. When Debra tells me they are both fifty-six, I frankly don't believe her. I'm not sure I would believe forty-six.

"They're in town just for the night," Allena tells me, "and I thought we'd all go out to dinner, with Paradox and Jenny and my boyfriend Jim."

I pile into Allena's car with her and Jim, a fellow who produces online bondage porn, and we drive a short distance to a seafood restaurant on the water. We sit at wooden tables and order beers.

Craig and Debra are unmarried swingers from Illinois briefly visiting Seattle on an extended trip that has included a visit to Paris and swing clubs there. The Wet Spot isn't really their typical scene, but both of them have set off on a sexual odyssey of their own and are trying new things.

Debra is a school psychologist in a small Illinois city. After she and her first husband divorced, she "saw the divorce as an opportunity to reinvent myself" and she did it partly through swinging. When she married again, she and her second husband began visiting a club called Executive North in Mount Prospect, Illinois. That was where she met Craig, a prominent businessman in the Chicago area, and his wife. The four of them became friends, but, she insists, that friendship had nothing to do with why either of them divorced their spouses. She and Craig aren't exactly exclusive now anyway—they don't even live very near to each other.

Swinging for Debra is a way to receive positive affirmation and feel good about herself and others. She's not a BDSM aficionado— "I am not into pain. I have a strict 'no pain' policy!" For her, swinging "is all about intimacy."

She says this like trading partners in a sex club and intimacy should seem naturally linked concepts in my mind, but I confess that I don't get it. Intimacy would seem to imply at least a little exclusivity for at least a little longer than two hours.

"When you are naked and sharing intimate parts of yourself, those experiences are very intimate to me. We all have a great need for intimacy. Our society," she continues, "works against intimacy." We are atomized and harried, technologically plugged, and humanly unplugged. "So this is about trust and respect. There is no other place where you are so vulnerable and others are vulnerable as well." This is why she prefers the nude environments of swing clubs like the ones in Paris.

Craig has undergone a profound change in his life, just as Debra has in hers. There came a moment, he tells me, about a decade ago, "when I realized that the culture would kill me if I did not become what I am now." I don't know what that means. What is he now?

In a world in which people are not touched nearly enough, he says, one in which the prevailing attitude is about restriction and regulation and sin, we have become starved for intimate contact with other human beings, one of those things that make us human in the first place. All his business dealings, his success, his religious background as a Lutheran, never once helped him become the loving, sensitive man he is today. Now he wants to share that intimate touching. He has become an advocate for polyamory, having multiple, simultaneous loving relationships. He also serves as a sex surrogate for middle-aged women. "Sex is something we give to other people," he says. Craig wants to be a very giving person.

Knowing she and Craig are from Illinois, and now reminded by her mention of Paris, I have to ask her about Jack Ryan, the former Republican nominee for the U.S. Senate in Illinois. If Barack Obama becomes the next president of the United States, he can thank those sex clubs in Paris. Ryan was running against Obama, and had a good chance of winning, too, but his candidacy crumbled after court papers filed in his divorce from actress Jeri Ryan indicated that he and Jeri—she apparently reluctantly—visited the clubs. Personally, I don't think visiting a sex club in Paris should disqualify anyone from public office. On the other hand, I feel this episode revealed a moral flaw in Ryan, not of sexual depravity but of greed. (Did I mention he was married to Jeri Ryan?) Neither Craig nor Debra believes they ever ran into Ryan, but they say I'd be surprised by the number of well-to-do prominent people who go to the clubs. Actually, I wouldn't be surprised. Maybe once. Not anymore.

Swinger clubs like the ones Debra and Craig have been telling me about have been around for a long time. The most famous in the United States, probably the world, was Plato's Retreat, a New York City club that opened in 1977 during the last spasm of sexual profligacy in disco-era Manhattan. It closed in the wake of AIDs.

Swinger clubs are making a comeback now. Las Vegas, San Francisco, Dallas—most major cities have several swing clubs and many smaller cities have at least one. There are swinger travel agencies arranging swinger vacations to destinations like Cancún and Jamaica, swinger hotels, swinger message boards on the Internet, swinger personals.

The parties at Fetish Con, held in public nightclubs, did not offer any penetrative or oral sex or display of genitals. In fact, at many fetish events, sex is frowned upon regardless of venue, sex being secondary to the scene and a possible violation of a code of etiquette within the fetish community that discourages sex in "play spaces." The swinger clubs are different. Sex is the point. At

Miami Velvet, in South Florida, couples can even perform for an audience in the club's "Luvnasium."

With their emphasis on sex, swinger clubs are considered somewhat old-fashioned by many in the fetish and BDSM world. Some refer to swingers as "lifestylers," a name that evokes overweight, middle-aged people wearing gold chains and thong bikinis and cruising swimming pools in Las Vegas. But a new breed of swinger—younger and prettier—has arrived. Trained on raunchy MySpace party photos, Bang Bus, and hooking up, many are singles who just want hot, fast NSA (no strings attached) sex.

The Wet Spot is something different. It was founded in 1999 by six people who wanted to promote sexuality awareness and freedom. At the time, Allena was a well-known community activist and café owner who sometimes held BDSM "play parties" in the café's basement. The founders hired Allena to take charge. She has been the director ever since. While one can certainly "hook up" at the Wet Spot, there is a self-conscious exploration of sexuality as a way of life that the founders and Allena have tried to foster. That was what attracted Debra and Craig and why they wanted to stop by on their travels.

As soon as we return to the Wet Spot, Craig drops his pants. He goes wandering around in his gray man briefs and his socks, checking out some of the students from the earlier class who are practicing their fire play. When I look again, he is lying down on a table getting a massage from another man. Nearby, a woman is lying naked on a similar table with a flame erupting from the middle of her back. Her male partner is working like an intense Frankenstein concocting new variations, assembling his ingredients on a side stand, plotting his next creation.

Allena and I have arranged for a day of perv shopping in Seattle. First, though, just like two girls fortifying themselves for a day in the city, we meet one of her best friends for lunch at a downtown bistro. Allena wants to prove to me that completely normal, every-day people are having sex that we used to think was deviant and strange, something I proved to myself a long time ago, but Allena herself still finds it amazing after all these years promoting a sex-positive culture that it really is true. She enjoys hearing the stories of seemingly vanilla people over and over again.

So we sit with Pamela Kruger, a forty-three-year-old president of her own industrial supply company. Pamela doesn't care if I use her full real name or tell you exactly how she became a self-described pervert, a term she uses sarcastically as a way of tweaking what she believes is a national hypocrisy.

Pamela is a handsome woman in that strong, pioneer sort of way. She has a prominent chin, short blond hair, and a robust build. My first thought upon meeting her is that she reminds me a little of the actor Brian Dennehy, only prettier, and when I tell her so, she laughs loudly because as a child she had a major crush on Brian Dennehy. She used to masturbate to a poster of him that she hung in her room.

Most mothers want their children to become smart, educated, and responsible young people, and Pamela's was no different. Every week, when Pamela was twelve, her mom took her to the local public library in the suburb where they lived. It was always Pamela's assignment to check out a new book to read or to discover a new interest she wanted to explore. But Pamela's mother was also a member of the Doubleday Book Club. Every few weeks, the club mailed flyers to members highlighting new selections. Some of the titles included small asterisks. That meant the book was "sexually explicit." Unbeknownst to her mother, Pamela used this as a reading list.

"I would go to the library and seek out those books. One day, I found Anaïs Nin's *Delta of Venus*. That was my most influential book. A whole world opened up to me." Every week, her mother would take her to the library, and every week Pamela would head for the engineering section where she had hidden *Delta of Venus* so nobody would ever check it out. "I read more and more—Mom probably thought I wanted to be an engineer—until I eventually stole it."

Pamela's fantasies, sparked by Anaïs Nin, led to masturbation. "Discovering masturbation was huge! It was a big change in my life." Even after she married, she couldn't wait for her husband to go to work, "so I could lay around all day and masturbate like a fiend. I had that thing about Brian Dennehy, you know."

Once you break one taboo, others fall more easily. Having started at age twelve, breaking what she figured had to be a pretty big taboo reading that book, and then stealing it, taught Pamela how much heat could be generated by sin. So she kept pushing, until, today, there isn't much she refuses to try. I tell her about a dominatrix I met at Fetish Con, down in the lobby bar of the hotel, who had just come from an appointment with a client.

"What was he into?" I asked the domme.

"Scat. He likes scat."

I looked at her blankly, not because I didn't know what scat was, but because she took me by surprise. I was expecting spanking or something.

"You know, I shit on him."

"Well, yeah, I won't do scat," Pamela tells me. "I do like golden showers, though." Once she was lying on her back patio and a man was peeing on her and she's pretty sure the neighbors could see, because they've been looking at her funny ever since. She has become a regular at BDSM parties thrown by a neighbor in the small town north of Seattle where she lives. He's a sixty-one-year-old guy with some of the best BDSM equipment in the Pacific Northwest, including a roomful of medical gear. Once, an overenthusiastic Pamela tried to use the heart defibrillator. "'It's just for show!' he yelled at me. Stopped me at the last second," she recalls, laughing.

The first time she went to the Wet Spot, she says, she was terrified to come out of the bathroom. She wore a very short skirt without panties, "so I was basically bottomless." But after a few minutes she realized everyone else there was in some way exposing themselves, too.

"Do you ever feel abused or used, you know, as a woman?" I ask.

"Oh, I hope so!" she says, laughing at me. I have got to learn to stop asking these phony sensitive feminist questions. Starting with the firefighter back in Arizona, not one of the women I have encountered in my travels equated their own sexual indulgences as having anything to do with what is normally thought of as first-wave feminism. They all felt perfectly free to give and receive as much sex, in whatever variety they chose, as they wanted, which was supposed to be the point of feminism, as far as they were concerned. Why hoard one's sexuality as some sort of prize? they reasoned. I want what I want, and if I want to be peed on by a man and have a three-way with a man and a woman, who cares how anybody else wants to interpret that?

"I had a threesome with a guy and another woman recently," she says, and the girl came in, like, twenty-nine seconds, squirting all over him, and I'm, like, 'You bitch! Now I feel so inadequate.' Then she says, 'Well, I was faking it'!"

When I turn to my quest and ask if Pamela has any generalizations she'd like to share about why she thinks America has become a more wide-open country sexually, which seems to defy the common wisdom that we're becoming more buttoned up, she tells me she agrees that sexual experimentation like hers is becoming much more common. "And that's a shame." Pamela is the first person to say such a thing to me and I think she is the first person who has been completely honest about this. Everyone else has told me how happy they are that experimental sex and porn and toys are gaining acceptance, but I have always doubted them. Pamela derives pleasure from rule breaking, so "it is so sad that fetish wear is so mainstream now."

What if taboo—sin—did not exist? In the absence of sin, in a world devoid of condemnation, what fuel could Pamela use for heat? I have often joked with friends that I owe the Catholic Church a great debt for making sex dirty and therefore much more fun. I'm not sure how I could function, sexually speaking, if I didn't think I was committing a sin, somehow.

Art from the *Decameron* to *The Blue Angel* has celebrated the concept of sin as excitement. Condemnation may be the biggest favor any religious or political moralist could do for sex, especially now that sex is available anywhere and therefore no longer controllable.

But what happens when we kill sin and make sex akin to buying new snow tires? I ask Allena, who has made acceptance of sexual exploration a major part of her life's work.

"You need the religious right to condemn you, don't you?"

"Oh, yeah," she says. It was no accident that the sex-positive center was founded in 1999 and has grown since. "Both sides need each other. We give them people to be afraid of." This is why, she suggests, the two seemingly mutually exclusive strains of American life are happening at the same time. The more condemnation there is, in an age of unprecedented sexual availability, the more people will be seduced by the thrill of disobeying. The more deviancy the sexual moralists find, the more ammo they have to justify their argument that the nation is facing a values meltdown.

If perversion became bourgeois, what fun would the Wet Spot be? In fact, I don't think it is an accident that most of the Wet Spot members I have met so far are over thirty, many middle aged. The kids don't need a center to give them permission. They just do it on their own.

Allena drives a beat-up Suzuki stuffed with knickknacks. A small note on the dash says "Allena is well loved." As far as I can tell she is. A black leather rose surrounded by barbed wire is tucked up against the windshield, a memento from a BDSM conference.

First we stop at the Crypt, a place mainly for gay men, where I decide that I am not a leather kilt sort of guy, and that no matter how deeply discounted they may be, I am not going to wear a pair of black leather boy hot pants. Allena becomes more amused with every one of my vetoes. Next we drive back downtown to an adult store, but the clothes are for women and though a young man with multiple facial piercing tries to convince me I might look good in a body stocking, I veto that, too.

As she drives, Allena talks more about this idea of mainstreaming perversion, an oxymoron, but neither of us can think of another phrase. Now that she's thinking about it, she recalls a time when she was giving a fisting seminar, lessons on the sexual joy to be experienced by women who learn how to have a lover insert their entire fist into the vagina. The seminar was being given in a hotel.

"And there was a wedding rehearsal there and some of the bridesmaids peeked into the room and asked what we were doing. When I told them, they were all, 'Ewww!' but then I told them how much fun it could be and before you know it, they were lying down on the table, these cute little chicks with their dresses up over their heads, getting fisted. People just aren't afraid to try things anymore."

Finally, Allena drives us toward the city's Capital Hill neighborhood. We stop into Babeland, founded by one of Joani Blank's two interns, and see their selection of vibrators, including a new computerized thing a woman can program with preset routines. It seems like a long time ago that I worked at Fascinations and visited the women in Missouri. Then we drive a few more blocks and park across the street from a store called Metro, a goth palace.

A very pretty, tall, young woman with short black hair and glasses is sitting behind the counter reading a book when we walk in. Her name is Keda. She is wearing a camisole and black pants and a stainless-steel collar with a padlock in front. I also notice lines of deep diagonal scars on her chest, forearms, and wrists.

We're there a few minutes when Allena pulls a pair of black shiny pants off a rack.

"Oh, these would be perfect! You'll look hot!"

They are extraordinarily narrow pants.

"Let's get you a shirt, too" she says as if there is no question about the pants. A few minutes later she has selected the T-shirt with the skull.

In the mirror of the dressing room I look all the world like a shiny, older Joey Ramone.

I walk up to the counter and hand the clothes to Keda. She is twenty-one years old, she says. "Were you a cutter?" I ask, referring to her scars.

"I was an angsty teenager," she replies. She was in and out of treatment for her habit of cutting herself and it worked, intermittently. She finally stopped altogether. "I am not allowed to cut myself anymore," she says, fingering her padlock. "Now I have somebody else do it."

Allena hands Keda a business card. "Call me," she says.

When we step outside, Allena explains that "many people in our community stop cutting once they get involved." I hadn't thought of the Wet Spot members as a community, but I suppose they are like any other ad hoc community in which people find a form of family and shelter. They have turned the sexual realm into a real-world place.

Allena runs into a young woman on our way back to the car, a woman I am going to call Sunshine. Sunshine has shaved half her head, though at first you can't tell because she has long hair that flows over her skull as if Sunshine hasn't really decided if she wants half her head shaved or not. Sunshine is a Wet Spot member, one of the youngest I have seen so far, and a friend of Allena's, though their relationship is really more like older sister to younger sister. Sunshine is a little wild, Allena explains. Sometimes Allena has to rein her in and provide some guidance.

I meet Sunshine again, later that evening, at a business-networking happy hour in a downtown bar. Allena, a whirlwind, organizes this monthly get-together for business owners and employees. Some are Wet Spot members, but others aren't. Sunshine is there because she runs her own massage service. When she sees me, she wants to ask if I'd like to interview her. Maybe we could go someplace? I want to stay and meet some other people, so I explain it's not possible. Will I be going to this weekend's party at the Wet Spot? she asks.

I spend most of my time talking to Janice and Peter. Janice, a legal secretary, is dressed in a knee-length skirt and long-sleeved blouse; she's just come from work. Her jewelry is tasteful, her brown hair cut short. She's pretty. She speaks in clipped, precise language, using an elevated vocabulary and a hint of hauteur.

Being in his rookie season as a sexual explorer, Peter is nervous about talking to me at all. He is a forty-two-year-old business consultant with an Ivy League MBA and some work for a renowned think tank in his background. He was divorced a few years ago and has a son, too, and you never know what an ex-wife might do in a court of law if she knew you were fucking several different women at a time and trying out your newfound interest in S&M on yourself.

Peter is an intense man. He was raised in a conservative fashion with a conservative ethnic background. If you were to see him in an airport, maybe Hong Kong or Shanghai or Bangkok, all places he flies to often, you would assume he is one of those youngish titans of business we are supposed to admire, the sort of guy we like because they break rules and make a lot of money doing it. Peter knows how to do all that—he's an expert, in fact—but he is just "dipping his toes" in the waters of sexual taboo.

"I have always been curious but fairly inhibited and never felt comfortable, really, at expressing to myself, and certainly not to other people, what I was interested in. I thought it was shameful." Like so many others, the digital world opened his eyes. "I did lots of online porn and knew what was out there." He found Internet bondage porn both "empowering and titillating." "But I never really had a chance to [experience it]. In Philly once, I came across a BDSM group and went to one of their meetings and stayed for a half hour and left. I was too overwhelmed with it."

It wasn't until he began dating a woman who happened to be a member of the Wet Spot that he truly began to explore in real life. "I have been going on and off for a couple of years now. I am comfortable there. I feel safe there."

Peter gives his newfound sexual life a great deal of thought. Even speaking to me, he says, is a deliberate act. "It is not something I am comfortable with, but it is a way for me to develop courage and to confront things I am afraid of and master them."

One of the things he always wanted to try, he says, is "ass play." Just the very idea of it made him feel wicked and shameful. He began to think about it in a conscious way, mentally rehearsing scenarios. Once, while standing in his apartment's kitchen, "I thought, 'Oh my God, now that I have opened this up, something really bad is going to happen.' I imagined all the knives and forks flying around attacking me for having these thoughts. I felt real shame and dread. 'How can you think of something like that?' But when I shared that with others, they said, 'Oh yeah, if you wanna try it, I would be willing,' and nothing bad happened."

Since then he has done everything from anal massage to being penetrated by strap-ons. If something occurs to him, he tries to find a way to make it happen and then decides if he likes it or not. Often he moves on, working his way down a cafeteria line of sexual dishes.

These days Peter has four sexual partners, all women. The variety, he has concluded, is natural. "There is this whole Judeo-Christian-rooted idea that you have a perfect other, but that is really unrealistic. Not to objectify women, but it's like eating Mexican food every day. It gets old."

Acting as the sub in some of his relationships, Peter tells me, is "a manifestation of integrity." "This is who I really am. I can be this passive, submissive person and told what to do and that's fine. There are no repercussions." Business, on the other hand, rewards aggression and decisiveness. "In my public persona, in the corporate world, to be successful, the company comes first. You put aside personal feelings, values. It is bottom-line driven, shareholder-value driven. That is very unnatural."

But Peter is not euphoric about what he also sees as the surge in American sexual exploration. Perhaps there is a backlash against this corporate philosophy and toward a more balanced work–life division that is driving the search for sexual sensation, but on the other hand, he argues, American culture glorifies sex. "So we are conditioned to overvalue sex."

Could be, he thinks, that we are seeking community and trying to find it through sexual gratification, the intimacies Debra says she feels even if fleetingly in swinger clubs, or the ad hoc family Allena has created at the Wet Spot, or the shared codes of the fetish world.

I think of a conversation I had months ago with Joe Beam. Isn't it possible, Joe, I asked him, that faced with our culture, people are looking for some sort of refuge or a new reality in sexual expression they are not finding in other areas of their lives? That you and other fundamentalist Christians, who find refuge in religion, have more in common with rubberists or swingers or shibari masters than might be comfortable to admit? That you are looking for the same thing?

"I think you are right," he answered. "We marry people we feel our parents will accept, or our social group accepts, and somebody who rates closely to you on the attractiveness scale. So while we think we are picking our own, we really aren't. And in the church it is even worse. 'We are going to control you.' That is our culture. Sex can be the one true place to be absolutely creative and totally expressive, totally uninhibited and be you. But in my opinion, from what I find in our seminars, most Americas don't have sex like that because we are hung up on our beliefs, or we aren't close to our partners . . . I think you are right, but I'm not sure if we know what that answer is. Some connection with other human beings. Otherwise we would all just masturbate. It's more efficient."

Peter worries about this. He has studied Marcus Aurelius, the Roman stoic who believed "that which is good must be something useful, and the perfect good man should look after it. But no such man would ever repent of having refused any sensual pleasure. Pleasure then is neither good nor useful." Abandoning moderation in all things, pleasure seeking, leads to weakness not just of the person, but of the state.

Still, Peter says, "One could make the argument that happier people are more productive people, especially in an information economy. When people plowed fields, if they didn't plow, you got no food, right?" But most of us don't plow anymore. We don't work in big scrap-metal yards or glass factories or appliance plants. We don't know the customer who comes into the small department store in the small town because she shops in the mall. We sit in front of computers. "It might be that we are having such a great time, it encourages more creativity and so more value-added services."

Now, there is an interesting economic theory. Raising the gross national product through sex.

"Isn't it possible, though, that we're just bored?" I ask.

Peter does not disagree.

Janice picks me up at my hotel. We're going to stop at a little Italian place she knows in her neighborhood for a light dinner and then I am going to change into my new pants and my shirt for a night at the Wet Spot.

The Italian place defines the term *hole-in-the-wall*. I'd like to tell you its name, because I loved it, but I can't. You'll see why in a moment. Janice and I walk in and the owner greets her warmly. She eats here a few times a week, and there is nothing quite so welcoming as the proprietor of a restaurant or bar where they know you well. Janice looks forward to the welcome and the sense of belonging.

Janice possesses a certain melancholy I can't identify, but as we talk she tells me about being an unmarried young woman and giving up a baby for adoption knowing that she could never do that child justice the way a loving adoptive family could. Janice's mother has never forgiven her that. Her father wasn't much help. He never particularly cared for Janice, though Janice doesn't know why.

She was married once. She still owns half the house where she and her ex-husband lived. Janice has a tattoo on her shoulder, one that is always hidden by her professional work clothes, of a rising Phoenix being reborn from the flames, a pictorial description of the reinvention Debra felt after her divorce and the self-creation Janice has embarked upon since hers. Her life, Janice says, is what she has made it. These words, said with smiles and gentleness, float on an underlying fierceness.

Currently, Janice lives with a man, a lawyer she loves, but she has also had a secondary sex partner in what she describes as a polyamorous relationship. Sometimes she and her primary partner "play" with others together. Janice likes the BDSM and "poly" life because she gets to be the bottom, mostly. Being the bottom means somebody is paying attention to you. Somebody cares. Every stroke with the lash, or every slap or shock or new bondage position, means somebody has taken the time to think just about you.

"I gotta tell you, Janice," I say. "These things sound like a helluva lot of work."

She laughs. They are work, she says. A pain in the ass sometimes. But they develop trust. "And trust is huge with me. I have trouble trusting." *Trust* is a word I have heard from many people. Is that what we are seeking, trust? Whom do you trust? Whom can you trust? In relationships like Janice's everything is elaborately negotiated. That is the advantage of BDSM or polyamory, you have to talk the way most couples never do. You have to lay it all out, strip off the desires you sometimes hide even from yourself.

Breaking the terms of the agreement is a capital offense. In a high-stakes relationship in which you might suspend somebody from your ceiling in a rope or use electrical devices or light them on fire, for crying out loud, not to mention risk a sexual disease by some unauthorized diddling with another person, how, why, would you ever trust somebody who broke the contract?

Janice won't. Yesterday, she broke it off with her secondary partner. He wasn't where he said he was going to be, and where he was was with a woman Janice knew nothing about. She cut him loose.

The owner comes over to see how our cocktails are tasting and Janice whispers into his ear.

"Sure," he says.

So Janice tells me the story of how, when a girlfriend was about to be married, a lot of her pals threw a bachelorette party by kidnapping her, forcing a hood over her head, tying her up, and bringing her here. When they all stumbled in, giggling and laughing, and sat down at the bar, Janice thought she detected a look from the owner toward the kidnapped bride-to-be. Something about the knots and the skillful way they were tied. And the hood. Janice and the owner exchanged some knowing glances before telling each other about their mutual membership at the Wet Spot.

"That happens all the time," she tells me. "I'm always running into people I recognize from the Spot. Sometimes I think half the city goes there."

Because I am dreading putting on those pants, I have tried to keep the conversation flowing. But we've eaten some ravioli and had a drink. It's time. Janice excuses herself and goes to the restroom to change out of her conservative clothes and into her Wet

Spot clothes. When she returns, she is wearing a long black gown with diagonal see-through strips through which it is virtually impossible to see. It's pretty, hardly the exotic costume I was anticipating.

Ravioli was not the best dinner to have before putting on absurdly tight PVC pants. You may also be interested to know, in case you find yourself choosing between PVC and a nice gabardine, that PVC pants conduct cold. I hadn't thought about this until I sat on Janice's car seats.

Being a weekend night, there's a good crowd at the Spot when Janice and I arrive. Allena, in the same long, woolen cape as the day we went shopping, greets us warmly and introduces me to a few regulars. Some people are dancing with all their clothes on, some are in their underwear, some women are topless, and a few people in the play space are naked. The back room is filled with subs and doms using the equipment. One woman rolls a huge trunk out of the room filled with all of her personal BDSM gear.

Though I don't notice at first, as I am standing by the play space observing somebody being flogged, I see a naked woman in a tiny cage at my feet. She is looking up at me like a puppy in the pound. After everything I have seen, every conversation I have had all over the country with all kinds of people, this is the first time I feel disturbed. If only she would smile. But she is not smiling. She is looking sad and reacts to my stare like a beaten dog reacts to an abusive owner. She squeezes herself to the back of the cage, curls into a ball with her hands to her face. She may be in her "sub space" and I don't doubt she is there willingly, but still, I'm bugged. I am tempted to crack open the cage and let her out.

Allena would say this is my own rescue fantasy. Am I like Dave Gibson? Think hard enough about sexuality, talk to enough people, and you start imagining there is a little bit of all of them in you.

Ten minutes later, a man opens the cage. "Are you going to be good?" he asks the woman. She nods. "Okay." She stands up, crookedly at first, and they walk off together.

When I turn to watch them I notice that directly behind me, a foot away, a man and a woman have been screwing on a couch. She has slipped her panties off from under a short pleated skirt and opened his fly, and now she is bouncing up and down on his lap.

Meanwhile, the head of the woman who is being fisted and punched in the thighs bangs into the man's knee every time the other woman's fist shoves into her vagina.

"Hi!" Sunshine says out of nowhere, distracting me from the action on the couch and oblivious to it herself. Sunshine has dressed cyber-style with huge colored dreadlocks and a short skirt, black lipstick, and enormous black boots with thick soles like some exoplanetary trooper. "Let's talk!"

"It's a little loud," I shout over the metal.

"Come on!"

She leads me to the after-care room and we sit down on the futon. "You look great!" she exclaims. "Nice pants."

I want Sunshine's story like I want everybody's story, and she obliges with a tale about growing up in Alaska and how her mom set her up with a guy in his thirties, some car enthusiast, when Sunshine was sixteen. Maybe she did that to get her away from Sunshine's dad, who used to dance "inappropriately" with her and "had anger issues." But as she speaks, I sense Sunshine has more on her mind than her story. She keeps looking at my wedding ring. There is a sign outside the entry forbidding sex in the after-care room and I am thankful for it. Sunshine is an attractive girl, but even if I were single, I wouldn't. She seems vulnerable and I have a code.

Sunshine sometimes dates women, but mainly she'd really like to find a man. The problem, though, is that she just "can't take a vanilla boy." Anastasia Pierce, the BDSM model I met at Fetish Con, told me that once you go fetish you can never go back, and I guess that's true for Sunshine.

In the absence of a good relationship, she is focused on her massage business. She wants to grow it, turn it into something serious

and pure, but she keeps giving happy endings to a few male customers when they ask really nicely. She can't help herself. But this
defeats the spirituality of massage, damages its integrity, you
know?

She puts her hand on my chest. "I really want to hug you right
now, but I don't know what you and your wife have negotiated." I
can't help it. I laugh, hard. It just bursts out because I am imagining how supremely abbreviated any such negotiation would be.

"Let's just say that's not part of our deal."

Sunshine's story goes pretty quickly after that and we leave the
after-care room. Five minutes later, I see Sunshine trussed up in a
shibari suspension, her large breasts hanging down from an opening in the ropes. A man on his knees is sucking them.

I meet up with Janice again. She has found a friend, a young
woman in a short, tight PVC dress, who spends her days working
for another set of lawyers. Neither of them knew the other was a
member. "See what I mean?" Janice says.

The thin, frail-looking man with the white hair and beard is
naked, strapped onto the big wooden X-shaped structure in the
middle of the play space. A man and woman have stripped down
to their underwear. She is topless. He's a portly fellow in a pair of
brown briefs and black socks and glasses.

The man and the woman work over the sub for half an hour.
They slap him, whip him, stroke him, whisper to him. When it is
all over, Mr. Portly wraps him up in a blanket, picks him up into
his arms like a child, and carries him across the threshold of the
play space to the couch where the woman is seated and waiting.
The sub puts his hand to his face as if about to suck his thumb. Mr.
Portly lays him down into the woman's lap and she strokes him
and he coos and goes fetal, and I am disgusted.

I am going to have to spend some time thinking about why this
particular sight, of these other sights, has affected me this way.

Janice is ready to leave. I'm not sorry. If you aren't going to get
wet, there's not much point in hanging around the pool. I find

Allena, who is now strolling through the Wet Spot with just her wool cape draped over her bare torso, and I smile and give her a hug. She says what a lot of people on this quest have said, "Hope we didn't shock you."

"No, you didn't shock me," I reply, for I am not shocked. I say good-bye to a few other Wet Spot members who have taken time to talk, and then Janice and I walk outside and I feel the cold air on the PVC.

On the way back to my hotel, Janice says "Okay, what do you really think?"

"I think we live in a very sick culture."

"Yes, we do," she says.

"But it's not sick because people are having sex. I don't care how people have sex. I think—" But then I stop, because I also have a code about talking out of my ass without having a couple of drinks first.

"It is sick," she says again. "People are looking for love, but who can you trust? My mother said she'd love me forever, too."

CHAPTER 9

America, Unzipped

Life as she saw it was quite simple. You wanted a good time; "they," meaning the party, wanted to stop you from having it; you broke the rules as best you could.

—George Orwell, *1984*, 1948

What I find so fascinating is that there is this huge sex industry, billions of dollars, and what it all comes down to is you. It comes down to one person: you. Everybody has their own story.

—Kim Airs, 2007

The plane takes off heading over Puget Sound and I am thinking I wouldn't mind having a conversation that does not include the words *dildo, fisting, squirting, orgasm, vibrator, latex, fucking, shibari,* or *three-way*.

At least I now know that the readers of my column are not an extraordinary group of especially perverted people. Their questions are American questions, their curiosity part of the country's conversation. In fact, I've spent so much time on the road talking sex that if I didn't know better, I'd swear June Cleaver was wearing crotchless panties under those dresses, and Ward had a Prince Albert hiding behind his flannel trousers, and instead of playing bridge with the Rutherfords, they were playing same-room swing. Immersion has a way of altering your outlook.

It can also skew your outlook, of course, and I have to remind myself that many people in the United States do not use sex toys. Most do not enter into polyamorous relationships, have probably never heard of shibari, and might think bukkake is a beer from Japan. Surveys tend to show that most of us get married, try to stay married, that half of us divorce anyway, that we think monogamy is still the ideal. Nevertheless sexual experimentation, sometimes radical experimentation, has become a mainstream pursuit.

I did not start out completely naive. I knew things had changed in the country; that's why I set out months ago armed with facts and statistics. I wanted to put some faces and words to what few numbers and facts existed. But I have been surprised at how profound the change is in the way many people live their sex lives.

This was not supposed to be the case. A generation ago, Jerry Falwell founded the Moral Majority and took credit for changing the sexual climate in the country. "More than 100,000 pastors, priests and rabbis and nearly seven million families joined hands and hearts to reclaim America for God," Falwell wrote shortly before he died in 2007. "Many historians believe the result was the election of Ronald Reagan in 1980 and the genesis of what the media calls the 'religious right.'"

The object of the Moral Majority, which was reborn in 2004 as the Moral Majority Coalition, was to agitate for a nation based on the idea found in verse fourteen, chapter seven, of the second book of Chronicles: "If my people, which are called by my name, shall humble themselves, and pray, and seek my face, and turn from their wicked ways; then will I hear from heaven, and will forgive their sin, and will heal their land."

While we elected Ronald Reagan, and George W. Bush (at least once), we have clearly not turned from our wicked ways as defined by the likes of Falwell. We have ballooned the porn industry into a multibillion-dollar enterprise, flooded into adult stores and retail websites to buy sex toys, helped Phil Harvey give away more condoms than ever. More of us have started having anal sex, oral sex is now considered foreplay by kids like Trista Windels, the number of sex clubs is expanding and so is the number of fetishists.

In the sex election, Americans have voted. In 2006, by the estimate of AVN Media Network, we spent $2 billion at exotic dance clubs. We spent $1.7 billion for cable TV porn, $2.8 billion on Internet porn, and another $1.7 billion on sex toys.

Falwell was forced to admit defeat in 2006, writing, "It is obvious that we are losing the cultural battle in many ways, especially with our young people."

If *cultural battle* means "sex," and it often does, Falwell was correct, except that from what I have seen I would replace *losing* with *lost.*

It's over. It's been over for a long time, but so much attention has been paid to the loudest voices condemning sexual exploration that we haven't listened to those who have pursued it. While there is obviously a vocal gay rights movement, there isn't much of a porn rights movement, or swinger rights movement, or sex toy buyers' movement, or fetish liberation movement. There is an organization called the National Coalition for Sexual Freedom, founded in 1997, that is focused mainly on keeping S&M enthusiasts out of jail and conventions from being shut down by local authorities, but I don't think there will soon be marches featuring vibrator-wielding women in Montgomery, Alabama.

This is not because they are ashamed. I have yet to meet a single person—with the possible exception of Don, who is clearly troubled about meeting strangers for sex in hotel rooms—who expresses any shame at all. Rather, they think that what they do sexually really isn't anybody's business and that they shouldn't have to reveal the details of their sex lives to the world in order to pursue them.

But this reticence gives the mistaken impression that Americans are not as interested in sexual variation as we are. Thirty years ago, pollsters asked people in Lexington, Kentucky, about pornography and a majority said they thought erotica ought to be available for adults. These people also assumed they were in the minority. The minority who felt there should be strict control of porn were sure they were the majority. We are more sexually laissez-faire than we think.

Over the past months I have met many people who are married, monogamous, and churchgoing and enjoy sex toys and porn. I have met psychologists who swing, nurses who show off online and act out bisexual fantasies, sub and dom businesspeople, Republican bondage fetishists, soldiers who play superhero (and not the kind you see at a kid's birthday party either). None of these people were scary. They are you and me and our neighbors.

Falwell has been proven wrong, Dobson proven wrong, the entire anti-sexual-freedom harangue proven wrong, and from what I can see the country is no worse off because a middle-aged housewife in Tempe buys a Pyrex dildo or because Peter experiments with "ass play." What does matter, and what I think we ought to worry about, is why there is so much sexual experimentation now and if anybody is finding any happiness doing it.

Sex, being a prime human instinct, has always been the weak point of social control. It provides a refuge where people can retreat to carve out a bit of autonomy, forge a bond with other human beings, and in a small way try to fulfill their own desires on their terms. George Orwell knew this, making Julia, Winston's lover in *1984*, an insincere member of the Junior Anti-Sex League who made her living censoring porn to be released to the proles. Phil Harvey knows it, too, and thinks that may be one reason why sex, and depictions of sex, are feared. Conservative religions have always known it.

More than eleven hundred years ago, Hincmar, archbishop of Reims, a powerful ecclesiastical and political counselor to several kings, described how some women "are reported to use certain

instruments of diabolical operation to excite desire. Thus they
sin . . . by committing fornication against their own bodies." In
ninth-century Europe, such a thing was not just a sin, it was a crime.
Church and state were siblings and each enforced the laws of the
other. Punishments could be severe, including the wearing of
sackcloth and ashes, public prostration, fasting, and other depriva-
tions that could go on for years at a time.

And yet women still used dildos. There wasn't much of an
"adult industry" to sell them, nor any adult stores or a thousand
Internet sites promoting them. The media did not inspire them.
The combined force of rigid church and state teaching was
required to keep sexuality in the shadows, and even then some
people, maybe many, defied the edicts.

Pope Paul VI recognized the necessity of threat to control sex in
the face of human nature. "Responsible men can become more
deeply convinced of the truth of the doctrine laid down by the
Church on this issue if they reflect on the consequences of
methods and plans for artificial birth control," he wrote in his
1968 encyclical *Humanae Vitae.* "Let them first consider how easily this course of action could open wide the way for marital infidelity and a general lowering of moral standards. Not much
experience is needed to be fully aware of human weakness and
to understand that human beings—and especially the young,
who are so exposed to temptation—need incentives to keep the
moral law, and it is an evil thing to make it easy for them to break
that law."

The risk of getting your girlfriend pregnant and finding yourself bagging groceries instead of going to college was a very real
threat to me, I can tell you, much more incentive than Catholic
teaching ever was. It was the hammer over my head accounting
for my late sexual start. (I wonder what I would have done if those
two girls in the swimming pool had told me they were taking
birth control.)

But Anne, the new convert to Roman Catholicism in Missouri,

takes birth control and clearly feels the church's authority over her sexual life is more advisory than mandate. She has made up her own parallel sexual morality and seized control of her own sexual destiny. Many of us do just that.

We have never been very good at taking direction when it comes to sex, and we are much less so now. There is just too much information streaming across our computers and televisions and magazines to put sex back in a closet. Every person now makes up his or her own mind, choosing from a cafeteria of possibility.

The younger the person, the truer this is. My younger Fascinations customers expressed surprise at some of the questions I asked them, as if asking questions about watching porn or buying the Rabbit Pearl vibrator betrayed my own quaintness. Like the teenage girl in Missouri who attended the Passion Party with her mom and sister, school and church are not places to learn about sex. They assume the messages they receive there are unreliable and stilted. Sex is not a moral issue, a religious issue, or a political issue. It is a personal issue.

I think Joe Beam and the other Christian sex advisers understand this. Joe does not want conservative Christians to have to choose between their churches and sex. He knows sex can be more powerful than church; it was for him. So by telling the faithful that they can have most of the sexual menu items they wish within the boundaries of heterosexual marriage, Beam and the others are attempting to reach a truce in the culture war over sex, even if—in my view—they have to bend the biblical literature to do it.

If this is so, however, what accounts for the rise of the hypersexual culture even while America is supposedly rediscovering its religiously restricted carnal outlook?

American sexual hypocrisy is a cliché and an old one at that. Ted Haggard's fall from grace and Senator David Vitter's prostitution scandal are just recent examples. But hypocrisy is fading. Every day I worked at Fascinations, we made, or nearly made, our sales goals. Average, taxpaying, solid citizens are shopping there and in the hundreds of other adult stores around the country. Over and over again, I heard how happy they are to have such a store that is so unlike the grungy places of the past. They can finally feel free to walk through the doors.

So I don't think the apparent contradiction is hypocrisy. After I began asking people to tell me their political affiliations, the split was close, slightly favoring Republicans and Independents, especially at Fetish Con. Melissa voted for George W. Bush because she liked his views on taxes and national defense. She thoroughly disapproves of his stances on social and sexual issues. I heard the same comments from most other people, liberal and conservative, religious and areligious.

Throughout my journey, I considered the assertion Susan Montani made to me about being rebellious and supporting "the cause." I have to confess that though I did not recognize it at the time, and though her comment made me uncomfortable, I suppose I do support "the cause" if the cause is defined as freedom for adults who want to have sex with other consenting adults even if that sex seems unusual to the rest of us.

But the fact is, people by and large do have that freedom. Make no mistake, there are plenty of hateful expressions, lots of repressive talk, and no doubt some of us would like to re-create the fictional asexuality depicted on early sitcoms, as Dobson suggested with his allusion to Mayberry. But I experienced nary a raised eyebrow. The cop in Rossville, Kansas, was nonchalant when I mentioned Passion Parties, the Hyatt sales manager in Tampa was cheerful and cooperative with the fetish conventioneers, Marty Tucker had never been in a legal fight over his sex products. Peter Acworth operates freely in San Francisco. PHE's epic battle started nearly a generation ago. When I told desk clerks, cabdrivers, flight attendants, and friends what I was doing, I heard, "Sounds like fun!" "Can't wait to hear about it," and a couple of noncommittal "interesting"s.

Community pressure does exist, just not to the degree one might assume from the rhetoric. What we have, I think, is a dispute about packaging. As far as I can tell, people are not opposed to adult stores as much as they are opposed to a big garish sign with a girl in a nightie looming over their house. According to a 2005 Harris poll, most people don't believe porn should be banned; they just want it kept away from kids. Most people don't seem to care how other people have sex either, but they don't necessarily want to watch them do it.

There is a self-conscious rebelliousness in the people I have met, however, not just among the fetishists or the denizens of the Wet Spot but even among the sex shop customers, the sex toy party ladies, and Joe Beam's audience. Like the majority in Lexington, Kentucky, thirty years ago, they believe they are going against the grain and they enjoy doing it. But I wonder if in some cases what looks like rebellion is really escape, a way to make that private realm more tangible and separate from the main current of American life.

Feeling rebellious accomplishes something important. It helps create a sense of community bonding with other rebellious people, the camaraderie Phil Harvey talks about that exists in his company. The parallels with the Christian revival movement are uncanny and go a long way toward explaining how both trends can exist at the same time.

Visit Christian websites or listen to Christian radio, and you will hear about how persecuted Christian conservatives are in the United States despite the fact that their man, George W. Bush, occupied the White House for eight years, they had significant representation in Congress and in statehouses, and politicians of all parties have suddenly started bending over backward to declare how godly they are. Nevertheless, "For 40 years, the anti-God Left has been using America's courts to impose an anti-religion, anti-family agenda on America," declares the Traditional Values Coalition.

This is a statement against the culture. In fact, there is no significant repression of Christians in this country just as there is no significant repression of sexual adventurers as long as they aren't using a violet wand on your front lawn. I think the true rebellion is against an increasingly atomized, technological, impersonal culture in which people feel crushed and out of control.

Instead of state or religious oppression of sexuality, there is increasingly a repression of sense of community, of intimacy, family loyalties, cohesiveness, and of self-control by the juggernaut of technological change, consumerism, niche marketing, the global economy. The landscape of Shawnee, Kansas, expresses it, with its strip malls, chain stores, and freeway bypasses. I don't think it is any accident that many of the people I met in Seattle worked in the area's high-tech industry where they help create one culture by day and escape into the opposite of that culture by night. Michael, a technical master in his work life, trades that in for skin-to-skin contact with Susan and their playmates. Don, a world-traveling businessman, spends many hours peering through a computer screen, reaching out for a facsimile of human contact.

Likewise, megachurches are communities unto themselves with their own rules and regulations and common beliefs that serve as a refuge. Your fellow congregation members are your brothers and sisters in Christ. The "war" rhetoric used by the likes of Dobson works just as it does at PHE to forge bonds among people who perceive themselves under attack.

In the fetish world and the BDSM world, there are many rules and regulations and points of etiquette. At first I was puzzled by them; it seems oxymoronic that sexual libertines would establish elaborate codes and the more radical the sex, the more rigid the codes. Everything is negotiated. Some negotiation recognizes the power of sex and the possible dangers—as Paradox explains, when you play with fire, you need some rules. But after watching the scenes at Fetish Con and the Wet Spot I think there is something else at work.

Janice said, "My mother said she'd love me forever." But her mother did not love her forever. So now Janice negotiates love and sex and feels safe in that web of rules. This superstructure of government creates the invisible borders for each person's custom-made sexual "realm." Within the realm you can exert control over your penis, vagina, fingers, mouth, toys, ropes, whatever you want. At Fetish Con, I met with two couples who lived dom-sub life-styles, and as a "lifestyle master" cum real estate agent explained, "What a lot of people in the vanilla world do not understand is that this entails an extreme amount of trust. It is a trust that goes beyond what a lot of people in everyday vanilla relationships have. Left and right they are lying to each other, doing things behind each other's back. A lot of that does not happen here."

Do you notice how many people on my quest have told me they want to feel something? How many say they want to experience intimacy? How many use the word *trust*? In an unzipped world, they are trying to zip themselves to something they can make real on their own. They could join a church, but sex seems more intense and a lot more fun.

Susan and Michael, Bob and Melissa, can find each other on the Internet, share explicit pictures, meet, explore their enthusiasm for kink, even fall in love. A woman in Shreveport can learn she is not the only person in the world who wants to be spanked, that the world is full of people like her. Madison Young can explore her own rope fetish, make money, and push the boundaries of sexual "feeling" so far that most any kink you have imagined can seem tame by comparison and therefore more possible. The online world is a giant virtual space of mutual support. And then, once you feel the tangible normalcy of it all, you can, as Michael says, "make it real" and feel the intensity in real life.

The more radical the exploration, the tighter the bond, the more one can "feel" in a culture gone numb. For many of the people with whom I have spent the last year, their experiences of sex are the most real things in their lives, just as fundamentalist

Christians will often say that their experience of Jesus is the most real thing in theirs.

Sex is true. You can feel a strap-on. You can feel a female ejaculation. You either come or you do not, and when you do it is the most elemental of human pleasures. There is no spin.

When I took my first steps on this trail, I wanted to know if these people were finding happiness, and now I am sure that some of them are. Joe Beam's audience is very happy—thrilled, really—now that he has lifted the shroud of guilt from their shoulders. I think many of the women in Missouri are happier than they were, having taken steps toward expanding their sexual lives. Melissa and Bob tell me they are happy, and I believe them. I am keeping my fingers crossed for Susan and Michael. I am not so sure about others I have met. I suppose some are and some are not, about the same answer Phil Harvey gave me, but what I am sure of is that seeking one's own sexual place is one of the more rational responses to an impoverished culture that often seems more virtual than real and that the search is theirs to make.

Which is not to say I am sanguine about every attempt to flee the culture we have built. I am haunted by the face of the guy in the Wet Spot, the one who nuzzled into his surrogate mommy as if trying to crawl up into her vagina and stay there for good. On the one hand, I can't really blame the guy for mewling and cuddling into his domme's lap any more than I can blame the future teen anal queen for her ambition.

But I resented him, I suppose, for hiding in "sub space." I felt humiliated on his behalf. I wanted him to reclaim his dignity. I am betraying my own prejudice here, I know. (BDSMers would say I have not figured out how to let go, that I am blocked.) As I say, I support the freedom of people to make whatever sexual choices they wish. But the sight of him crystallized a nagging thought I have had almost since the beginning, the one I expressed at PHE about what might happen if we killed taboo.

Phil Harvey argues that he and his fellow adult-industry titans are not creating "consumer slaves." I think he is correct, and that Kim Airs is correct, too, when she says that even with the marketing power of the sex industry we make our own sexual decisions, as we make sexual decisions in the face of government, religious, or social condemnation.

Still, we are sold sex the way we are sold giant flat-screen TVs, computers, and beer. Trista did not simply discover squirting out of thin air; she saw it on a DVD. The Sinclair Institute shows the use of sex toys not just because sex toys can enhance a sexual experience, but because it sells sex toys. JimmyJane has turned them into fashion. Anal sex has boomed in popularity in recent years, according to Mark Schoen and other experts, because almost every porn video now has at least one anal sex scene. Same with threesomes, bondage, and fetish. Somebody is having more fun than we are, we learn, and we want it, too.

This turns the quest to carve one's own sexual identity out of a banal culture into an ironic statement on the way everything becomes just another part of that banal culture. So Pamela Kruger is right to worry about how widely accepted fetish and alternative sex in general have become. Acceptance dampens the frisson that makes taboo delicious. Looking for *Delta of Venus* would hardly be any fun if it weren't forbidden. You can keep moving the boundaries, but just about everything that was once sexually taboo has shot right through mainstream and now landed in kitschy banality.

Sex, porn, bondage, S&M—none of it is transgressive anymore. There is no danger in it. It feels scripted and oftentimes it is. Sex is like Times Square, filled with Sephora and Disney and Nike and Virgin, and if you fly to Paris and walk down the Champs-Elysées you will find Sephora and Disney and Nike and Virgin. We live in a kitschy world. Sex has now been completely subsumed into it, used as an entertaining distraction the way toned-down porn was used to distract the proles in *1984.*

There is no danger, so of course Selina Raven is bored, and Peter worries about being bored. Kim Airs, the most enthusiastic sexual explorer I have ever met, admits to experiencing boredom. "Sometimes I do get bored," she says. "I'd be lying if I said I did not. It's kinda like, well, I don't want to say, 'Been there, done that,' but yeah sometimes."

This is why I think the sex explosion is just about over. People will still watch porn, and we will certainly still have sex, and some people will still want to be tied up as some people always have, but the hypersaturation of it all is about to fizzle. "We keep trying to push the envelope and get more outrageous," Candida Royalle, who is very smart and funny and something of a porn philosopher, told me in North Carolina, referring not to her own productions but to the new generation of pornographers. "But the real art is about pulling back and discovering the nuances. Do we have to swing from the chandeliers to be exciting?"

This comment reminded me of a photograph I admire greatly because it scares me just a little. *Woman in Moroccan Palace,* made by Irving Penn in 1951, is an image of Lisa Fonssagrives-Penn. She sits on a floor, swaddled in robes, a turban on her head, before a tea service set on a low table. Fonssagrives is beautiful in it. She is always beautiful with her carved face and tulip-stem neck, but in this image she has a slightly subversive look in her eyes, challenging and dangerous, teetering on the edge between heartbreak and ecstasy, both outcomes seemingly just as possible.

ACKNOWLEDGMENTS

Writing books would be impossible without a set of enablers. I must thank mine.

My wife, Shelley, deserves an award of some sort. If you have to ask why, you haven't read this book.

Julia Pastore, who edited this volume, believed in it from the beginning and kept that faith. She got me, got the idea, and then called me out if I got lazy to make sure I didn't forget it.

The debonair Joe Regal, an agent out of the old school, believed in it, and in me, even before Julia. I am grateful for his continuing trust and faith.

I dragooned Francesca Hayslett into the unenviable job of reading and critiquing early drafts of most chapters. Yet she worked like an enthusiastic volunteer.

It was Jacqueline Stenson who called me that day as I sat in the Atlanta airport. Over the next several years, Jackie provided an obscene amount of support not only for the MSNBC column, but for this book. I also appreciate the support of Julia Sommerfeld, Jane Weaver, Danny Defreitas, and Jennifer Sizemore of MSNBC, who let me delve much deeper into America's sexual heart than I had any right to expect.

The editors at *Glamour* magazine, especially Jill Herzig—who has been a longtime patron of mine for reasons known only to her—Wendy Naugle, Genevieve Field, and Cindi Leive, displayed enormous patience and tolerance. I owe them.

Alex Heard, part colleague, part mentor, part inspiration, continues to give me valuable encouragement and advice.

Jane Hahn demanded I write a book about sex. I wish she were here to see it.

Two volumes provided important context for my own journey: *The Social Organization of Sexuality*, by Edward O. Laumann, John H. Gagnon, Robert T. Michael, and Stuart Michaels; and *Handbook of Medieval Sexuality*, edited by Vern L. Bullough and James A. Brundage, from which I took the quote from Hincmar.

This book depends utterly on the willingness of those people who appear in it to allow me entry into the most intimate parts of their lives. I am humbled by their openness, honesty, and graciousness.

And finally, thank you Montana Wildhack.

ABOUT THE AUTHOR

BRIAN ALEXANDER hails from a small town in central Ohio where he served as both a Catholic altar boy and president of the county's Teenage Republicans. He was once voted "most likely to become president of the United States" in junior high school, but opted for the prodigal life of writer and journalist. Now a contributing editor at *Glamour* magazine and a columnist for MSNBC.com, he has written for the *New York Times, The New York Times Magazine, The Los Angeles Times Magazine, Esquire, Outside, Wired, Details,* and many other publications. He has made appearances on *Charlie Rose, Today, The Early Show,* CNN, ESPN, and other television and radio programs.

www.AmericaUnzipped.com